THE *Champion*
REAL ESTATE TEAM™

THE Champion REAL ESTATE TEAM™

*A Proven Plan for
Executing High Performance
and Increasing Profits*

Dirk Zeller

New York   Chicago   San Francisco   Lisbon
London   Madrid   Mexico City   Milan   New Delhi
San Juan   Seoul   Singapore   Sydney   Toronto

The Champion Real Estate Team is a trademark of Sales Champions, Inc.

1 2 3 4 5 6 7 8 9 0   FGR/FGR   0 9 8 7

ISBN-13: 978-0-07-149901-9
ISBN-10: 0-07-149901-6

This publication is designed to provide accurate and authoritative information in regard to the subject matter covered. It is sold with the understanding that the publisher is not engaged in rendering legal, accounting, or other professional service. If legal advice or other expert assistance is required, the services of a competent professional person should be sought.
—*From a Declaration of Principles Jointly Adopted by a Committee of the American Bar Association and a Committee of Publishers and Associations*

McGraw-Hill books are available at special discounts to use as premiums and sales promotions, or for use in corporate training programs. For more information, please write to the Director of Special Sales, Professional Publishing, McGraw-Hill, Two Penn Plaza, New York, NY 10121-2298. Or contact your local bookstore.

This book is printed on acid-free paper.

Library of Congress Cataloging-in-Publication Data
Zeller, Dirk.
 The champion real estate team / by Dirk Zeller.
     p. cm.
 Includes index.
 ISBN-13: 978-0-07-149901-9 (pbk. : alk. paper)
 ISBN-10: 0-07-149901-6
 1. Real estate business. 2. Real estate agents. I. Title.
HD1375.Z448 2007
333.33068--dc22
                                   2007023049

Dedication

This book is dedicated to a Champion Team—my team at Real Estate Champions. The excellence that the members of this team exhibit each day is truly amazing. As in most Champion Teams, there are people behind the scenes who do a large amount of work so that a few can receive recognition. The few who receive the recognition are always indebted to the others. That is certainly the blessing I receive from these team members each day.

This dynamic team of people, from the sales staff led by Roger Marti, Director of Sales, to the coaching staff led by Don Cunningham, Director of Coaching, to Judy Cox, Office Manager, to Julie Porfirio, Vice President of Operations, who takes on the tough assignments that no one else can handle, to Dan Matejsek, Senior Vice President of Marketing, and his team, who deliver our message to the world, changes the lives of thousands of people each day.

Thanks. You and your teams have played an integral part of forging the Champion Team at Real Estate Champions!

Contents

PART III: TEAM LEAD GENERATION

PART IV: TAKING YOUR TEAM TO THE CHAMPION LEVEL

Preface

The buzz-word in today's real estate world is *teams*. Everyone is focused on building a team. I talk to agents who have less than six months' experience in the business, and they already have a team of people. They have already produced the marketing materials and Web sites that give them the appearance of having a team. The problem is that they haven't established the sales skills, time management skills, and business skills that will lead to success. They don't have an activity management plan, time management plan, personal management plan, team management plan, business management plan, or financial management plan. The truth is, in almost all cases, they and their teams are doomed.

I read a story to Wesley, my five-year-old son, the other night that reminds me of many of these people who are feverishly building teams, yet are so new in the business. It's a story about a ruler who had to have the finest of everything. He had the need to be recognized by all of the people as the ruler, with exclusive powers and privileges. He had to have the best of everything, especially in his clothes. He employed tailors to make him exquisite garments, but nothing was quite good enough. I am sure you all know what story I am talking about by now. Of course, it's *The Emperor's New Clothes*. The emperor paraded around naked with his head held high. I believe that there are a lot of people in real estate who are trying to build teams but are doing the same thing as the emperor—parading around naked. It took a small child to eventually say, "The emperor has no clothes on." What will it take for agents to realize the same thing?

Building a Champion Team doesn't happen overnight or instantly (or, for some, ever). It doesn't happen because of luck, the breaks, "the secret," or some new revolutionary technique or strategy. It's the result of a deliberate, planned, constantly vigilant, correcting, and demanding process of personal, business, and team member development that culminates in a clear vision and action plans that all team members must embrace. It also creates a culture of love, respect, and passion. When this culture catches on, your team members will have the passion to improve themselves to the Champion level.

I watched a wonderful movie a few days ago called *Facing Giants*. It was a low-budget movie made by Hollywood outsiders, but it carries a powerful message for someone who is aspiring to be a Champion or to create a Champion Team. There is a scene in the movie that encapsulates what needs to happen to each player on the team.

A high school football team is beginning its sixth losing season in a row. The team's best player has just transferred to another school for his senior season. The players are questioning whether they will win anything this season. The coach takes his best play player (his tough guy middle linebacker) and makes him do a "death crawl" in front of the team. The "death crawl" involved crawling low on all fours with another player on your back—back to back. The coach asks his tough guy leader who is questioning himself and the team how far he thinks he can go. How far can he do the "death crawl"? The tough guy player says 30 yards. The coach says he wants 50 yards, and he knows the guy can do it. The coach then utters the key words, "I want you to do your best; just give me your best."

The coach then blindfolds the player because he doesn't want circumstances, distractions, or doubt to affect his performance. He doesn't want the player to be limited by his vision of where he currently is. The coach wants the player to focus only on his hands, his feet, his will, and the goal of giving it his all. The player begins the death crawl and asks the coach, after about 20 yards, where he is and how close he is to the 50. The coach's response is, "Don't focus on that; you said you would give me your best!" The player then says that he doesn't know if he can make it. The player's doubts continue to rush out of his mouth.

The camera then shows you the coach and the player side by side, but you can't tell where they are on the field because the shot is a close-up. The coach is walking every step of the way with his player. When it gets tough, the coach gets on his hands and knees, face to face with the player, and begins shouting encouragement at him: "You can do it, don't quit, give me your best, don't quit until you have nothing left, all I want is your best, I want everything you've got." The scene crescendos with the player laboring and straining to go on, while the coach is encouraging him: give me 20 more steps, 10 more steps, 1 more step. Finally the player collapses in a heap. He has truly given it his best and his all. The coach then lies down on the field with his face about a foot away from the player's face and tells him that he is in the end zone!

The player found out that his best was a whole lot more than he had ever imagined. That's a Champion Coach who helped a player become a Champion Player, which is the cornerstone of building a Champion Team. You must have the passion to become a Champion Coach and lead your players beyond what they believe they can do. You are the one with the vision for the team. Your team members must catch that vision. You need to push their performance.

While the journey and realization of building a Champion Team isn't reached quickly, the decision to make the commitment you need as the Champion Coach and first Champion Player happens in a moment. You have to decide right now if you are willing to give it your very best, to not stop until you have nothing left, to never quit. The truth is that, as your coach right now through the written word, "I want everything you've got." Because that's what Champion Coaches expect, and that's what Champion Agents do. Champion Agents are the only ones who can build Champion Teams.

Now that you are one of my coaching clients, I will pray the same thing for you that I pray for all of my coaching clients:

Play all out, give it everything you've got, play to the best of your ability, give it your very best, and leave it all on the field before the game is done. Then you will walk away a Champion!

Acknowledgments

Creating a piece of work as significant and timely for the real estate industry as *The Champion Real Estate Team* requires the orchestration of many ideas and efforts that have culminated in the complete product you enjoy.

To Dianne Wheeler, my editor at McGraw-Hill, it was a pleasure to work with you again. You are the consummate professional. Your patience and dedication to the project, myself, and my challenging schedule do not go unnoticed.

To Rachelle Cotton, who endured another book project of mine (this makes our third together), your patience in laboring over my writing, ideas out of the blue, and changes in course and scope is much appreciated. These books would not exist without Rachelle. A special thanks to Caryn Yates-Clowers, an incredibly talented coach at Real Estate Champions, who reviewed and edited the manuscript of this book.

To John Gualtieri and Dean and Missy Vanderbilt, previous coaching clients who helped me construct our Team Performance Coaching program and who now coach that program with excellence, your contributions to helping agents build Champion Real Estate Teams are unmatched in the real estate industry.

Finally, to my home team, my wife of 18 years, Joan, my five-year-old son, Wesley, and my two-year-old daughter, Annabelle, of all the teams I have played for, played with, and built, our home team is the best. Keeping the home team at the Champion level is the true passion in my life.

Introduction

This book is really a step-by-step blueprint for establishing a well-run team. It is packed with how-tos, systems, strategies, processes, and ideas for implementation that will transform your business. Having personally established one of the first multi-assistant teams in my region, I have watched the evolution of real estate teams for over 15 years. My experience in applying these strategies both in my own business and in hundreds of other agents' team practices that I have coached in the last nearly 10 years has led to this book.

This book, *The Champion Real Estate Team*, is written from the same perspective as my previous book, *The Champion Real Estate Agent*. It reveals the pathway and steps to take to reach the pinnacle of real estate sales using a team. It isn't written from the perspective of, "I've made it." That type of book would have a limited audience. I answer the question: what did someone do, say, think, create, market, monitor, prospect, manage, coach, and perfect to reach the peak in real estate sales by leveraging his efforts through a team?

This book has four distinct parts. The first part closes the gap between the Champion Agent and the Champion Team. It really takes a quick look at you first. It also goes into the how, where, and why of building a Champion Team. The second part takes dead aim at designing your team, hiring and monitoring the people, and training the members of both your administrative staff and your sales staff. This area is where most agents fail miserably when trying to increase their business and their quality of life by building teams. You might want to read this section multiple times. The third part explores different strategies and tactics for lead generation and lead conversion when using a team structure. The creation, conversion, and monitoring of the cause-and-effect relationship between the leads that are created and the revenue that is generated is paramount for the success of your team. The final part takes your team to the Champion level. It digs deep to find the "secret" that separates marginally performing teams from Champion Performing Teams. You can build a good team without this section, but you can't build a great team. Your ability to achieve the level of Champion Team will enable you to achieve more time off, more income, and a better quality of life. You will also be building an asset that can be sold.

Chapter 1: The Champion Team's Business.   In this chapter, I address the history of real estate teams and explore the positive and negative aspects of having a team. I help you establish your first model for building your real estate team and help you explore the right questions to ask in determining the size and scope of your ideal team structure.

Chapter 2: First You and Then Them.   I explode the myth that more is better; only better is better. If you think you can hire a bunch of people and put your feet up, think again. This chapter goes deeply into how to improve your odds of success and how to use the four proven paths to increase production. Before you build a team, you must look honestly at yourself.

Chapter 3: What Is a Champion Team?   This chapter identifies your company's business vision. It examines the core values, core purpose, and envisioned future of your team. It also probes the six characteristics of Champion Teams, so that you can establish those attributes in your team.

Chapter 4: Three Steps to Building Your Ideal Team.   This chapter focuses you on developing written clarity for your long-term goals and team structure. You will select the most important positions, establish the order for hiring people to fill them, step clear of the hurdles, and take action on your plan.

Chapter 5: Designing the Positions and Hiring the Players.   Here I look each step of the hiring process, from the ads you run to attract applicants to interviews in person and over the phone. I also look at the trend toward family real estate businesses and how to make this work for all parties.

Chapter 6: I Hired Him—Now What?   You need to focus on training and monitoring both yourself and your team members. I share with you a checklist for training, to-do lists, meetings, telephone procedures, job responsibilities, communication strategies, and other such tools. This is a chapter that you will want to devour over and over.

Chapter 7: Expanding Your Sales Team.   In this chapter, I look at the potential sales or revenue-creating positions on your team. It covers the when, where, how, and who of hiring to increase sales. I also explain, in detail, how to establish a fair compensation structure for your sales team and yourself.

Chapter 8: Use Assessments to Improve Your Odds.   This chapter helps you to understand why large companies all use assessments to make better employee hires. You will learn solid assessment techniques and be given resources that you can use to increase the odds of success dramatically. For most teams, staff turnover is a huge expense.

Chapter 9: Hiring Buyer's Agents.   This chapter evaluates the use of buyer's agents, hiring practices for adding them to your team, and techniques of buyer's agents. I teach you the three key evaluations when hiring a buyer's agent. The chapter also covers the differences between and pros and cons of hiring new versus experienced agents as buyer's agents. When most agents think of a real estate team, they think of an agent who has buyer's agents. You won't want to miss this chapter.

Chapter 10: Training the Buyer's Agent.   Here I explore how to create an exceptionally performing and highly trained buyer's agent. Not only do I reveal the steps for training a buyer's agent, but I also help you avoid the biggest mistakes agents make when training buyer's agents.

Chapter 11: Set Performance Standards.   This chapter delves into establishing benchmarks, goals, and standards for your team. I give you systems and strategies for getting the best performance from each member of your team.

Chapter 12: Tried-and-True Lead-Generation Techniques.   This chapter takes a focused look at lead generation through ad calls, sign calls, and open houses. These should bring in significant amounts of revenue for a team, but they rarely do because the systems, scripts, and strategies of most teams are faulty. I give you the most advanced techniques to increase your conversion rate dramatically.

Chapter 13: Using Technology to Generate Leads.   The information in this chapter is based on years of using technology to increase lead volume in the teams I have coached. I share with you how to increase your leads through the Internet, interactive voice response, and voice broadcast media.

Chapter 14: Generate Leads through Live Events.   This chapter deals with the many types of live events you can hold to increase your leads. I coach you through buyer seminars, investment seminars, and client events (the most preferred type of event). You will also learn how to set an effective agenda and how to select the right affinity partners to help you deliver more value and defray some of the costs.

Chapter 15: Turning Leads into Dollars. Finally, in this chapter, I give you a master's degree in lead follow-up, lead categorization, and lead conversion. Learning to create more leads is easier than managing and converting leads well. You will learn the secrets of a Champion Team's high conversion ratios on leads.

Chapter 16: Effective Marketing Strategies for the Team. This chapter enables you to create a larger-than-life image for yourself and your team. Giving you these core marketing messages and techniques for positioning yourself as an expert will transform your business. Teaching you to evaluate your strengths, weaknesses, opportunities, and threats allows you to refine your marketing message to dominate the competition.

Chapter 17: Your Team Members Must Master the Telephone. Here I instruct you in mastering one of the most difficult challenges for any sales organization: the telephone. You will learn to demonstrate your value and the team's value within 10 seconds of your initial phone call.

Chapter 18: Building High-Performance Teams. This chapter reveals how to establish a "play to the limit" culture in your team. You will learn the difference between education, training, and coaching, so that you can increase your coaching and improve the results from your team. I coach you on how to coach your team members.

Without question, this book will become your premier resource for building your team or raising the performance of your team. You will find that you need to come back to it again and again to reharvest the knowledge contained inside it. It is designed to be a resource for your whole real estate career. Don't try to implement everything this week or even this year. There is too much. We are taking the first step toward building your Champion Team together. I promise you, I will coach you every step of the way through the written words of this book until you reach the Champion Level.

THE

Champion

REAL
ESTATE
TEAM™

PART I

CLOSING THE GAP BETWEEN CHAMPION AGENT AND CHAMPION TEAM

1

The Champion Team's Business

The buzzword in real estate today is *teams*. I see more agents trying to establish teams in their practices than ever before, and they are trying to create these teams much earlier in their careers. I even see marginally successful agents with less than one year in the business who are trying to attract others to work with them in that unstable environment. Because of this new "business plan *du jour*," I regularly see agents developing marketing materials and Web sites that give the illusion that the agent has a team. Many agents are using names like "The Joe Smith Home Selling Team" or www.joesmithteam.com to promote the idea that they are larger than life.

For too many people who are doing this, team building is premature. Many agents don't have the sales, marketing, leadership, and business skills to be successful, but are still trying to create teams. If your sales and lead generation are inconsistent, building a team will not solve your problems. If you don't have a powerful administrative assistant, hiring a bunch of inexperienced buyer's agents won't solve your revenue problem. In fact, it will make your revenue problem worse. The buyer's agents will divert your attention from the revenue-generating activities that you must do. You will end up spending much of your time helping the buyer's agents manage their transactions and shepherd them to closing. You will gain a portion of their production, but you will lose most of yours in order to do it. That certainly isn't the path to building a Champion Team.

The Birth of Real Estate Teams

The birth of real estate teams really occurred in the early 1990s. Agents were trying to leverage themselves through other people who could help them serve their clients better. To deal with some of the more repetitive activities of the business that generated little new revenue, administrative assistants were hired. A few years later, successful agents began to expand or leverage themselves by hiring sales assistants to work on the buyer side of the transaction. These successful agents had buyer's agents (or buyer's specialists) to handle the buyer side of the business, which is more labor-intensive.

I hired my first administrative assistant in 1991. I had no idea what I was doing, and neither did she. In those early days, there wasn't a blueprint to follow. Almost everyone, including me, learned the hard way—through trial and error. I messed up a lot, but eventually I figured it out. I created a mountain of success on top of piles of failure. Fortunately, you don't have to learn that way. You can be the beneficiary of my experience, allowing you to vastly reduce your mistakes. You have in your hands the blueprint or road map to greater success. Before you dive into creating your new team, however, I really believe you have to answer some key questions about yourself and your business:

1. Am I really prepared to lead people?
2. Do I have enough leads to support a team?
3. What size team do I see having five years from now?
4. What sales volume do I expect in five years?
5. Am I willing to increase my prospecting now?

The Pros and Cons of Having a Team

For most agents who are considering expanding their business by creating a team, the positives are easy to spot. It's easy to put on rose-colored glasses when evaluating the possibility of establishing a team.

One positive is certainly that you will have more people working to service your clients and prospects—even if you are just adding an administrative assistant. Your level of service with a well-trained, professional administrative assistant will be higher than a single agent can provide. All of the administrative functions, such as feedback from agent showings, sending copies of advertisements to sellers, and creating marketing flyers and brochures, can be done more quickly, better, and more efficiently with an assistant than by a single agent.

You will also be able to achieve a better balance between your business and your family time by leveraging yourself through a team. Being able to have weekends off for your family is a large benefit, in my view. I truly believe that my effectiveness as a sales-person and business owner was enhanced because I didn't work Friday, Saturday, or Sunday—as most agents did. I was able to be "on vacation" each weekend to enjoy the fruits of my labor with my wife, Joan. This would be even more important for me today, since I now have children to raise and enjoy.

As the lead agent, you will have a larger amount of time to invest in direct income-producing activities (DIPA). That's where most lead agents who are building teams fall off the path to success. They fail to increase their DIPA time to increase their revenue.

With a team, you gain the ability to delegate what I view as the worst aspect of real estate sales—dealing with the emotional roller-coaster ride that clients often take you on. This roller coaster of emotion can last through the entire listing process and requires hand-holding, extra service, and dealing with the high expectations of many clients. These clients are often on the razor's edge of emotion. We need to service them well, but their worst fears and problems can often send even the most seasoned, experienced agent into an activity funk. When you achieve a sale, you will often start back up the roller coaster again. Having a skilled team can protect you from these emotional swings, peaks, and valleys. A great team or a great assistant can help protect you from a client's challenges that could wipe you out and keep you from revenue-producing activities.

One trait of Champion Lead Agents is the ability to avoid being taken off the track toward their goals. The arrows of running a service-based business don't cause these agents to go down for the rest of the week or even the day.

The downside of developing a team is the inevitable trial and error that change creates. Even when you have a complete blueprint to success (as you have with this book), errors will occur. Change is a constant.

> **Coach's Tip:** *A champion is someone who, when he goes off track, doesn't allow that period of frustration or lack of focus and intensity to be more than a few minutes, rather than hours, days, or weeks.*

As I speak to, and coach, agents from around the world, one constant emerges. There is apprehension about the radical changes that are constantly going on around us. We have seen more changes in real estate in the last 5 years than we saw in the previous 35 years. We have seen massive consolidations. We have seen the strong influence of technology on our business, such as the Internet, stronger contact management software, and the advent of one-telephone-number systems that follow us everywhere. The changes have only begun. We need to embrace these changes and act upon them in the six inches between our ears. I think that R. D. Laing described this current time exceedingly well, even though he died in 1989. He said that we live in a moment of history where change has speeded up so much that we begin to see the present only when it is already disappearing.

Let me give you a few steps to help ease the process of change.

1. *Create your future.* Some people make the future; most people wait for the future to come to them.

   We have to create the future. If we are simply waiting for the phone calls of life, they will never come. We have to break down what we need to do each and every day in order to move up the mountain of success. Then we must go and do it. Too many of us are waiting for other people to lead us to success. We cannot afford to wait.

   > **Coach's Tip:** *The measure of a truly successful person is the ability to evaluate and to act decisively. Let me repeat that, so that it sinks in—the biggest waste of time in life is the period between the moment you know that a decision must be made and the moment when you finally make that decision and act on it.*

   Create your future by adhering to your daily business disciplines. These disciplines include prospecting, lead follow-up, listing appointments, showing property, writing, and negotiating contracts. If you carry out these activities, and if you are really diligent in prospecting and lead follow-up, you will always create the future you desire.

2. *Enhance change.* If you're not riding the wave of change, you'll find yourself beneath it. Spend time daily, weekly, and monthly evaluating and analyzing the change in the real estate industry. You need to invest time in understanding new technology that you can implement in your business. How effective are you in using your contact manager (i.e., Top Producer, On Line Agent, GoldMine, or ACT)? Do you have the ability to use these tools to their full capacity? Do you have a Web site that generates activity, or is your Web site just an electronic business card? You must spend time daily embracing and mastering the technology curve.

3. *Envision the future of your business and your life.* Invest time in planning for your eventual success. You have to have an idea of what the future will hold for you. You must create the target at which to take dead aim.

Walt Disney said, "The future is not the result of choices among alternative paths offered in the present. It is a place that is created—created first in the mind and the will, created next in the activity." Walt had the vision for Disneyland and Disney World long before they were built. When you look out ahead at your life and your real estate business, what do you see? If you see nothing, that's what you will get. If you have a sharp picture of the future and where you are going, that's what you will get. The first step is the picture. The next is to do the things that will make the picture a reality. Change is a major part of creating that picture; embrace it, enjoy it, and attack it. Implement the mindset of change, and you will implement a grand future.

There are certainly cons to hiring more people. The management, motivation, and coaching of staff is both a blessing and a curse. There is nothing more gratifying in life than assisting and guiding people in growth. There is also nothing more frustrating in life than assisting and guiding people in growth. The management challenges grow exponentially with each person you add to your team. Your skills as the leader, coach, and motivator need to grow as well.

If you hire talented people, your biggest challenge will be staying ahead of them in terms of your learning and skills. The most challenging aspect of my job is staying ahead of my staff, my clients, my coaches, and the real estate industry. It takes a tremendous expenditure of time, emotion, and energy to accomplish that.

Why Do You Want a Team?

The most important questions in life begin with *why*. Too many people get caught up in the how of reaching the goal. They spend little time focusing on the clarity of the why. Why we want something is clearly the power source. If the why is large enough, the how becomes easy. We often focus on the wrong end of the equation. Why do you want to be financially independent? Why do you want to build a real estate sales business to a large scale? Why do you want a team? Why does having a team connect with your life goals? What will a team provide for you?

I don't think there are hundreds of whys in our lives. I think there are a handful of whys that interconnect our goals and our dreams. This small handful of whys creates the power source in our life, enabling us to become a Champion Lead Agent, Champion Parent, or Champion Spouse and creating a Champion Legacy for our life.

Five Reasons Most Agents Want to Build a Team

Your individual reasons for wanting a team may not be among these top five. These are the reasons that I hear from agents most frequently when I ask them why they want to build a team. I have not listed them in order or frequency. I have merely selected the top five responses.

1. *To increase their income.* Increased income is achieved by increasing gross revenue. Many lead agents who are trying to build a team for the first time increase their gross revenue, but they often don't increase their net revenue. Agents want to expand their team in order to increase the number of dollars in their pocket, but most agents who are in the early stages of team building increase only their gross revenue. I personally have coached hundreds of agents who started to build a team before I began coaching them. When we

looked at the costs, revenues, time invested, and net profit of their first attempt at building a team, they netted less per month than when they were individual agents on their own.

2. *Quality of life.*   The desire to move from being an agent in demand to an agent in command is a great objective. Having a practice that allows you to control your schedule, so that you have more normal business hours, is a wonderful goal. Being an agent in demand who is at the beck and call of your clients and prospects doesn't make for a very good quality of life. Having to return calls and meet clients at night and on weekends will lead to burnout and family resentment for the career you have chosen.

Becoming an agent who is in command of his schedule, lead generation, client service systems, and accessibility is more easily done through the team format—that is, provided you have the skills, abilities, and systems at a reasonable level when building your individual agent's practice.

As the lead agent, you will need to train your other agents to command their value, schedule, servicing, and client interaction. The truth is, if the agents on your team already had those skills, they would not be interested in joining your team. They would be successful on their own.

3. *Stability of income.*   Agents often build teams to try to smooth out the swings in income that happen in the real estate business. They feel that if they had a few buyer's agents, their income would be more consistent from month to month. One of the battles for most agents is the feast or famine nature of their practice. They have a couple of stellar income months, followed by a couple of months with low income or no income. These income cycles make it difficult for most agents to control their cash flow, spending, and saving. They cause agents to overspend in the good months and have limited funds left for the bad months.

4. *Leverage.*   Having people working with you toward a common goal or common sales production creates leverage. The ability for sales to be made without your personal effort creates leverage.

_____

I remember my father, who was a dentist, always working to balance his time off with his practice needs and income needs. When we went to Hawaii as a family for a week to 10 days every Christmas, he didn't make any money. In fact, he lost money. There wasn't any drilling, filling, or billing taking place while he was gone. The fixed costs of the mortgage on his office building still needed to be paid, however. His staff still received their salaries, even when new revenue wasn't being created.

_____

Most individual agents still have overhead and expenses (both business and personal) to cover while they are away. A team will soften the net loss or even allow you to turn a small profit while you are resting and relaxing.

5. *The ability to do only what you want to do.*   This reason takes a number of different forms. The most prevalent is the "I don't have to prospect anymore" philosophy. Many lead agents want to build a team so that they don't ever have to prospect again. Too often, the things they want to delegate to others are the activities that they, quite frankly, need to continue to do.

Too often, these lead agents who are trying to build a team view the role of a team leader or the owner of a company as being able to put your feet up on your desk. My experience is that the owner of a well-run company is probably the hardest-working person in that company. If what you want to do is put your feet up, I would encourage you to rethink your philosophy. You may be able to pull back when you have refined your team to the Champion's edge. However, until then, you will have to be the hardest worker if your desire is to build a Champion Team.

What Price Are You Willing to Pay?

A Champion Lead Agent realizes that there is a price to be paid. Nothing comes to someone who has climbed to the Champion level that hasn't been earned or paid for. The pathway to becoming a Champion isn't a downhill path. You know you are on the path to becoming a Champion because it's uphill all the way.

Once you are a Champion Agent, the opportunities come more frequently and easily. Because you have arrived at the Champion level, everyone (buyers and sellers) wants to work for and work with you. Generally, in the real estate market, it costs the same to work with a marginal agent as it does to work with a Champion Agent or Champion Team.

We all want to be successful. I have never in my life met anyone who didn't want success. The question is: what are we willing to do to acquire it? Success does not care who acquires her. Success is available to anyone who is willing to pay the price that she requires. There are some examples we can all recognize where the price was a little less for some people than for others. I admit my good fortune in being the son of Norm and Becky Zeller, who lowered the price for me to achieve success because of the environment they provided, their philosophy, the work ethic they demonstrated, and the education they afforded me. All of those factors, and others, advanced me up the success ladder faster than others who didn't have the incredible model parents that I had. Nevertheless, I still had to pay a price for success. We all must come to grips with the fact that there is a price to be paid.

The price of being a Champion is measured in both time and resources. You must be willing to invest larger amounts of time than other agents in DIPA: prospecting, lead follow-up, buyer interview appointments and listing appointments, showing property, writing and negotiating contracts, and personal development.

Personal Development.   The edge for a Champion is created through the investment of personal development time. Champions have the passion and invest the time to improve their mindset, skills, and business systems. They invest their time in reading, seminars, training CDs, coaching, and any other form of personal development available. You will need to establish a culture on your team of personal learning and development.

═══════════════════

In 1996, when Joan and I completed our vacation home in Bend, my personal development time kicked into another gear. I had always read and studied success from my first day in real estate sales. I attended countless seminars and listened to countless tape series in the pursuit of success. Now I hit a new level of investment in personal development because I had a newfound freedom and a location away from the distractions of life and business where I could immerse myself in personal development time. I spent many evenings in the library in that home in front of the fireplace with Joan, both of us in our leather wingback chairs devouring a good book—mine usually on business, sales, leadership, management, or finance.

═══════════════════

Now, I must admit that, with a five-year-old son, Wesley, and a two-year-old daughter, Annabelle, the challenge of carving out enough personal development time to continue to grow and stay ahead of our clients and competition is greater than ever. A Champion is willing to stay up late or get up early when the house is quiet to stay at the top of her game.

Because of the competitive nature of business, whatever brought you to the level of success you have reached today will not be enough to keep you there. To maintain your level of success, you must learn, advance, and grow. The members of your team must have the same philosophy. The competition will always get better. The marketplace will always be adjusting. If you don't have a passion for learning and improving, you'd better get one fast. If you have to study and learn just to keep pace, imagine what you must do in order to grow, expand, and get ahead. To grow, you must spend at least an hour a day on your personal development.

Most agents invest too little in their personal development; that causes their team members to be deficient as well. Think of books, CD series, teleseminars, online seminars, and coaching as buying or investing in new equipment for your company. That new equipment will help you make sales in larger quantities, faster, and more efficiently than ever before. Your investment in personal development will pay the largest dividend in your business—larger than a new computer, new marketing strategy, new Web site, or anything else.

There is another area that I have identified where lack of investment is a huge limitation and a barrier to massive success for most agents and their teams in the real estate business. Until this lack is overcome, all the other changes, adjustments, and gyrations will have limited results. This area is sales skills!

Too many agents, even those who are trying to build teams, have invested little time in improving their individual sales skills. New agents coming out of sales careers where they have received exceptional fundamental sales training earn a large income early in their careers. For most agents, there is a direct correlation between sales skills and gross commissions. A true Champion Lead Agent has impeccable sales skills. Now, before you assume that you're in that category, let's make an honest evaluation of your real sales skills.

How good are your scripts and dialogues for generating leads and driving those leads to appointments? What are your conversion ratios? How strong is your listing presentation, especially when you are competing against a good agent? How long is your presentation: are you there for over an hour? Can you get the buyer to come into your office for a consultation? Does the buyer sign the agency contract every time after your consultation? How are you at responding to objections in sales? Can you clearly convey the benefits of doing business with you? Is your 30-second elevator speech dialed? Do you really close on the client at the end of every presentation, or do you wait for clients to close themselves?

One of the key areas in which you invest your time needs to be sales skills development. I have met too many agents who are somewhat successful or even moderately successful, but whose sales skills are atrocious. You will also need to invest large amounts of time in developing the sales skills of your team members. This is clearly one segment of the price one must pay to be a Champion Lead Agent who has a Champion Team.

Prospect Consistency. It doesn't take a Champion to prospect and look for business when she is broke. Anyone (even a poor performer) does a little prospecting when she is broke and has no listings or sales or good leads that can be converted to dollars soon. True Champions prospect consistently, even when they are busy. They find the time and structure it, rather than make the time each day to generate new leads. You have to invest your time resources to create more revenue and success. A Champion Team Leader mandates that all of her sales assistants prospect consistently. She monitors and manages those prospecting standards in terms of contacts, leads, appointments, and conversion ratios.

The real question is: are you willing to pay the price? Deep down inside, you know some of what you need to do. The question is: are you willing to do it? Are you willing to invest the time, energy, emotion, and money to become a Champion Lead Agent? Are your people willing to invest with you—side by side—to become Champions as well?

> **Champion Rule:**   *A Champion is ready and willing to make the sacrifice that is necessary.*

The challenge for most people climbing the ladder of success to become a Champion Team Leader is knowing when and how much sacrifice is necessary. The key is making the right amount of sacrifice needed for the situation. Too often, agents who want to build a team expect to give up too much. I was speaking with an agent the other day who wanted to be one of the top agents in his marketplace. Based on his comments, I realized that he thought the only path to real estate sales success was being a workaholic. As we spoke further, he began to understand there were better avenues to success than a 70-hour work-week; that he could achieve a large, successful sales practice by putting forth the effort of sacrifice plus a little bit more.

I don't believe people need to work 70-hour weeks to achieve success. Doing so only demonstrates how inefficient they are in the use of their time. It also indicates a lack of the skills that create revenue. Conversely, I do not believe that people achieve wealth and success by working a typical 40-hour week, as most workers do. I know that to achieve success and wealth and quality of life, you have to sacrifice by putting in a little more effort than the next guy. Once you have increased your skill to the Champion's level, you can go well below a 40-hour workweek and still earn a large income. It's the climb up the success mountain that too many people either don't give enough or give too much to. In terms of working hours, if you are in a growth stage of your business, I believe around 50 hours a week is required.

Too many of us stop short of what is needed. Because we have allocated fewer resources than are required, our results are guaranteed to fall short of our expectations. Others sacrifice more than is needed, which is a waste of resources. You can kill a fly with a bomb, but that really takes more sacrifice, resources, and power than is necessary. The question is, are you currently making the right amount of sacrifice to be a Champion Lead Agent and to be prepared to build a Champion Team?

It's Easy to Get Faked Out

To be a Champion Lead Agent, you have to be focused on the facts and on reality. A Champion Lead Agent is willing to search for the truth concerning his skills, the marketplace, and his results, and to evaluate this with a keen eye.

The real estate business can be a big show. It is often the big show of egos and gross income. As an agent who is trying to achieve Champion-level performance, you can be easily swayed by other agents who have "made it." I want to share a word of caution, so that you avoid the mistakes of others.

Rule 1.   *If it seems too good to be true, it usually is.* Easy-money marketing strategies, easy lead generation, building a large team, and heading to the beach to sip mai tais—there are many trainers and agents who profess philosophies contrary to the laws of success in life. Tread carefully, because you might achieve what they have in life, and you might not want it.

It's easy to project a larger-than-life image through overspending, not paying your taxes, and borrowing money. It's easy to always talk about gross commission income and sales volume and winning awards based on those factors. In real estate sales, awards and recognition are given to people on the basis of their sales volume and income, not the quality of their business, their service to clients, or their net profit after expenses. I know of an agent team that is among the top five agents in the country for a large national firm, but this team discounts its commissions heavily. Would all the agents who respect this team for its sales volume feel the same way if they really knew how the team acquired the business?

Check the claims, look under the hood, and evaluate your options carefully. Following someone who gives the appearance of having found the "secret to success," or who claims to have developed a system that allows success to be achieved easily without work, will eventually lead you to destruction. You will fall far short of the Champion level of success in your business.

Rule 2.   *Objects in the mirror may appear closer than they actually are.* Because of the egos, the recognition that all agents want, and the rewards of real estate sales, it is easy to assume that someone is doing well when in fact she often is not. We see agents who dress well, drive fancy cars, and live in large houses, giving the appearance of wealth and success. This doesn't mean they are Champion Agents. The fact that someone has a large team of assistants and large sales numbers doesn't mean that she is a Champion Lead Agent.

The truth is, unpaid taxes, poor fiscal management, and living beyond one's means, both in business and in one's personal life, can make bankruptcy appear in the mirror, rather than financial independence.

Just because someone is on the superstar agent panel doesn't mean that she has a profitable business model. Nor does it mean that she understands how she generates her leads; where her transactions, leads, appointments, and commission income come from; what she's spending on marketing; and what marketing really works and the return on investment for it.

I recently began working with a lead agent of a team who had bought a moving truck to supply to his clients. I asked him why he had done it. He said proudly that he had done it because the truck would bring him business and referrals. I asked him how he was going to track the cost versus return. How many transactions did he need to do annually to cover the payments, insurance, gas, maintenance, cleaning, and equipment for the moving van? How much of his time or his staff's time would it take to manage, organize, and oversee the use of the moving van? The truth is, before I asked these valid business questions, I knew that he had no idea how to answer any of them—and he didn't.

He finally admitted that he had heard about this tactic from a "very successful" agent and thought it was a great idea. What a great way to get his name out there and promote himself! He was swayed by a big show that drew him into thinking that, with limited work and some expense, he could generate tons of leads. What he really got was an extra expense, an administrative nightmare, and increased liability with a low return on investment. He also got his name and face plastered on the side of a panel moving van to feed his ego.

Studies have shown that most people will do almost anything for recognition. For most people, being recognized or getting their ego stroked is more important than income. This type of ego can also lead agents to try to build teams. Many do so because they are falling below production recognition levels in their company. They are not getting the top sales awards because others have significantly more staff and assistants.

I have told hundreds of thousands of agents this truth: "You can build your business for income or build it for your ego, but you can't do both at the same time." You must choose which is most important to you. You must choose which is going to be the driving factor enabling you to play at the Champion level in your business.

Consciously or unconsciously, we are choosing one of those paths, ego or income, every time we invest in marketing, select clients to work with, invest in our business, invest our time, expand our lead generation, and change our sales or presentation process.

Does your ego drive you and your business, or are they driven by your desire for a certain income level or net profit level? Which one of those controls your thinking, your actions, and your decision making for a greater percentage of the time? The answer to this question will really determine your net profit, the personal time you invest in the business, and the quality of life for you and your family. Most agents never come to grips with this challenge and can't move beyond it—to be a Champion.

Big Teams Do Not Always Mean Big Money

A number of years ago, I was speaking to a high-powered group of agents in Houston, Texas. I was sharing with them the seven key numbers in a real estate agent's practice that the agent must monitor, watch, evaluate, and, in most cases, change. These seven numbers, because I controlled them well, enabled me to sell over 150 homes annually while working only Monday through Thursday and taking Friday, Saturday, and Sunday off. I didn't answer the phone, fax, or e-mail on those days. I was off with my family. In fact, for most of those days, I was a three-hour drive away at my vacation home. These numbers allowed me to build a business with a high net profit where I netted well over 60 percent of the gross revenue I created each year. You don't need to gross $2,400,000 in revenue to net over a million dollars in profit, as some experts will try to convince you. A Champion will cast an evaluating eye on that model.

While I was coaching this group of agents on these seven key numbers, I was sharing with them the idea that most agents know nothing about these numbers. This is also true for lead agents who either are working to build large teams or already have large teams. They also have these seven numbers way out of alignment. The reality is, they have these numbers so far out of alignment that the net profit is poor. This is especially true for many agents with "superstar" status in real estate. They achieve large gross incomes but low net profit numbers, and they often live, spend, and have a lifestyle as if their gross income were their net income.

I was on a superstar panel in the 1990s where a prominent agent (one of the first to break the million dollar a year gross commission income barrier), who is now a speaker, admitted (after getting off the stage and getting real) that he was broke. He had nothing to show for the million-dollar gross income he had earned that year. I can assure you that he wasn't projecting the image of being broke on the stage.

As I shared these concepts and stories in Houston that day, a beautiful blonde lady in back stood up. She was the "perfect Realtor." You can easily picture her clean, professional suit and the diamonds dripping off her fingers, wrist, and neck. She had the brooch as well as the hat. She graciously raised her hand to make a statement that I will never forget. She said, "Excuse me, Dirk. We have a saying for that type of person here in Texas. We call them 'Big Hat… …No Cattle.'" She described the truth perfectly for many superstar agents or lead agents of large teams. They are often big hat… no cattle. I want to state emphatically that building a Champion Team is the way to go in the real estate business. The problem is that so few agents who have large teams currently know what steps to take and the order in which to take them. Too many are left with a business that is worse or only marginally better than before.

Coaching Tip: *Focus on quality rather than quantity when considering the size of your team. Focus on potential productivity, profitability, and sustainability, so you can build a scaleable and then sellable practice.*

A Champion Lead Agent recognizes that the truth about your income, your earnings, and the quality of your business is contained on line 32 of your 1040. The Champion's score isn't measured by gross income, production awards, sales volume, number of assistants, or name recognition. You can achieve a number of those outcomes, especially the production awards, because you have a larger number of bodies on your team than the next guy. One of the key measures of the effectiveness of your team is to divide the units of production by the number of people on the team. What is the per-staff-member production of the team? What is the per-sales-team or per-agent average production? If you are producing less than 20 units per staff member, your efficiency is pretty low. If your per-agent average is less than 30 units, you are not getting the proper efficiency from your salespeople and yourself. You should be pulling that 30-per-agent average up with your unit production. A champion's score, when we are talking about money, is measured by his tax return, specifically line 32 of the 1040 form. Line 32 is your adjusted gross income (AGI). This is the number that you have to live on, save, invest, and spend. It's the number that any bank will look at to determine whether to lend you money for the investment property that all of us in real estate want to buy to build our net worth.

Reality is found on line 32. Jack Welch, the former CEO of GE, has six famous rules for business success. The first is to face reality as it is, not as you wish it to be. Too often, we hedge, adjust, evade, and concoct a new reality that is more optimistic than reality is. Champion Lead Agents don't concoct new, false realities to make themselves feel better. They deal with the truth and change the outcome. There is nothing more based in reality, with regard to earned income, than line 32 of your tax return. Nothing is more black and white with regard to earnings than line 32.

A Champion Lead Agent's scorecard encompasses far more than just money. The reason I started with the money is that this is what we generally recognize in real estate sales circles. It is also easy to count and see how we are doing. When evaluating the other areas of life, the results are more difficult to observe and gauge.

The most challenging and certainly the most meaningful area of development and growth is the relationships in your life: investing the time to have vibrant relationships with your spouse or significant other, your children, your parents, and your friends. One advantage that the business and income of a Champion Lead Agent provide is the opportunity to earn more in less time, so that you have additional time to invest in life's more meaningful pursuits. If you are to become a Champion Performer, balancing career, money, family, health, and spiritual areas of life must be your aim. You don't have to be a Champion to earn a large income and bankrupt the other areas of your life while doing so. I am not greatly impressed by people who do. It doesn't take any particular skill to work too many hours, earn a large income, and blow up your family in the process. You get an A for income and an F for family. Your GPA is a C or less.

Seven Questions to Ask to Determine the Right Size Team for You

You must be willing to get out of the answers and into the questions. You have to really know the size and scope of the team you need before you hire the first member of that team. That doesn't mean that you won't make some changes or adjustments along the way. It only means that you must be proactive, not reactive, in your planning and your strategy.

1. *How much do you want to sell in units and sales volume as a team and individually?* The key is really transaction units. To me, what makes a Champion Team's business is an annual increase in unit volume. Did you grow the number of units sold in a year by 20, 30, or 40 percent? You can increase sales volume by raising your average sales price more easily as an individual agent than you can by building a team from the ground up.

   A Champion Team has the goals and objectives of raising units sold as well as sales price. As an individual agent, you might be at capacity in terms of number of units sold, or at least at the point of diminishing returns. For a team, a focus on increasing the number of units sold yields more income stability and greater referral value in the future.

2. *What does your business look like in five years?* Being able to envision your production, sales volume, percentage of revenue from buyers and sellers, transaction units, sources of leads, conversion rate of leads, and net profit goals will help you achieve a clearer picture of the size of the team you need. It will allow you to build a team to a fixed point of reference in the future. Then you can create a plan of action points and strategic steps to arrive at your desired result.

3. *How long do you plan on being a real estate agent?* You might not want to waste a lot of energy and mistakes in building a large team if your answer is a few years (fewer than five). You would be better served by being lean and mean in your size and approach. Establishing a team of one or two administrative people with a buyer's agent

or two would take you a few years. The extra effort and risk might not provide a large enough return. Your time would be better invested in deepening your relationships with your past clients and working to generate more referrals and higher-quality referrals out of your database. Investing your time in readying your business for sale would be the highest and best use of that time.

4. *Do you have other business interests, either now or in the future?* I fell squarely into this category. I am often asked, "Why did you stop growing your business at 150 units per year?" It was because I had other business interests. I was faced with the fact that in order to go beyond 150 units, I would need to add additional staff, refine my systems, do further marketing, and either train and educate or hire someone who could manage the whole sales operation at its increased size. There were really a number of evaluations, challenges, and problems that would need to be addressed in order to achieve additional growth. I wasn't willing to take on new risk, reduce my net profit in the short run, and invest more of my time.

    For me, it was really a business and life decision: how did I want to spend some discretionary time that I had acquired through the proper care and execution of my business plan? I chose to select two areas that I was interested in, and that I felt would be far more lucrative for myself and my family in the long run than adding another 50 or 100 units of production. I invested more of my time in land development, home building (Joan had a construction company), and building investment property for our personal portfolio. I am not saying that not growing beyond a certain point would be the right decision for you. It was the right one for me and my family.

5. *Where do you see your income coming from in 10 years?* Is it from sales commissions earned by you and your team? Is it from owning a brokerage business where you are the broker/owner with 20 agents, 200 agents, or 2,000 agents working for you? Is it from investment properties? If it's from a combination of these, what percentage comes from each source?

    Each of us has a limited amount of energy that he can invest daily, weekly, monthly, and annually. For you, what creates the greatest return in personal satisfaction and income based on your goals, your desires, and how you are wired?

6. *What's the size of your marketplace?* If your marketplace is on the small side, you building a large team will be challenging. You will have to acquire a large segment of the marketplace. In a small town of, say, 75,000 people, unless it's a resort area, building a large team would require you to own 30 percent of the sales that happen annually in that small marketplace. For an individual team to own 30 percent of the marketplace is a rare occurrence. I have a few clients who have achieved this in small markets, but it has been a challenge at each step. They could have achieved the same number of units far more easily in a larger marketplace.

The advantage when they got there was that they knew that no one would ever be able to take it away from them. No one will be willing to work as hard as they did to get there. It also makes their practice more valuable at the time of sale.

7. *Are you a good teacher, manager, and coach?*   Being a great leader and coach is more important than being a good manager. Competent managers are really a dime a dozen. A good leader is truly priceless.

> *Do people work with passion for your vision of success?*
> *Are you able to hold people accountable to standards and set actions?*
> *Do you have the ability to stay calm when the entire world is falling apart?*
> *Are you willing to correct wrong thinking, behaviors, and actions?*
> *Are you able to encourage others to raise their performance?*

Ensure Your Success

There are as many models, trainers, and philosophies of how to be successful in real estate as there are people. Each one of these people, including myself, has strong beliefs concerning the path that one must take in order to be successful. The truth is, there isn't just one pathway to achieving success in real estate sales. There isn't one way to build a team. There are a number of ways to prosper in the business. That is one of the exciting aspects of real estate sales. If anyone (agent, trainer, manager, or sales guru) tells you that her way is the only way, run in the other direction.

The real question is: what will be your way? There is a right model or right pathway for you to use to build your team based on your experience, database size, market, commitment level, behavioral style, sales skills, and competitive nature. The way to ensure your success is to evaluate yourself based on the factors I just listed and build your business and your team in a complementary way.

For example, for the last eight years, we have been the leader in behavior assessments in the real estate industry. Through working with thousands of agents and benchmarking their behavioral style, we have discovered patterns for how people with different behavior styles can build a business that is effective and comfortable for them. Not everyone should call for sale by owners (FSBOs) and expired listings, as some trainers profess. In fact, there are a few behavioral styles whose success rate in prospecting to those sources is so dismal that trying to do so would be counterproductive. There are other behavioral styles that are so competitive and focused that they struggle to create referral-based relationships even after they have gone to numerous seminars to learn referral techniques. Some agents sell more effectively when they use facts and figures, while others use emotional connection and emotional techniques.

Being able to build your business around your natural gifts and the natural skills that were given to you at birth and that you have spent years perfecting is the mark of a Champion. Using behavioral analysis to select, manage, train, structure, coach, and position team members will strengthen any team. If you want to learn more about yourself and your team, go to www.RealEstateChampions.com/FreeDISC and take a free assessment that will reveal how you are wired for success.

Establish Your System

The way to ensure your success is to find your system, strategy, tactics, and lead generation and conversion sources. Too many lead agents and teams are looking for an off-the-rack solution in a tailor-fit world. We need to be willing to pause—to evaluate, research, and design the right long-term solution. We need to design the right team. Anyone can do something that he finds incongruent with his behavioral style for a short period of time, especially if he is broke. You can get staff members to do jobs that are incongruent with their behavioral skills for that short time frame. However, if you expect them to completely transform themselves, they will eventually leave or be asked to leave. The problem is that this type of behavior is not sustainable. When we have made enough money or feel comfortable, we stop doing activities we don't want to.

Searching for your system and attempting to perfect that system will ensure your success. You still need to attend seminars and training, listen to CDs, read books, and participate in coaching. If you work with a coaching company that is focused on helping you uncover your system, rather than forcing you into its system, you have a higher probability of long-term success once the coaching is completed. There is no one system or one way to be successful in the real estate sales business.

Choose Your Lead Source

The second step to ensure your success happens once you have made the best decision on how you are going to generate leads. For example, will you get them from past clients; your sphere of influence; strategic alliances with other professionals like accountants, financial planners, and family law attorneys; community involvement; FSBOs; expireds; or bank real estate owned (REO) properties? There are unlimited sources to choose from. Once you have made a final decision, stick with it. A Champion Lead Agent tests new strategies for a long enough period of time to modify them a few times and test and monitor all of the results. A huge error that I see most agents make is the error of impatience. They change strategies and tactics so quickly that they never get past the steepest part of the learning curve. They are moving from one ice mountain to the next, trying to find the secret path to the top. It isn't there; you have to climb to the top.

Most agents try a farm for three to four months, don't get any business, and scrap the farm. They try sending a new newsletter to their past clients and sphere of influence for three to four months and decide that doesn't work. They will call FSBOs or expireds for a few weeks, not achieve the result level they want, and stop that practice. In order to know whether something new that you are trying works, you have to try it for at least six months. It takes that long to gauge the return on investment. It takes that long to tweak and perfect the strategy. You won't get all the facts you need to make an informed decision on whether the strategy works or not in less than a six-month period of time.

Don't Lose Your Sales Focus

When I think of a Champion Lead Agent, I think of a Champion Salesperson—someone who understands, accepts, and embraces the fact that sales and sales skills are the name of the game. The essence of selling in real estate is to create leads that you convert to clients and then to commission checks.

I often ask agents, "If you had to choose to be exceptional in one of two areas of your business, and those two areas were creating clients and keeping clients, which one would you choose?" More than 75 percent of them will tell me keeping clients. Before I go any further, I want to state clearly that I think you have to do both well to have a Champion Team. You have to be able to both create and serve clients successfully. However, the question was worded "if you could do only one" for a reason. One of these alternatives is really a sales function: creating clients. The other is customer service: keeping clients.

Most lead agents select the wrong one when given the choice between the two. The correct answer is creating clients. Again, I am not advocating such a narrow-minded approach, but we do need to establish priorities as businesspeople. We need to work on the strategic skills that will create the greatest return for us. The truth is, you won't have anyone to serve if you aren't able to create clients with regularity and consistency. You can't serve clients if you don't create clients in the first place. Client service excellence is the direct result of a client's service experience, so client creation is a necessary prerequisite to outstanding client service.

Client creation is harder than client servicing. It requires sales skills, consistency, and persistent prospecting for clients. You must acquire a level of sales skill and confidence that enables you to pick up the phone, call people you know and people you don't know, and ask them for the opportunity to do business with them. You need to be able to train that level of competence and confidence to all of your sales staff as well. You also need to develop and train the skills of asking your clients to refer you to others who might benefit from your service. Selling is really the name of the game.

CHAPTER

2

First You and Then Them

There has been a big push in the real estate industry for agents to establish teams. The number of agents using listing coordinators, transaction coordinators, marketing coordinators, runners, buyer's agents, and listing agents has increased dramatically in the last few years.

I was one of the first agents in my sales area of Portland, Oregon, to elicit the help of assistants to build a larger, better practice. I hired my first assistant before I had completed my first year in real estate sales. I added more administrative help, and more sales help in the form of buyer's agents, in my second full year in the business. I speak from experience, having made a tremendous number of mistakes in hiring, firing, accountability, time management, organization, structure, implementation, and systems development in those early years. Building a great team takes much more than hiring a few people. It takes much more than hiring great people. The initial step starts with you.

Having coached and trained hundreds of thousands of agents (thousands of whom had teams), I have found that even the most successful agents do not approach establishing a team by taking the right steps in the proper order. To achieve lasting success in business, it's not enough to know the steps that you need to take. Taking the right steps in the wrong order will lead to disaster. You may be able to fend off the looming catastrophe longer, but it will come soon enough. Similarly, taking the wrong steps in the right order will also send you crashing to the rocks. The combination of the correct steps and the correct order is the only way to avoid disaster.

Your Success... It's Up to You

Having a team will not make up for deficiencies in your core skills. The core skills in real estate are time management, prospecting, sales skills, qualifying, presentation skills for buyers and sellers, objection-handling skills, and closing skills. On a larger scale, those skills that are directly linked to lead creation, lead conversion, and prospect commitment must be at the Champion Agent level before you can even hope to build a Champion Team. You will rarely be able to hire people who already possess these skills. You will have to instill and train these skills in the people you hire.

Coaching Tip: *Your personal productivity is the engine that drives the train in your team's success. Do not let any team member, circumstance, singular transaction, problem client, or competitive agent affect that fact.*

When building a team, most agents let their direct income-producing activities (DIPA) slide. DIPA are prospecting, lead follow-up, listing appointments, buyer interviews, showing property, writing and negotiating contracts, and even personal development. All of these activities are directly connected to income. That's why they are DIPA. Most agents, when they establish a team, have a tendency to reduce the number of hours they invest in DIPA. The areas of DIPA that get hit hardest are prospecting and lead follow-up. Many agents, when they bring on staff to expand their team, cease carrying out these two activities.

There are two core reasons why prospecting and lead follow-up drop heavily when an agent is establishing or expanding her team. The first is that the agent wants the team to prospect and do the lead follow-up for her. She wants the team members to do these things so that she doesn't have to—ever again. Too many agents want to have a team so that they can avoid prospecting. That is the wrong reason to create a team-based business. If you manage to hire someone who is exceptional at prospecting, it won't take long before he figures out how to go out on his own. He can easily calculate how much money he is bringing into the team. When the number gets large enough for him to feel that he can make more on his own because he knows how to generate leads, he will move down the road or across the hall and become your newest competition, with inside information about you and your business. You can't stop prospecting. In fact, you may have to increase your prospecting time so that you can increase your volume of leads to ensure that you have the cash flow to help capitalize your new or growing team.

The second core reason why prospecting and lead follow-up drop is that the agent has a new focus on systems development and increased management responsibilities. Now that you are adding staff, whether these people are administrative or sales producing, you need to devote some of your time to monitoring, managing, and coaching them. You will also need to establish checklists, task and priority lists, job descriptions, and many other items that fall under the buzzword of systems. If only we could just download all the skills, knowledge, and information we have acquired in the business to new staff members in minutes by connecting a cable between our brains and hitting the download button.

Better Is Better—More Is *Not* Better

Too many agents have the view, which is driven by their ego, that the larger the team, the better. Bigger doesn't mean better. With every person you add to the team, you increase the management and monitoring required, personal problems that come to work, interstaff politics, distractions, and disruptions. My grandmother, Bobbi, had a saying about productivity and people that I must have heard a thousand times. It was, "At work, one boy is a whole boy, two boys are a half, and three boys are no boys at all." If you focus only on the volume of people or the size of the team, you can end up with no team at all.

Adding administrative staff members must enable you to provide your clients with a higher level of service that they can recognize and appreciate. With the right consistent prospecting and marketing approach, this can lead to an increase in referrals as well. Adding staff members such as buyer's agents and listing agents should directly increase revenue because these people are salespeople. Overall, the added staff members should create a better quality of life for you. You are able to relinquish lower-value activities, increase your time off and frequency of vacations, and make it to more t-ball games and date nights. However you define quality of life, it is improved.

Having more of anything in life just for the sake of having more doesn't lead to success. If you have a poor business model with a low volume of leads, adding more staff will only bring your poor business model and lead deficiencies to light faster. A person who is a jerk who acquires more money only becomes more of a jerk, as the increased options her money affords her give her more opportunities to show off her true nature.

What Is Your Primary Job?

I often ask agents, "If you had to segment your business into two sections, what would they be?" Most of them initially want to negotiate for more segments. They don't want to look at their business in such black-and-white terms. Here are the two sections that I feel the business breaks up into: creating customers and servicing customers. Those are the two major functions in a sales business. I then ask, "If you had the option of being exceptional in only one of these areas, which one would you choose?" Many agents, again, really don't want to look at the option of being excellent in only one. One of the marks of a Champion Agent or a Champion Team is excellence in both. I would contend that few agents and few teams achieve this. When confronted with this tough decision, most agents would rather achieve excellence in customer service. They feel that this is the pathway to a growing, sustainable business.

In my many years in real estate sales and real estate training and coaching, I have encountered few agents who reach the upper echelon of real estate sales with an exclusive focus on customer service. Before you jump to conclusions concerning my viewpoint, let me remind you that it is essential that you excel at both customer creation and customer service in order to become a Champion Agent or the leader of a Champion Team. However, while you are trying to climb the mountain of success, one of these disciplines will be secondary to the other. Your investment of time and energy will be greater in one than in the other. Your staff will pick up on your signals regarding which discipline is more important to you, and will adopt that prioritization as well. The decisions you make in this one area will determine how quickly you execute your success plan.

In terms of earnings and income, I have met many agents who earn large sums of money who are world-class at client creation and downright poor at customer service. While these agents don't generate the referrals they should because of their lack of customer service, they have developed viable businesses because of their top-notch skills in client creation. Again, I want to emphasize that this is not the ideal platform for success. Still, it is better than a limited focus exclusively on customer service. In the end, you must achieve a balance between these two areas. While climbing the ladder of success, however, your focus must be tilted toward customer creation.

I have used the phrase "customer creation" to wrap up the real word in a fancy wrapper to make it more palatable. It's like the exterior coating they put on aspirin, so that it doesn't upset our stomachs as much. Let me peel off the coating and call customer creation what it really is: prospecting.

As the leader of the team, your primary job is to be a Champion example, to be the model that all the members of your administrative and sales staff will follow. You need to set the example by prospecting on a daily basis. Let's have a real moment of truth in our relationship. The truth is, you are in sales, right? Sales is a profession where we have to find prospects to whom we sell our services.

Coaching Tip: Prospecting is the first step in the sales process. You are in sales; you need to prospect. You must decide and commit to the course of prospecting for your whole career. You must also establish a culture of prospecting for your team to have success.

If you don't prospect, you won't find prospects. If you don't find prospects, you won't be able to make presentations to prospects to create customers. If you don't have customers, there won't be anyone for you to serve. You won't be able to deliver exceptional service, so you won't be able to create clients. These clients you don't have won't be able to send you referrals so that you can acquire new prospects more easily.

We really have an unlimited supply of areas where we can prospect. Webster defines prospecting as "seeking a potential customer; seeking with a vision of success." This definition doesn't say waiting for the phone to ring, sending out postcards, or hoping someone calls you. It clearly says that prospecting is a seeking activity. Let me share a guarantee from ancient scripture: "Seek, and you shall find." The guarantee is that if you seek, you will find. I hear all the time from people, "Well, what if it doesn't work?" You can be assured that it will work because seekers become finders.

The second element of this definition says that we need to seek "with a vision of success." Webster must have worked in a real estate office. He knows how other agents can try to pull you down or away from prospecting. You may even have brokers who try to belittle you because of your prospecting. Webster was saying, get your mind to positive, expect good results; focus on that, and you will succeed. Don't let others negatively influence your vision of success.

The quandary isn't whether you should or shouldn't prospect. It's what method you should use and how much prospecting you need to do each day to achieve your sales, income, and net profit goals. What standard do you need to set for your team? What sources do you need to invest your time in prospecting? What sources are most effective based on the conditions in your market? What source creates the greatest short-term revenue? What source creates the most significant long-term revenue? These are all questions that you need to ask before you begin the disciplined process of prospecting.

List on Purpose; Make Sales by Accident

The focus of the lead agent's prospecting should be on generating listing prospects. You are not in the business of generating just any old lead. As the lead agent of a Champion Team, your focus must be on listings. The buyer's agents can generate buyer leads with the right system. They will even generate listing leads occasionally. Your time, energy, and focus must be devoted to generating and converting listing prospects.

The best way to ensure your buyer's agents' success is to have a large inventory of listings. Buyer's agents often starve and fail because the lead agent didn't establish a large enough listing inventory. Listings will always have an unfair power to create exponential business through ad calls, sign calls, open house opportunities, Internet leads, call capture opportunities, and many other passive sources of lead generation. Some of these will happen magically while you and your team are asleep in your beds. *You have to list on purpose.*

The selling by accident part of this section heading means just that—you will sell other homes by accident. You may even sell the homes you have listed by accident through another agent, yourself, or your team. When I am coaching one of my Champion Agent clients, I really focus on the number of listings that the client needs to take that month and that quarter. Since we create such a complete business plan for the client's year, we clearly know the benchmarks for each month and quarter. When an agent fall behind on the number of listings sold, it bothers her more than it bothers me. As long as she continues to secure the number of new listings per month that her plan requires, and prices them competitively, the sales will come.

Most markets will experience four to five major sales spurts during the course of the year. These sales spurts usually cannot be predicted; they just happen. As a lead agent, your objective is to develop a bank of listings that will enable you to take advantage of these sales spurts and still have some inventory after each spurt is over. You will know that you are in a spurt when showings increase rapidly, you start to receive offers, and the urgency of the buyers seems to have increased.

If you have only a handful of listings (e.g., fewer than five), you could come out of the spurt with five sales but no inventory of listings to generate leads from in the future. If you are behind in listings sold for the year, don't panic until you look at your active listing inventory. If you are on track toward your goal in listings taken, sometimes all you will need to do is wait. All this assumes that your listings are the best-priced inventory (with the best value) in the marketplace. If you don't have the best price and the best value, the upcoming spurt will influence your sales to a lesser degree. You must reposition the properties in terms of pricing to take advantage of the next spurt.

The Greatest Leverage in Real Estate

There is a growing belief that having a large team of producing agents under you gives you the best leverage in the business. There are more agents today than ever before who are trying to create their leverage through people. While I agree that this approach is valid, you must ask yourself some important questions. Are you personally ready to build and use that team? Most importantly, have you used the easiest and greatest form of leverage in real estate before you start exploring people leverage?

The greatest, easiest, and most profitable leverage in real estate sales comes from becoming a listing agent. Too many of us are not using this leverage to establish the foundation for our success. We are getting drawn into the more-people-bigger-team mentality before we dominate as listing agents. Once you have the skills and production of a Champion Listing Agent, you can build a team of producing agents more easily.

Being a Champion Listing Agent spawns opportunities that offer new risks and high rewards. As a Champion Listing Agent, you will enjoy these benefits:

1. *Gain leverage by employing numerous people to work for you at no cost.*   How many licensed agents are in your Board of Realtors? That will be the number of people you will be employing to sell your inventory each day. The best part is that having all of these people working for you costs you nothing! There are no wages, withholdings, taxes, insurance, workers' comp., or equipment changes (telephone, desks, and office supplies). There are no expenses of any kind. Now, I know that many of you are saying that the company covers all that for the buyer's agents who work for you. That may be true, but you still have to manage these people and deal with their personal problems,

their mistakes, their low motivation at times, and interpersonal office politics. All of those things still need to be controlled and managed, and you need to exert leadership to produce a result.

If you focus on being a great listing agent first, you don't have to manage and lead any of the agents who are out selling your property until they actually write a contract to present. You are employing all these agents with little investment of time, no cost, and no risk. When you have producing agents on your team, you are taking a risk in terms of your leads and how they convert them. You must invest large amounts of your time to train them, coach them, and direct them to success. Champion Listing Agents eliminate the risk and receive the reward.

I want to stress, again, that I am not anti-team or anti-buyer's agent. I do, however, believe that in their desire to create a Champion Team real estate practice, agents can take on higher risk and receive a lower net reward because they heard an "expert" claim success, or because they really didn't evaluate the return on investment or evaluate the risk/reward equation.

2. *Generate multiple streams of income.*   The residual value of a listing develops leverage in the form of additional business creation, brand recognition growth, market share, and market presence. By taking a listing, you are, in effect, creating a storefront from which to sell your services. A listing creates sign calls, ad calls, and Internet leads that you can convert to both buyers and sellers. It allows you to raise your personal profile in a neighborhood to generate future business. An agent who works with buyers almost exclusively has no profile.

What is a listing worth to you beyond just making a commission from the sale? One of the numbers I tracked was additional revenue and additional transactions created through securing a listing. For me, the average was 1.68 transactions for every listing I took. By pounding a sign in someone's yard instead of working with a buyer, I enjoyed the leverage of another 0.68 of a transaction. Track the buyers generated and converted from your listings, the sellers who buy through you, and the additional listings you generate because you sold the house down the street. I am sure that you will find that you gain leverage from every listing you take. I am sure your ratios will be as good as or better than mine.

3. *Maintain a client even if the transaction fails.*   When you are representing a seller, if a pending transaction fails to close, you still have a client. You can put the home back on the market, salvage the relationship, and sell the home. If you are representing the buyer, she has the option of not doing business with you in the future. She can decide to use someone else to represent her on her purchase. Representing the seller provides more security for your income should something fail to close or go smoothly.

4. *Gain control of your life.*   As a listing agent, you will be able to create a business that does not require working weekends and multiple nights, as most agents must. You can build a business that is more family friendly for your children and your spouse. While you are away, you will still be creating growing activity on offers if you are a listing agent.

   I remember very few Monday mornings (after a nice long weekend with Joan at our vacation home) when there wasn't a contract on one of my sellers' homes waiting for me. I didn't know about it until I walked in the door on Monday morning.

5. *Invest less time per transaction.*   It takes less time to represent a seller than to represent a buyer. There will be a transaction every so often that will be the exception to that rule, but in general, representing the seller clearly requires a lower investment of time. Because the seller uses smaller amounts of your time, you are able to invest that time elsewhere to create more income.

I believe that your focus as the lead agent or chief rainmaker of a Champion Team shouldn't be on achieving a 50/50 mix of buyers and sellers. The objective should be to be weighted toward the seller side. The only time your mix should be at 50/50 is if you have two or more buyer's agents working for you. Listing agents, ultimately, dictate the marketplace. They set the terms, conditions, and control level of the marketplace. You need to be established as a strong listing agent before you hire your first producing agent assistant like a buyer's agent.

Manage Your Resources to Increase Your Return

Whether you are a sole agent or an agent leading a large team, you must expand the resources in your business. Resources are things that you invest and use to generate a return. The most successful business owners understand the correlation and connection between the resources they expend and the return they anticipate receiving. The resources and return should be something you can determine in advance and monitor for a repeat pattern or formula.

Resources are not in unlimited supply, so their value is extremely high. You and I don't have an unlimited supply of time. Our time is limited to 24 hours a day—that's 86,400 seconds. Sleeping takes eight hours, so fully one-third of our day is taken up with resting and recharging our bodies. We invest our time, money, emotion, and energy (all of which are finite) to receive our return. Our knowledge and skill, while not finite, are at a set level until we invest more time to acquire greater knowledge and skill. Champion Agents who lead Champion Teams use their resources wisely.

The return we expect is the needed result or scorecard of how we and our team used our resources. We are all trying to acquire greater amounts of money. We are in real estate to achieve a level of financial independence. I have yet to meet a real estate agent who didn't want to become financially independent through the acquisition, ownership, and selling of property. An agent who is attempting to build a team wants to achieve all this and more. The forward-thinking agent also wants to build a business asset that can be sold in the future. Most agents want to establish a 100 percent referral-based business, which they falsely believe means that they will never have to prospect again. I view referrals in the desired return column as merely future money (Figure 2.1). It is an expected return in the form of income growth in the future based on your large use of resources today with an ongoing small use of resources applied consistently over time to serve your clients through frequent personal contact.

Resources	Return
Time	Quality of Life
Money	Money
Energy	Financial Independence
Emotion	Satisfaction of a job well done
Knowledge	
Skill	Referrals

Figure 2.1 Resources versus returns grid.

Creating a Championship Performance

The pathway to excellence is not easy. This is one of the key reasons that most people never achieve excellence. They aren't willing to apply themselves with enough focus, force, and consistency to overcome the challenges and hurdles that litter the small, narrow, rocky pathway to super success!

Discipline—The Magic Word

A number of years ago, I started to plan out what I wanted to teach my son, Wesley. What were the tools, skills, characteristics, knowledge, and attitudes that I wanted to instill in him? He is, in effect, "on loan" to Joan and me for 18 years. I want the loan to be at full maturity when it comes due in 13 more years. Once I had completed my plan, I asked this question: if I could ensure that he got only one of these things because my life was cut short, which one would I select? It took me a few minutes to decide which one. My decision was discipline.

Now, you might have selected something else from the list for your child. The reason I selected discipline was that, if he had discipline, he could acquire any of the other things in my plan when he needed them. If he really needed something later in life, his discipline would give him the basic building block to achieve it. I also recognized at that moment that if he learned and acted in a disciplined way, his success was guaranteed. This doesn't mean that he won't have hardships and challenges; it means that he will have the primary skill necessary to work through them. A Champion Listing Agent is no different. To really be at that Champion level, you have to acquire discipline.

Discipline is the most fundamental building block for success in life. Nothing of significance can be accomplished in life without first developing and then mastering the skill of discipline in a key area. It enables you to capture your motion and wisdom and translate them into action. Discipline is the bridge between thought and accomplishment—between inspiration and achievement—between necessity and productivity.

Here is your challenge in life: you must do things that you don't want to do so that you can have the things you want to have. It is the process of purposeful delayed gratification. An immediate reward for lack of discipline is a Friday at the golf course. A future reward for discipline is owning the golf course. It's not a matter of if, but of when. If it is later, the price is greater. You will pay a greater price for your success if you put off taking disciplined action to achieve that success.

> *Life is a series of problems.*
> *Discipline is a basic set of tools*
> *that are required to solve life's problems.*
> *—M. Scott Peck*

Success is not something that you pursue. Success is something that you attract by being the person you become. Our mandate is to develop the disciplines of success in ourselves first, and then to help others members of the team acquire those disciplines as well.

Establish Discipline in Your Life

Most people develop a long list of undisciplined habits. We all know the things that we do that lead to our demise. We resolve over and over again to remove those undisciplined habits from our life. We resolve to quit smoking, quit eating certain foods, or quit eating too much food. We try to attack and wipe out the negatives in our lives.

However, most of us can focus too much on what we aren't doing in a disciplined manner. That can lead to disappointment, lack of motivation, and, in extreme cases, hopelessness. Too much focus on the "have-nots" rather than the "haves" is really the wrong approach to a disciplined life. The correct approach is to focus on something new, to establish a new habit or discipline. We need to have good feelings and good rewards from starting and sticking with something new that is beneficial to us. We need to deal with the bad habits by establishing new, good ones.

Focus on walking around the block, making a couple of calls to your past clients each day, and practicing your scripts and dialogues daily. These will all enable you to establish more discipline and success in your life.

Monkey See... Monkey Do

Most of what we learn in life comes from observed behavior. This observed behavior happens in all environments, from work to home.

A few months ago, my wife, Joan, came to me because of observed behavior that Wesley, our five-year-old son, had picked up. Joan was driving home from doing errands with Wesley in the car. She was following a slow-moving car in front of her, and Wesley asked her why she was going so slowly. Joan told him that she couldn't go any faster because there was a slow-moving car in front of her. Wesley asked her, "Why don't you just honk the horn? That's what Daddy does." I was busted! In Wesley's mind, based on observation, a slow-moving car means that you should honk the horn.

Your staff, especially the sales staff, will learn from you through observed behavior. They will learn how to prospect, how frequently they need to prospect, and how long they must prospect. They will learn how valuable leads are to your team, how to treat leads, and what to do with those leads. They will also learn what the performance standards are through observed behavior. The members of your team will be able to observe how closely you are really monitoring them. They will observe whether there is consistency between your rhetoric and your actions.

Champion Team Rule: *People will do consistently only those things that you expect and inspect.*

If you are unwilling to set clear expectations, inspect the progress toward them, and inspect the results, the outcome for your team will be far below your goals for your team. If the members of your team know what is important to you and your business, and they know that you are watching or monitoring them, your probability of success increases considerably.

A word of caution: team members won't react favorably to, "Do as I say, not as I do." If you want them to prospect consistently, you will have to set a personal example of consistency in this area. They will need to see you prospecting and making sales that are linked to your prospecting activities. If they are to work the leads, treat them as valuable, and qualify them effectively, they will need to see you doing the same. If you want them to have a sense of urgency in dealing the leads, you will need to have that sense of urgency in dealing with the leads as well. Becoming a successful leader of your team is accomplished only through the proverbial *monkey see… monkey do*!

Use the Four Requirements for of Success

The four requirements are knowledge, skill, attitude, and activities. When you work to improve or increase any of these, you increase the odds of your becoming more successful and wealthy, improving your relationships, and improving your health. Everything in life is governed by these four requirements.

Because everything in life is also governed by priorities, one of these four requirements will always be more important than the other three. There is an order in which to attack and improve these four requirements for success. Before you read on, I want you to rank or prioritize the requirements:

Write a 1, 2, 3, or 4 next to each of these. Don't proceed until you have completed the exercise.

_____Knowledge
_____Skill
_____Attitude
_____Activities

I have used this exercise with hundreds of audiences during my speaking and training career. The breakdown never changes much. About 5 percent of people believe that knowledge, skill, or activities is the first priority. About 85 percent of people say that attitude is the number one influencer of increased success. I think one could make a valid case for attitude being the highest priority, as without a good attitude, your growth will be stunted, as will your earnings and quality of life. Like many others, I believe this is a logical argument.

My research through working with thousands of successful people has led me to another conclusion, however. Most successful people have a good enough attitude to be producing at a much higher level than they currently are. The barrier that must be climbed to get to the Champion Agent or Champion Team level isn't attitude, but activities. It's engaging in success-producing activities with focus and consistency and allowing your attitude, skills, and knowledge to produce the results you desire.

Too many people want their attitude to get better before they start to engage in a challenging task. One of the fundamental questions that a person who is trying to rise to the Champion level in life must ask is: does my attitude influence my activities more than my activities influence my attitude? (Read that statement again.)

Simply stated, does how I feel control what I do? If you answered yes, then there is a barrier between you and your goals and dreams in life. This barrier will stop you from becoming a Champion Agent who can lead a Champion Team. If you are waiting for your attitude to improve before you begin doing some of the tougher things that you know you need to do as a salesperson, you could be waiting a long time. You're like the person who stands in front of the stove and says, "Give me some heat, and then I will put wood in." We have to put the wood in before we can experience the heat. There is a direct link between your activities and your income. There is also a direct link between your activities and an improved attitude. You can't let whether you feel like doing something that needs to be done control whether you will be successful.

Four Ways to Increase Sales Production

A Champion Agent who is trying to build a Champion Team focuses on performing the activities that create revenue for his business a greater amount of the time than a good agent or a low-producing agent does. Put your emphasis on connecting with people in a personal, direct, and focused way. When you break down a real estate agent's business, there are only four ways to increase production:

1. Increase the number of sales contacts
2. Improve the method of making contact
3. Increase the quality of the prospects
4. Increase the quality of the message

When you begin working on any one of these things, you have taken a step toward becoming a Champion Agent. Once you have raised your level of performance in each of these areas, you can call yourself a Champion!

Increase the Number of Sales Contacts

Whether we like it or not, real estate sales is a full-contact sport. Too many agents try to devise ways to avoid making personal contact with people. We use massive mailing programs to raise our image and "build our brand." We develop elaborate Web sites and e-mail contact systems so that we can hide behind the computer every waking hour of the day. Some of us do this because we don't interact well with people. Some of us do it because we feel that "prospecting" for business is beneath us. Others do it because someone told them that this is what they should do. In the end, what matters is the number of contacts.

My definition of a contact is probably different from most other people's. I define a contact as talking to someone over the age of 21 about real estate. This person must have the capacity to buy or sell or be able to refer you to someone who can. A contact can be face to face or over the phone. For the purpose of my definition, a contact is not an e-mail address or a mailing piece that you send. It must be face to face or phone to phone. You can make a contact at an open house, during floor time, at the grocery store, or at your child's soccer game, provided you really make it a contact by discussing real estate and discussing referrals.

Life is a series of numbers, or, in essence, a numbers game. It's the number of t-ball games you make or miss or how frequently you have a date night with your spouse or significant other. You can have numbers in your life that you don't like. A few years ago, I had a cholesterol count of about 200—not a good number. I could ignore that number or work to change it. I decided I needed to take action to change it.

Numbers matter, both in life and in business. One of the ways to know the health of your business is to know your sales ratios. If you know your sales and conversion ratios, you can determine your income before the year, quarter, or even month begins. One of the most powerful tools we have is our sales ratios, but only the Champion Agent knows what they really are.

Within the first year of my real estate practice, I understood my sales ratios of contacts to leads, leads to appointments, appointments to representation contracts, and contracts to closings. Because I clearly knew my ratios, I was able to create a plan that I could follow to earn what I wanted to earn.

The reason that such a high percentage of our clients at Real Estate Champions earn what they want to earn is that we teach them that contacts matter and that sales ratios are king. A word of caution: you can't just track these ratios once and then stop tracking them. You must embrace tracking your sales ratios for the rest of your career. Your sales ratios will usually improve because your skills will improve: your skill and ability to ask for referrals, to ask for appointments, and to conduct Champion-level buyer and seller interviews. A Champion Agent should see regular improvement in his sales ratios if he is working on his sales and business skills. A Champion Team operates in the same manner by tracking everything.

There is one exception to the rule that your sales ratios will generally improve over time. Your sales ratios can change negatively or adversely if the market changes adversely. You might see, as some of our clients have, the number of contacts needed to create a lead go up and the number of leads needed to generate an appointment go up as well. In some markets, the number of appointments rises because the sellers are unwilling to do what is necessary in terms of price to be competitive.

You might have to walk away, as some of our clients have, from a few more listings. When that happens, you have to have an attitude of acceptance and a commitment to doing what it takes. Jack Welch, the famous retired CEO of General Electric, has six rules for business success. One of the rules is, "Face reality as it is, not as you wish it to be." Champion Agents have that attitude and commitment. When the marketplace dictates that sales ratios will change and things will get tougher, they deal with the reality of the marketplace's influence on their business. They recognize and accept that influence and increase their number of contacts to reflect the new sales ratios that will enable them to reach their goals.

Improve the Method of Making Contacts

How we choose to make contact with people will determine our success level or outcome. Having been in the real estate business for the better part of 18 years, I can say that, in the last 8 years, we have moved away from the face-to-face, belly-to-belly, phone-to-phone business that I started in. I would contend that we are less personal today in business than ever before.

As agents, we are relying more on communication via e-mail and mail than ever before. We are relying on the Internet to create leads, convert prospects, and sell homes. I believe the Internet and e-mail are wonderful tools. They make marketing communication easy. They fall far short, however, of the standard for making sales. If you believe that you are going to drip your way to high-volume sales and high net profit, then your thinking is pure folly. Personal service, counsel, expertise, and especially sales will never be removed from the business.

In the late 1990s, there were a large number of Internet prognosticators who put forth a vision of selling real estate via the Internet. Through Web sites, pay-per-click ads, organic traffic, and virtual tours, we were all going to sell homes easily. People would come to these magical Web sites, watch the virtual tours of the homes, and click the "buy it" button at the bottom of the page. We would have just then sold a home!

What all the Internet prognosticators missed was the fact that people would never make such a large personal and financial decision for their family based on a few digital pictures and a click. The public still wants the personal service, expert counsel, market knowledge, and market interpretation of trends that a Champion Agent provides. The problem is that we as an industry bought into some of the malarkey that was being presented to us. We have become less personal and less intimate with our clients and prospects since that time.

When you look at the method in conjunction with the number of contacts, the pathway to success seems obvious. The number of contacts you need to make decreases as the method you select becomes warmer and more personal. You would need more than 1,000 mail pieces to create a few leads. In direct mail, companies are looking for only a couple of percentage points of return. When using the telephone, you drop down into the low hundreds level for cold calling. I am not an advocate of cold calling; the odds of achieving a satisfactory result are still too long. (I define cold calling as using a crisscross directory or some other untargeted list to call people randomly.) At best, you might work geographically to improve your odds.

When the method changes to target groups, the ratios improve to making around 50 contacts to produce a few leads. Calling absentee owners, people in a particular geographic area that you mail to, a school directory list, orphaned past clients of other agents who have left your company, or any other group that you can create that you can target with a combination of mail and phone works. The results improve when you combine mail and phone and maintain contact over a period of time. This is not a one-and-done strategy. You want to select targets that you can work with profitably over the long run.

The last category is warm prospects. When you work to create revenue through this method of contact, you increase your ratios to 25 contacts for a few leads. The contact points are your current clients, your past clients, and the sphere of influence people in your database. Most agents merely mail these people something periodically; they never call them. When the method of contact is exclusively mail, the results move back up to the thousands level when they should be in the teens. I would also place expired listings and FSBOs in this 25 or less category. Because of these people's demonstrated motivation, your odds of lead generation and lead conversion to appointments are markedly better.

As would-be leaders of Champion Teams, we need to understand that the method of contact is directly related to our success in real estate sales. We must work to create a business that takes advantage of the way the odds can swing in our favor if we use our contact method appropriately.

Increase the Quality of the Prospects

The quality of their prospects is something that really separates non-Champion Performers from Champion Performers. Your ability to separate the wheat from the chaff will lead to a dramatic increase in your value per hour and gross income, a low frustration level, better clients, and more and better referrals.

The natural tendency for most salespeople is to work with leads, rather than prospect for new leads. Most salespeople, especially in real estate, do primarily lead follow-up, rather than prospecting or lead creation. The problem with this approach is the possibility that your leads aren't any good. Most agents have a group of bad leads that they are trying to convince to be good leads so that they don't have to prospect. Let me give you a hint: you can be the greatest salesperson in the world, but you will rarely convince a bad lead to convert to a good lead. You are far better off investing your time in finding better leads. We hold onto these marginal or bad leads so that we can avoid prospecting. We know that if we don't have enough leads, we will be forced to prospect.

It takes less effort, time, emotion, and frustration to convert and serve high-quality leads. The question is, how do we determine whether the prospect we just created is a high-quality lead? I frequently ask agents that question. I get a variety of answers, including asking prospects qualifying questions, evaluating the source of the lead, and many others. The Champion's technique is to ask the prospect for a face-to-face appointment. By asking her for an appointment, you can cut through the smoke to see whether she is real. The last place on earth that a prospect with low motivation wants to be is in front of a salesperson.

If you didn't have a reasonable level of motivation to purchase a car, what is the last place you would want to be? Correct, at a car dealership, getting "hotboxed" by a salesperson and his sales manager. The same is true with a real estate prospect. The best way to determine the quality and motivation of a lead is to ask for an appointment. This will be the choke point for your buyer's agents. Their ability to drive prospects to face-to-face presentations will be the biggest factor determining their success. The buyer's agents who can do that will sell three to four homes a month or more. The ones who are ineffective will sell one or two homes a month or less. There will be an increase in sales of 100 percent from leads of the same quality.

There are many prospects whose sales resistance goes up in direct proportion to the length of your litany of prequalifying questions. Questions, even well-scripted and directed ones, can lead to sales resistance. I am not saying that you shouldn't ask questions; you need to do so to keep the discussion flowing, so that you can ask for an appointment again in a minute or two. The most efficient way to determine the viability of the prospect is to determine her willingness to meet with you.

There is an age-old rule that governs success and people. This rule was created in 1895 by a man in Italy named Wilfred Pareto. He observed that, at that time, most people had little influence, power, or money in the marketplace. He called this group of people the "trivial many." He decided that these people made up about 80 percent of the population. He then theorized that the remaining 20 percent had all of the influence, power, and capital of society. He called them the "vital few." He created the 80/20 Rule, which has governed success for more than 100 years. The 80/20 Rule applies to your prospects as well.

According to this rule, 80 percent of the prospects you work with will create 20 percent of your income. The amount of time, effort, and energy required to work with these prospects is disproportionately not in your favor. The odds of becoming a Champion Agent by working with this group are long indeed. The devastating part of working with this group is that you are spending 80 percent of your time, capital, effort, energy, and emotion to create a 20 percent return on investment. The numbers are not in line with a successful business.

A Champion Team works with the elite 20 percent of the population that creates an 80 percent return on investment because this gives the team an added return or unequal return on its investment. Working with this elite 20 percent doesn't mean that you are working only with those who would be defined as the upper crust of society, although working with high-priced buyers and sellers certainly can have a positive effect on your income. In evaluating the quality of the prospect, you need to determine that she has a high level of motivation, has sufficient financial capacity, is easy to work with, and has realistic expectations of service and of what she can purchase. I have met high-priced buyers and sellers who were also high maintenance; I placed them in the 80 percent category, not the 20 percent category. The question you must wrestle with quickly is, does this prospect fit into the 80 percent or the 20 percent?

You have limited resources of time, effort, energy, emotions, and dollars to invest. Your objective is to select clients who require low levels of resources but produce high levels of return. That is what a 20 percent prospect provides. The common school of thought in real estate is that sales is a volume game, that if we raise the volume of production, we raise the income. I believe this school of thought is poorly conceived and simplistic for a sales-oriented business. One of my competitors, who is a "magic marketing" guy, has a saying, "You can't go broke making money." He is absolutely wrong. Many successful companies and real estate agents have gone broke making money. Increasing gross sales volume has merit, but not at the expense of cost of sales and net profit.

If you are running a company that makes widgets, and it costs you $8.00 to make a widget, but you sell it for $7.00, you will go broke fast. In fact, even if you sell that widget for $10.00, you could still go broke because the cost of sales, marketing, and serving the client might be more than the $2.00 profit from the sale.

Champion Team Rule: *Sales is a margins game, not a volume game.*

What you must focus on is the sales margins, not just the sales volume. Your objective is to enhance or expand the margin between the resources you expend and the return you get. When you are working with a team, your expenses are higher. You may create more sales, but those sales have a higher cost because you have to pay the buyer's agents to create them. One way to influence your margins is by selecting better prospects to serve. You must reduce the resources, in the form of your time, effort, energy, emotion, and dollars, that you invest to receive the return of money, job satisfaction, and future revenue in the form of referrals and repeat business. Better prospects create better margins. Don't be fooled by the sales volume game. The margins in business and life are what really count.

Without strong margins in my business, I would not have been able to work only four days a week; have Friday, Saturday, and Sunday off each week; sell 150 homes a year; fund the initial start-up of my wife's construction company; develop subdivision land; buy investment property; and fully fund our retirement accounts beginning in my first year in real estate sales. I was actually in tune with those margins as I added both nonproducing and producing team members. I rarely engaged in a transaction that didn't have a clear, objective opportunity to return a reasonable net profit. There are lower risks in running a high-margin business. You are better able to weather the storms of life and business that will come. It's easier to adjust to market changes.

I had a client a number of years ago who was one of the best agents in her marketplace. She was in the top five in gross income and sales volume in a major metropolitan city. She had a large team of both nonproducing and producing assistants. She had a large marketing budget, as well, to create leads. The truth was, her revenues relative to her expenses and the sales performance of her team were dangerously low, but she was a big name in the market in terms of sales.

I could see when I started to work with this client that she was in trouble. This great lady had zero margins in her business. Her staff and marketing expenses were too high to support her gross revenue. She sold, on average, about 10 homes a month, but she was in trouble. She had operated this way for years, and she had little to show for it in personal assets because there was no net left after all her work. Given the change in the marketplace, I could tell that she had about 180 days left before she would be gone. When I say gone, I mean out of business, which would mean that she and her team would be out of income and jobs.

I couldn't get her to see what I saw. To this day (about eight years later), that still haunts me. She struggled for another 120 days and was forced to take a corporate training position with a large local company. She made more net money doing that than she had made from her real estate practice because of her poor margins. She was one of the nicest people I have ever worked with. I was really sorry that she couldn't make the transition. That's what happens when the margins get out of whack.

The quality of your prospects dramatically influences your margins in your business.

The 20 Percent. There is one last principle or rule that I want to share with you to help you improve the quality of your prospects and your business margins. It's the 20/50/30 Rule. The 20/50/30 Rule breaks down prospects into three distinctive categories. These categories determine your approach and actions.

The 20 percent are people who are easy to work with. They convert and trust you easily. They will decide quickly because their motivation is high. They treat service providers with respect. They are really the golden group. Your marketing and prospecting should be focused on generating more of these prospects. Most trainers will try to tell you that the only way to get people in this group is to work your referral system. That's a load of hogwash. You can secure prospects that fit into this group from any source. I have personally gotten prospects in this group from referrals, past clients, FSBOs, expired listings, ad calls, sign calls, open houses, divorce attorneys, other agent referrals, and countless other sources.

My best advice for dealing with this group is to get out of their way. Let them trust you; lead them and sell them. Tell them when a home is right for them as the buyer. Ask them to make a decision and to make it now. Don't be afraid to guide them to the culmination of the sale. For example, suppose you have a buyer who is in this 20 percent, and you see that the home you are standing in is the right home for him (it has all the amenities, location, and features that he wants) and has an emotional connection for him. Buying signals are flying. Don't show this person another home; sell him this one… get out of his way. Far too often, I see agents miss the emotional buying moment and confuse a prospect (especially one in this 20 percent) by showing him more homes, giving him more options, and driving him to confusion.

The 50 Percent.   This is the group that Champion Agents convert at a higher rate than other agents. This is the group that your team members need to improve conversion on as well. Anyone, even a new agent, can convert a 20 percent quality prospect eventually. It's this 50 percent group that Champion Agents and Champion Teams excel at.

The first observation is that this group is large. It's disastrous if you can't convert this group. The problem is, these people need convincing. They need to clearly understand the benefits and service advantages of working with you and your team rather than with any of the other agents they could choose. To convert these people who are on the fence, you must convince them that the grass is greener on your side. The only way to do this is through a compelling, benefits-driven presentation that is first delivered over the phone to set a face-to-face meeting. Then, the face-to-face meeting must clearly answer the basic question of why the prospect should hire you.

This is a competitive group to work with, unlike the 20 percent. People in this group will not roll over and sign an exclusive right to represent agreement without knowing the facts. Once you begin to service members of this group, it is possible to move them up into the 20 percent, but you have to convince them to do this. With greater competition in the real estate market because of more agents, more company options, more service models, and greater media exposure, you need to be ready to compete.

My belief is that the real estate community doesn't dramatically influence the number of transactions that are done annually in the marketplace. In 2004, a record number of transactions were completed in the United States—about 6.8 million sales. In 2005, there were 7.2 million sales. The real estate community didn't cause the 400,000 increase in sales from 2004 to 2005. The market conditions, interest rates, and law of supply and demand influenced the upward motion of the sales.

The only way for us, as agents and companies, to increase sales is to take sales and market share from others—from other agents, other teams, and other companies. Now, some people don't like it when I say that, but what I am telling you is the truth. These people want us all to be cooperative and sing around the campfire together. Business doesn't work that way. Sometimes you have to play hardball to secure more prospects. When you are dealing with someone in this 50 percent group, you will have to compete with others to secure him as a client. Don't make the fatal error of assuming that you are the only agent or team who knows about this prospect's desire for real estate. You must instill this truth in your sales agents as well. When prospects are in this 50 percent group, you need to be prepared to compete for their business. In most cases, whoever secures a face-to-face presentation will be the victor!

The 30 Percent.   This is the group that can really gum up your business. When your sales agents waste time with these people, it can be disastrous for your team. You need only a few of these people to cause problems for your business. The quality of these prospects is so low that you need to move on quickly. I would affectionately call these people "toxic." They will suck the marrow of life out of you. They are death to your business. They will drain your battery fast. You will expend your energy and emotion on them in such large quantities that it will affect all other areas of your business and your life. Are you working with toxic clients right now? The only solution is to run away fast. You must screen these people out quickly and hope that they waste some other agent's time and energy.

There is an age-old law called the Law of Attraction. The Law of Attraction basically says that you will be attracted to what you are looking for. If you decide you are going to buy a new Jeep Grand Cherokee in black, whenever you drive down the road for the next few weeks, you will see black Grand Cherokees everywhere. Your mind will seek out things, situations, and people that are consistent with your focus.

The Law of Attraction applies to sales, as well, in two areas. The first is, people are attracted to people who are like themselves. When you evaluate your friends, you will find that they have values and beliefs similar to yours. People tend to congregate based on their values and beliefs. In sales, we are all trying to establish a referral base for our business. If people know, hang out with, and influence other people who are similar to them in values and beliefs, what types of referrals will you receive from the toxic 30 percent if you decide to arduously serve them? You will get a whole new batch of 30 percent prospects. My contention is that one is bad enough. I don't want any more. By working with clients in the 30 percent group, you wear yourself out physically and emotionally for a limited return and zero residual value in the relationship.

If you and your team focus on attracting the 20 percent by deliberately prospecting and marketing to this group, the Law of Attraction will enhance your referral business. It will lead to higher margins in your business. When you target the 20 percent, you will still receive a large quantity of prospects in the 50 percent category as well as a few of the toxic 30 percent variety. The quality of prospects in your sales business matters.

Improve the Quality of the Message

It is my belief that this is where the Champion Agent really excels over other agents and teams. The message you present is essential to your success. The message your team members present is essential to your team. What you say and how you deliver your message in tonality and body language influence the results you achieve. This is the edge that the sales agents of your team don't possess. If they were that skilled at sales, they probably would not be members of your team. You will need to address this issue aggressively and promptly when you bring any sales agent onto your team. I think we have become too far removed from the sales aspect of real estate sales. In the end, homes are not bought but sold. Professional representation services are not bought but sold. We have to sell to be at the Champion Team level. Most agents have never had formal sales training of any kind. They have had a couple of weeks of introduction to being a real estate salesperson that their broker provided—that's it. You need to realize that this is the background of the typical sales agent you have or will have on your team.

When sales skills go up, income goes up. There is a direct correlation between a person's sales skills and ability and that person's income. I know that a large number of the people reading this will be skeptics. Let me illustrate my point. To be successful at any profession, no matter what profession you select, you have to achieve mastery of the primary tool of that profession. There are other secondary tools that help, but the primary tool is the cornerstone for your success. Without mastery of it, you will always be brushing up against a ceiling of production; you will never explode through.

As a real estate salesperson, you have laptops, BlackBerries, Internet sites, lockboxes, lockbox keys, marketing pieces, mailings, flyers, customer relation management (CRM) software, computers, tracking forms, your car, your clothes, a Multiple Listing Service (MLS), and countless other secondary tools. But what is your primary tool as a real estate salesperson? It's the words that you say and how you deliver them. The message you present and convey either causes the prospect to work with you or repels her. All the other secondary tools will not make up for a lack of skill in the primary area—the words that you say and how you deliver them.

Most agents invest far more in their wardrobe than they do in themselves and their skills. This will almost certainly be true of your sales agents. You will have to require that they improve. I have listened to hundreds of very good agents' prospecting, lead follow-up, buyer consultation, and listing presentation tapes. I have never gotten one initially that I thought was awesome. The tapes I have listened to have come from some of the best agents in the world. That's why I can say confidently that the vast majority of you reading this book and all the members of your sales team, even if your team is doing a lot of production, have a message or presentation that is not very good. I am not trying to make you toss this book aside, never to pick it up again, by making such a bold comment. I am merely trying to get all of you to face the facts about how important your message is and what you need to do to change it to improve your business.

A client I worked with for a number of years was an excellent agent in Cleveland, Ohio, named Sheri Nasca. Sheri was one of the best salespeople I have ever worked with in terms of sales skills. She was forced to move to the Chicago area and restart her business. She closed 60 sales her first year in Chicago without knowing a soul. She was able to do this because of her superior sales skills. I think closing 60 units during your first year in production without market presence, a sphere of influence, or past clients is outstanding. Sheri did it because she is the consummate professional in her sales skills.

A professional football team will practice for 40 to 50 hours a week in preparation for a 60-minute game. How much time do you and the members of your sales team invest each week in practicing the craft of selling? Most agents will spend at least $500 on a good suit, $75 on a quality shirt, $75 on a nice tie, $12 on socks, and $200 on a quality pair of shoes. All told, they will invest nearly $850 to walk out the door dressed for success. Yet, they won't spend a dime on what matters most—their mind and the sales skills they need in order to create, convert, and service their customers well. The message you present and its quality are imperative.

How Are Your Sales Skills?

It's time for all real estate agents to embrace the fact that we are salespeople. Too many salespeople have what I describe as role rejection when it comes to their career and the activities that lead to success. We are in sales. We sell our representation services to prospective buyers and sellers. Too often, I encounter real estate salespeople who try to disguise the fact that they are in sales. Are you really skilled at sales? Are you able to effectively convey scripts and dialogues with power, intensity, and passion?

The ability to be introspective and to look at your strengths and weaknesses will help you achieve Champion-level performance in life. Far too many of us are too busy trying to

Coaching Tip: *Champion Performers are people who are able to be honest with themselves about their skills: the strengths and the weaknesses. Do not invest time trying to cover the tracks of your low results or deficiencies.*

cover our tracks to hide our deficiencies. To become a Champion, you must face your weaknesses, admit them, and search for help in strengthening them.

If you want an objective view of your ability, aptitude, and attitude toward sales, I have included an evaluation process, Figure 2.2 that I have used successfully to diagnose areas for improvement. You will want to use this yourself and have all of your sales agents use it as well. It incorporates the four requirements for success to establish areas of improvement. I want you to pause right now and rate your habits, disciplines, and viewpoint on the tasks given in the figure, which a real estate salesperson must perform regularly. Use a scale of 1 to 10 for each task, and give yourself a score for each task based on your knowledge, skill, attitude, and historic activity level.

Self-Evaluation of Personal Selling Tasks

Rate yourself for the following tasks on a scale of 1 - 10 in each of the four areas.

AREAS
1. Your **Knowledge** of the task.
2. Your **Skill** in performing the task.
3. Your **Attitude** in performing the task.
4. Your historic on-going **Activity** consistency in performing the task.

TASKS	RATING
1. Prospecting	K____ S____ A____ A____
2. Qualifying Sellers	K____ S____ A____ A____
3. Qualifying Buyers	K____ S____ A____ A____
4. Lead Follow-up	K____ S____ A____ A____
5. Listing Presentations	K____ S____ A____ A____
6. Showing Property	K____ S____ A____ A____
7. Handling Objections	K____ S____ A____ A____
8. Closing the Client	K____ S____ A____ A____
9. Identifying pro-active lead generation sources	K____ S____ A____ A____
10. Working sources/finding leads	K____ S____ A____ A____
11. Contacting leads/identifying prospects	K____ S____ A____ A____
12. Qualifying prospects	K____ S____ A____ A____
13. Avoiding & eliminating unqualified prospects	K____ S____ A____ A____
14. Getting meetings with qualified prospects	K____ S____ A____ A____
15. Making service presentations	K____ S____ A____ A____
16. Closing/asking for commitments	K____ S____ A____ A____
17. Overcoming objections/getting commitments	K____ S____ A____ A____

©2006 Real Estate Champions, Inc.

Figure 2.2 Self-evaluation of personal selling skills.

After you have scored all the tasks, take a look at your weakest areas, giving greater weight to the prospecting and lead follow-up tasks. You must give greater weight to those tasks because if you fail to produce leads, you won't be able to make sales presentations because you won't have any prospects to work with. Decide what you are going to do with this newfound truth. What areas and tasks must you attack ravenously to improve in the next 30 days? Establish clear-cut goals and timelines for raising your performance in key areas and key tasks where you are lacking. Repeat the process for all of your sales agents.

Earl Nightingale, the famous success trainer, said, "We will all be successful in life based on our ability to sell." He was not making a statement specifically to salespeople, but to everyone. His statement holds true for every profession imaginable. The most successful doctors, dentists, attorneys, or accountants are world-class salespeople. They are highly effective at selling their ideas, strategies, beliefs, and service to their prospects and clients. As a salesperson, your objective in sales is the same. You must be able to create prospects and sell them on the validity of your views, solutions, and service model to earn a commission check. The quality of your sales skills will determine the quality of your sales career.

Your sales skills will influence the four ways to increase production. They will influence the number of contacts you make. The better your skills, the more likely it is that you will increase your number of contacts over the competition. The better your sales skills, the more likely you are to select more personal and effective methods of making contact with potential prospects. You won't be as tempted to hope that your e-mail and direct-mail campaigns will become your biggest lead sources. The fear of periodic personal rejection will not stop you from making more effective personal contacts, either face to face or phone to phone. These more personal contacts have a much higher probability of success than any direct-mail or e-mail marketing campaign ever created. You want that attitude to permeate your team as well.

Because of your sales skills, the quality of your prospects will be much higher than most agents'. You won't waste your time with low-quality prospects. You will recognize the tire kickers much faster and remove them or disqualify them from wasting your time. Doing this won't cause you heartburn because you know clearly that you can create more leads regularly because of your sales skills. Imagine how unstoppable your team would be if all of your sales agents had that skill level and mindset.

Lastly, because of your sales skills, the quality of your message and your delivery of that message will be superior, meaning that you will convert a higher percentage of your presentations to income. This high success rate only feeds your confidence. When your confidence goes up, your competence goes up as well. Because of your increased confidence, you will close more effectively and more quickly, which means that you will have less time invested per sale and the opportunity to make more sales. These are all positive outcomes that salespeople experience when they focus on improving their sales skills. Want to join this elite group of Champion Agents and Champion Teams? There will always be room for more.

As the lead agent, you won't be able to teach, train, and coach what you have not mastered yourself. You owe it to your sales-oriented assistants, your buyer's agents, and your listing agents to have the highest level of sales skills so that they can learn from you. They won't learn these skills from any other source but you. They also will probably never be better than you. If you raise your level, you raise their level. When people can't learn, grow, and expand, they tend to leave. When one of the salespeople on your team becomes a better salesperson than you, expect her to leave. She has run her course with you.

3

What Is a Champion Team?

Few agents achieve the level of a Champion Agent in real estate. By that I mean that few have reached the point where they have established a well-run, balanced business; where they know how to produce a regular stream of leads that is sufficient to fund their business plans and their goals; and where they understand their commission ratios: leads to appointments, appointments to clients created, clients created to contracts, contracts to closings, closings to income, income to net profit, and net profit to personal wealth or financial independence. A true Champion Agent with a Champion Agent's practice knows the cost of her business in each major category, such as advertising, promotion, car expenses, phone expenses, client care, office supplies, assistant costs, and brokerage fees. This information allows the Champion Agent to project, in advance, her income and expenses and to monitor cash flows in her business.

My definition of a Champion Team is not dramatically different from the definition of a Champion Agent. A Champion Team must know all the sales ratios and business ratios that I shared earlier. It must know those ratios for each and every sales member on the team. The difference between the definition of a Champion Team

Coach's Tip: *Once you have personally entered the ranks of Champion Agents, you have the opportunity to build a Champion Team. If you haven't ascended to the Champion level as an agent, you won't be able to build a Champion Team.*

and that of an individual Champion Agent is that with a Champion Team, revenue, sales, processing, client care, closings, servicing, income, and net profit still go on even when the lead agent is away for a week or a month. Even in a Champion Team, however, the gross commission revenue will drop when the lead agent is away. To assume that you can take away the most skilled player on the team and maintain the same level of sales is foolish.

The Chicago Bulls, in all their championship years with Michael Jordan, would still have been a very good team without Michael. They would have won a lot of games and made the playoffs. However, no one would believe that they would have won even one championship, let alone six, without Air Jordan.

If all the functions of your successful real estate practice continue while you are absent—if new listings are taken, new buyer sales are made, transactions are negotiated, transactions are closed, the marketing and prospecting get done, you can pay your expenses and your salary, and there is a reasonable net profit left over for you (the owner)—then you have a Champion Team.

Your Definition of a Champion Team

I have shared with you my long version of what a Champion Team is. The truth is, it matters very little what my definition is. The real question is, what is your definition of a Champion Team? To be successful in life, we all have to reach our target. In order to achieve our objectives, goals, and dreams, we have to know what those objectives, goals, and dreams are. You have to be willing to ask yourself the tough questions to get at the right answers. You have to get out of the answers and into the questions.

Coaching Tip: **The right questions will lead you to the right answers. If you ask really exceptional truth-searching questions, you will receive Champion-level answers.**

It is my belief that, both in life and in business, the questions are more important than the answers. There is a connection between asking the right questions and the law of cause and effect. The law of cause and effect states that repeating certain actions over time will produce certain results. Eating five Big Mac hamburgers and five large orders of fries a day without exercise will lead to weight gain, high cholesterol, high fat, heart disease, and premature death. The same is true of asking oneself the right questions. If you ask the right questions, you will discover the answers. Let's look at a few personal questions that you must deal with in order to start defining the pieces of your Champion Team.

1. What are my strengths?
2. What are my weaknesses?
3. What new behaviors do I need to embrace to achieve a higher level of success?
4. What are the key abilities that I need to possess to unlock my true potential?
5. Why am I not taking the actions I need to take?

You have to be willing to look at yourself first before you can start the process of defining your Champion Team.

> **Champion Team Rule:** *Champion Agents and Champion Teams are most honest with themselves about where they fall short.*

Let me help you establish a target for your team.

1. Where do you want to be in five years in terms of units, volume, income, and net profit?
2. What's the mix of sellers and buyers in your business in units, volume, income, and net profit?
3. What sources are you going to use to generate the business (e.g., referrals, marketing, the Internet, expired listings, or other sources)?
4. What percentage of the business will each source produce?
5. What does your team need to look like in terms of people, skills, and positions to produce these results?
6. What will you need to do personally to build this team?
7. What will you need to do to maintain the team once you have built it?
8. What other outside resources could you use to help you accomplish these goals?
9. Where do you think your biggest challenges will come from?
10. Why do you want to build a team?
11. What will building a team do for you and your family?
12. You have accomplished your goals—now what?

Taking the time to personally define the who, what, where, when, how, and especially why will increase the odds that you will arrive where you want to be. Here is my promise to you: you will arrive somewhere in five years; the only question yet to be answered is where. Will you and your team arrive where you planned, or somewhere else? You are the one who does the choosing based on your clarity of purpose and definition. You will arrive; the only question is where.

Organizational Chart

Setting out your goals, dreams, production, service model, and sales team in an organizational chart creates a more organized flow to your business (Figure 3.1). It also helps you avoid something that most agents engage in; I call it real estate remodeling. The vast majority of agents who are building teams are in the process of real estate remodeling. Some are in that state constantly because they lack an organizational structure. Most are in it every year or every few years.

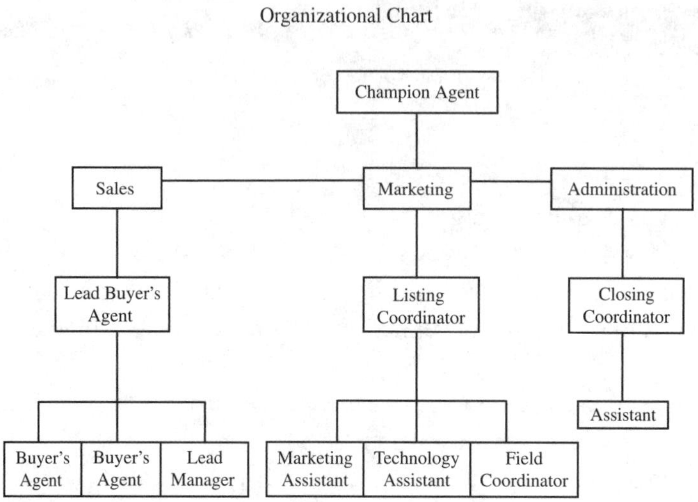

Organizational Chart

Figure 3.1 Organizational chart.

Real estate remodeling takes place when you make large, sweeping course and strategy changes in your business. You can make changes of this type in the sales process, marketing strategy, or client service, but they are most common in the team format, particularly with regard to people and organizational structure.

When you build your business based on your annual goals, as most agents do, you set yourself up for real estate remodeling. You select an income goal for the year. Then, if you are reasonably well organized, you create a rudimentary plan to achieve that income goal. All of your work, marketing, sales efforts, staffing, and structure are directed toward that goal. If your goal is $300,000 in income for the year, you build a structure, systems, and a team that can hit that $300,000 number. Whether you achieve the goal or not is almost immaterial to this discussion. Your attitude will be better if you hit the goal, but you will be facing the same problem whether you hit the goal or miss it. You have built an overall business with the systems, staffing, and services needed to gross $300,000 in sales.

When the calendar gets ready to turn to the New Year, you might decide that you want to earn $500,000 in the next year. You have to throw out almost all of the $300,000 model. It is really of little use to you because you and your team will need to change your activities, skills, management, coaching, marketing, lead conversion rates, lead volume, customer service, and many more items in order to reach the $500,000 mark. You are clearly engaging in real estate remodeling.

That's not the way it should be. Consider yourself the captain of a mighty sailing vessel. You are maneuvering the helm of this huge ship with a large crew on board in close quarters. You have well-verified charts and maps, and you are highly skilled with a sextant to determine your exact position by the stars. You know exactly where the seaport that you are sailing toward is located, and the seas are favorable and the winds brisk. The skies are clear, so you can see the stars, making it easy for you to use your sextant. You will be making only small corrections of a few degrees because you are so well prepared and your objective of reaching a certain port is so clear.

Business Vision Is Where It All Starts

Being able to establish a business vision for your company separates you from the other real estate agents. When building a team, you must pause and define your business vision. Enduring, successful people and successful companies establish their core values and core purpose. They then remain fixed on those core values and core purpose throughout their business life. The elements that change are their business strategy and tactics, as a result of changes in the marketplace and the competition.

Successful people and successful companies know that it is critically important to know who you are and what you stand for. In many cases, knowing who you are, as a team, is more important than knowing where you are going. We all change and adapt as our world changes and adapts. This change is inevitable. The only thing about change that is in question is whether it will be evolution or revolution.

Evolution is defined by Webster as "A process in which something passes by degrees to a different stage (especially a more advanced or mature stage)." We want to engage in small, gradual movement or change over a period of time. This type of change comes about only through clarity of values and purpose. More effort, energy, and resources can be used to increase success, sales, and production in an evolutionary mode, rather than a revolutionary mode.

Revolution is defined by Webster as "A drastic and far-reaching change in ways of thinking and behaving." The change that occurs in a revolution is more violent, sudden, and potentially damaging. The vast majority of resources will be used to keep up with the revolution at hand or to try to get out of the revolutionary process. The stress level is significantly higher in revolution, and the probability of success is much lower. By having well-defined core values and a core purpose, you can avoid the forces of revolution more effectively.

The Value of Mission Statements

For some time, the prevailing school of thought on the subject of mission statements has been that you have to build a mission statement for your team. When I ask many experts why they have that view, their answers are less than stellar: "Because good companies have them"; "You just do"; "Your people need something to guide them." There are a host of other answers that I have heard regularly.

I have personally coached hundreds of the most successful agents in the last almost 10 years. I always ask them if they have a mission statement. When they say, "Oh, yes," I ask them what it is. The phone always goes dead silent. Then I hear this rustling of papers as they try to find the document that has their mission statement on it. When they can't find it, they try to recite some garbled version of it from memory.

I personally feel that mission statements have little value, and that we should abolish their use. Most small business owners (like real estate agents) see their mission statement as something that you have to have or do, but you don't know why you have to have it or do it. Among small business owners, the most common method of building a mission statement is to copy something they like from a large company, like Nordstrom if you have a service mentality or Nike if you like competition or Wal-Mart if you want to serve the ordinary or disadvantaged consumer.

Most people don't build their mission statement from within, from their own views, tenets, and principles of excellence in life and business. They build their mission statement based on what sounds good, looks good on a brochure or marketing piece, or includes the components that another successful company articulates in its mission statement. My best advice is to scrap the whole exercise and start focusing on what you stand for.

What Do You Stand For?

You can't look for what you stand for in others. You have to discover it in yourself. It is not outside in the world around you; it is in your inner world, in your mind and heart. In order for what you stand for to be authentic, you have to search for it. You aren't asking yourself what you should stand for; you are asking yourself what you passionately stand for.

Champion Example

At Real Estate Champions, we stand for hard work and continuous self-improvement. We believe passionately that the quest for self-improvement, both personally and professionally, is one of the noblest callings in life. I personally toil long hours each week in the quest for self-improvement, building tools, training systems, scripts, materials, strategies, tactics, theories, coaching—the list is endless. I spend additional hours reading, writing, praying, and listening to CDs to keep my personal development in high gear. I have other people on my team as well who contribute to this effort.

No one in the real estate field has produced more high-quality systems, tools, strategies, skill improvement, and business mastery systems in the last 10 years than we have at Real Estate Champions. You can pick any name, speaker, trainer, or coach; most of them are still selling the same material they were selling 10 years ago! We have six distinctly different coaching programs, more than 50 different training programs and audio CDs, DVD training, Internet subscription-based training, and five books written on sales success, four of which have come out in the last 18 months.

We don't do this simply because it's good business; we create new intellectual property and deliver it in many different ways because that's what we stand for. It is born out of my personal core values and beliefs. We passionately believe that we need to engage in our own journey of personal self-improvement if we are to affect the world. Once we take on that challenge, we will be able to affect the world around us.

Define Your Core Values. Your core values are really a small set of guiding principles for your business. They are the essential beliefs of your organization. They will not change; they endure over time. Most successful companies and teams decide what their core values are without regard to market influences. Changes in the environment or in market conditions shouldn't change your core values. If the competition increases, your core values endure.

> *The core values embodied in our credo might be a competitive advantage, but that is not why we have them. We have them because they define for us what we stand for, and we would hold them even if they become a competitive disadvantage in certain situations.*
> *—Ralph S. Larsen, CEO of Johnson & Johnson*

You and your team won't have ten core values; you will have three, four, or maybe five. That number makes sense because you can't call something core if it is only one of ten things. The key question to ask yourself when evaluating what you are crafting is this: if the marketplace changed and my core values were a disadvantage, would I still keep them? If you don't say yes, then these aren't your core values. I can answer for myself that if the training, education, and coaching market changed, I would still believe in hard work and continuous self-improvement, even if this was a competitive disadvantage. The truth is, at times it is a competitive disadvantage; it would be easier to sell a magic pill program over and over to the masses of agents who secretly want to buy that type of material. There is a long list of sellers of magic pill programs. You won't find my name on that list... ever.

Other questions you might use to ferret out your core values from your internal vault are

1. What core values or core beliefs do you bring to work?
2. What core values did you learn from your parents?
3. Do you still believe that those core values are valid?
4. If you started another company, would your core values change?
5. Do you think these core values will be valid 50 years from now?
6. If you had enough money, would these core values still be important to you?

    Now, let me share the granddaddy of all questions for me. It's the one I use to separate the values that are really at my core.

7. What would you tell your children your core values are?

What that question is asking is what you want your children to learn through your modeling to them. My children and yours learn more through observation than through any other medium. All our lectures carry little weight when our actions are inconsistent with the rhetoric. These inconsistencies will appear at work as well. Your team and your staff will see them as clearly as your children do.

If you state that honesty and integrity are among your core values, what do you do when the waitress forgets to add a meal to the bill or when the clerk charges you for only one shirt, not the two that you bought, and you know about it? Do you call attention to the mistake even if you don't discover it until you have gotten home, or do you take your windfall and move on? I am not making a statement one way or the other as to what you should do. I know what I would do without hesitation, whether anyone was looking or not. It's part of my core values. It might not be part of yours, and that is a personal choice. The real question is: what would you do?

Having a firm set of core values will help you build a better team. Your job, as the lead agent, isn't to teach and coach your team members to adhere to your core values. It's to select people who share your core values—people who share a passion for the same areas and values for life.

Nordstrom doesn't hire people and then try to train them to be exceptional at customer service. It hires people who have a passion for customer service and trains them to refine and improve that service. If it hired people who didn't have a passion for customer service, there wouldn't be all of these legendary stories about Nordstrom taking back snow tires and other items that it doesn't even sell!

Your core values can be used effectively as a hiring and screening tool. You can use them to make better decisions about your team members and the clients you work with.

A few years ago, a client who was one of the top sales agents in Seattle called in, very frustrated. She was struggling with a particular client who brought a reasonable amount of business her way. We spent a session trying to create solutions to her challenging client. In the next session, the situation was no better, so I asked her one question: "Does your client share the same core values as you do?"

That question stopped her in her tracks. It didn't take long for her to determine that he didn't. Her struggle with this client became crystal clear to her. It wasn't a struggle over commission, honesty, or trust; it was a struggle over the fact that he did not have the same core values as she did. In fact, as she described it, they were not even on the same continent, let alone the United States, state of Washington, and city of Seattle.

My final question was: "Now that you know what you know, what are you going to do?" I will grant you that this is a tough question to face, but she did it without hesitation. "I need to fire him as a client," she said. I got an e-mail later that day telling what a positive experience it was firing this $600,000 seller. She explained it as one of the best moments of her 15-year real estate career.

Define Your Core Purpose. Your company's core purpose is the reason for its existence. What you are trying to do when you create a core purpose is to grasp the very soul of your company. The soul of your company (or any company) isn't just to make money or turn a profit; it goes well beyond the structure, income, sales, closings, leads, and people you serve.

The mark of a great team is its adherence to its purpose. It is important that each member of the team contribute to a common purpose that could not be achieved by separate individuals working independently. Your purpose for a company is like a piece of sheet music for a symphony. All the players in the symphony must know the music and play together for the magic to happen. If the trombones are out of rhythm, the music is compromised. There is a difference in the specific notes played by the different instruments and when they play, but not in the core purpose. The instruments combine for the grandiose symphony sound. The need for the sheet music will end when the composition being played is completed; the core purpose will not.

A true core purpose is really a guiding light for a company that can never be fulfilled. When companies have goals, tactics, strategies, and objectives, their desire is to complete or fulfill them. The purpose is never completed, and it does not change or alter. If you have captured your core purpose, it will guide you for your whole life. A true core purpose will inspire change in the organization but will not change itself.

Champion Example

My company, Real Estate Champions, has this core purpose: "To teach and inspire people to use their God-given gifts to achieve excellence in life." Nowhere in our core purpose is real estate mentioned. We certainly do the majority of our business in the real estate field, but that is not the purpose of our company. Our purpose is to help people like you tap into the hidden skills, talents, and attitudes that will enable you to achieve the exceptional life that you deserve and that is within your reach. Both you and the people on your team have the capacity to do so much more than you are doing. You have the God-given abilities to earn far greater sums of money than you do right now—or have ever imagined.

It's as if most human beings are a five-number combination lock, and they have only one or two numbers right. The lock won't open until you get all five. Having one or two has little value in a situation where you don't receive the reward until you get all five. Your life and business won't change much if you go from two numbers to three numbers. It's only when you get to five that the world is your oyster.

My core purpose and the core purpose of Real Estate Champions is to get you to that fifth number. Your objective as a business owner who is trying to build a team is to ground your core purpose on bedrock, so that your people rally around it, get passionate about it, and want to work toward fulfillment of it—even if you will never get there.

Your Business Vision Establishes Your Principles

The principles by which you run your business will be influenced by your core values and core purpose. If your core values and core purpose don't match, you will have incongruence in your business. The first people who will see it are the members of your team. You will lose credibility, and with it their trust, faith, passion, and commitment to you and your cause. They will begin to accept cutting the corners in your business that you allow yourself to cut.

The next group that will become aware of this incongruence is your customers. This is especially true if you publicly state your core purpose and core values, either orally or in your marketing pieces. Even if your customers don't read your statement or hear it personally, they will observe the incongruence. It is impossible to get away from the observable elements.

Clarity Often Leads to Change

Once you have established your core values and a core purpose, you may have to change. You may have to change yourself first. When a team has to change, the leader is usually the one who has to change the most. You may also have to change your systems, procedures, marketing, advertising, customer service, communication, lead generation, lead conversion, strategy, and tactics. There are numerous areas that might need to be addressed once you have clarity in your core values and core purpose.

You might also have to change the people on your team. It is my belief that you can't train people to adhere to and believe in your core values. Either they buy into them 100 percent or they don't. There really is no middle ground on this. As the lead agent and owner of the business, you do have to train the members of your team on your core values and purpose and the quantifiable actions that fulfill those values and purpose. You can't just hand them a piece of paper with your values and purpose on it and consider it done for good. You have to constantly educate them on the meaning of your core values and core purpose. Through training, education, and coaching on your core values and core purpose, you want your team members to internalize your values and purpose and apply them to decision making, so that you create adherence. If a staff member doesn't share your view, you can't change her; you can only improve her.

Champion Team Rule: *If you can't change people, you have to change people.*

You might have to read that a time or two for its meaning to sink in. It's always a better statement from the platform than on paper. What I am trying to say is that if someone on your team won't improve or change, you will have to find someone else for that position.

Your Business Vision Will Dictate Your Staff, Systems, and Clients

An effective business vision will help you make cogent decisions on staffing. Do you want to provide Lexus customer service or Kia customer service? Is your client's experience important, or is getting the job done professionally and well more important?

Look at Starbucks. Its whole vision and passion is about the experience. We pay almost $3 for a latte that costs the company less than $0.50 to make for us. It is getting a profit margin in excess of 80 percent at the cost-of-sales level in its business. This is all because of the experience. In fact, a recent memo from the CEO to all the employees expressed concern that since Starbucks had gone to totally automated machines, the experience at a Starbucks had suffered. The aroma of coffee is less noticeable, the grinding sounds are absent, and the barista measuring coffee and tamping it down (pounding out the used grounds) is now missing from the Starbucks coffeehouse experience.

For you as a business, if your core vision and core purpose define your service and the experience for your clients at this level, you'd better make the commitment to have enough staff to pull that off. You will need to guarantee that your systems are customer-oriented and that they are easy for your staff and your clients to understand. The clients you select can't be focused on the service model that Joe Cheap Discount Realtor uses. If the price you list the house for and the fee you charge are a client's most important concerns, this is probably the wrong client for you.

Six Characteristics of Champion Teams

Through years of research, working with teams, and coaching teams to the Champion Team level, I have found that there is a repeating pattern in what Champion Teams possess, implement, and do. They are focused on results and actions, unlike lower-performing teams.

Standards

There is a set of standards for production, performance, and conduct for each position on the team. These are established by position first at the Champion Performer level, so that each employee knows clearly what is expected of him. Team members have a target to shoot for, since most of them will not be there yet.

A second set of standards for staff members needs to establish a pathway to the Champion Performer level. What do staff members need to do, learn, and improve on? What responsibilities must they take over in what time frame? For production assistants, what sales, prospecting, lead generation, lead conversion, and sales ratios must they attain over time to hit the Champion standard?

Accountability

There should be an established system of accountability, with written reports that must be handed in at regular intervals, either daily for new or underperforming people or weekly for others who are on track or doing well.

Champion Team Rule: *Performance improves faster when it is measured and reported.*

You must measure and report the performance of your team members. They need to know that you are watching them and monitoring their activities. They must know that you are willing to hold them accountable for fulfilling their commitments.

Cooperation

Everyone needs to be working toward a common set of goals. All team members need to view the team win as the real win. They need to see that an individual win that increases one person's success or production at the expense of everyone else is a loss.

If there is an antagonist on the team, no matter how much she sells or produces in the administrative area, you must take corrective action. If someone lowers the motivation of other team members, a change is in order. If that person lowers your motivation, he needs to be gone—now!

Caring

People on the best teams really care about one another and about their clients. They cover, encourage, help, and support one another to achieve greater success. They care about the goals and objectives of the team and the other members, and they work for a win for everyone on the team, the company, and the clients. They also band together during times of adversity to overcome all obstacles. You will never hear, "That's not my job."

Competitiveness

The purpose of a Champion Team is to win. The members of the team love to compete in the game of real estate. All team members are competing to bring in more leads, provide greater levels of service to the clients, and position the team as the expert team and the only choice in the marketplace for real estate representation. Their philosophy is like that of Al Davis of the Raiders—just win, baby!

Shared Values

Everyone on the team is aligned with the team's values. All team members embrace the business vision, core values, and envisioned future of the team. They understand, agree with, and desire to live the values of the organization, both in their personal lives and in their business lives. It's as if the team is a tug-of-war team, pulling in perfect harmony and unison to win the tug-of-war.

Three Steps to Building Your Ideal Team

There are very few blueprints available for real estate agents who want to expand their business by building a team. The people who have built teams have done so predominantly through trial and error. My goal in this chapter is to give you the initial steps of that blueprint for success.

Step 1—Start with the Finish

Make sure you are clear about what you want your production in units and sales volume to be in the future. Go out at least five years (ten years would be even better). You have to cross the finish line in your mind before you can begin the race.

To really be effective in designing a plan for your team, you must start with the plan for your life. Far too many people who are trying to achieve success are focused only on business success, rather than life success. Develop the skill or art of living an exceptional life, rather than just achieving monetary success. To truly start with the finish, you must take a broader look at what you are trying to accomplish as a human being—a business owner, parent, spouse, friend, and so on.

Stephen Covey, in his book *Seven Habits of Highly Effective People*, introduced to the masses the concept of the need to start with the end in mind. Fundamentally, that is what we are doing when we set goals in writing. We are establishing the end before we write the chapters or the foreword of the book of our life. Many of the goal programs I have studied or evaluated have you write your obituary. That is certainly starting with the end in mind.

There is nothing on this earth that is farther out than your death. Picking a point in time somewhere in the future and working backward is an effective technique for establishing the road map for your success. What are the things that you want to accomplish on this earth before you take the final dirt nap? What's on your life list? What do you want to do and accomplish before you are all done?

I wanted to have two children—a boy and a girl. I decided this before all the pregnancy problems, fertility treatments, a miscarriage, and the eventual realization that Joan and I would be unable to have children as most couples do. Without our actively seeking an adoption, our son, Wesley, dropped into our laps like manna from heaven. Our daughter was not quite as abrupt but was an equally miraculous blessing. Goals and divine intervention are a powerful combination.

In developing goals, you should not consider the odds of your reaching them. Many of us are too conservative in our approach to goals. It's not about what you think you can have or what is reasonable. It's about what you want. If you let your imagination go, what would you desire? If you could have anything you wanted, what would it be? What would create joy, enjoyment, and pleasure for you? What do you want to be able to buy and own? What do you want to be recognized for? Where do you want to live? Do you need multiple homes? Where would they be? How would they be furnished? Where do you want to travel? What experiences do you want to have in life? What skills or abilities do you want to acquire? What do you want your business to look like? These are the types of questions you need to answer in order to craft your path in life.

Coach's Tip: _Take a clean sheet of paper and write out your goals, based on the questions I just asked. I want you to write at least 75 to 100 goals for the rest of your life. Write out your business goals, financial goals, family goals, relationship goals, and spiritual goals. Create a list of what you want to do, see, and accomplish in your lifetime._

Clarity Is Explosive

Small entrepreneurial business owners struggle with clarity. A real estate agent and even a real estate team is a small entrepreneurial business. Having clarity of purpose, goals, and team structure dramatically increases the likelihood that you will arrive at what you envision exactly the way you imagined it and on the timeline you established. The sharper the clarity as to who you are, what you desire, and what actions must be taken to get there, the faster you will achieve your goals, the greater your accomplishment will be, and the grander the life you will lead.

The truth is, clarity is everything. Lack of clarity is the key reason that most real estate teams fail, or at least fall short of their potential. The team leader didn't invest the time to acquire the clarity needed for everyone to be successful. Either you have clarity or you don't; it can't be faked. The question is, do you have it? If you don't, what are you going to do about it?

You might consider hiring a coach. This should be a company or an individual that has designed a program specifically for teams or for people who want to build teams. An integral component of the coaching program must be helping you create a clarity of purpose for your business. The coach must have been successful at creating and leading real estate teams in the past. If the coach has never done it, she can't coach it! Don't fall into the trap of hiring a generalist or a one-trick-pony type of coach. A generalist is someone who coaches all kinds of different people in all kinds of different fields. The one-trick-pony coach or coaching company primarily coaches in one area, such as relationships, referral business building, or technology coaching. If all that was necessary to be successful was skill at building relationships to generate referrals, wouldn't every agent and every team sell hundreds of homes a year?

If you have not been able to establish clarity up to this point, you may need some help. If you think coaching is a possible option, go to our Web site at www.realestatechampions.com. Ours is the only coaching company that has a specifically designed team coaching program. You owe it to yourself to at least check it out.

In order to create clarity, you first have to know what you want to accomplish. Then you have to identify the best route for achieving it. You have to be open to new information, techniques, and strategies. Once you find flaws in your approach, which you will, you need to elicit feedback and correct your course. You will most likely have to self-correct as well. Sometimes you may even have to abandon the majority of your plan and create and embrace another one. This change is often thrust upon you by outside circumstances or outside forces that you don't or won't control.

For example, if interest rates went to 18 percent, that would be an outside circumstance that a real estate agent or real estate team could not control. I have clients in Michigan who have been affected by the problems in the automobile industry. Their markets have been adversely affected by the economic conditions in their local market area and the number of people who have lost their jobs. Through clarity, coaching, and strategic adjustments, they have been able to grow their business even in these lean economic times.

Don't wait for clarity to arrive, because it never will. You must seek it out and acquire it. The more of it you possess, the greater your odds of success in your business and in your life.

Personal Performance

One of the mistakes that agents make in building a team is not monitoring their personal performance. The lead agent will sometimes set production goals for the team to achieve. However, he often fails to break those goals down to show what he is going to do. It's easy to leave the production goals at a group level and never hold yourself accountable for the number of listings and sales that you as an individual need to make in order to accomplish your overall goals for the team.

- What level of performance standard are you holding yourself to?
- How many listings do you personally need to commit to taking?
- How many sales do you personally need to commit to making?
- How much prospecting will you do monthly, weekly, and daily?
- How many books will you read; how many CDs will you listen to; how many seminars will you attend this year?
- How many hours of role playing will you do monthly?

It's easy to look to others to raise the company's production, but what are you willing to do now? What are you willing to commit to doing in the future? Focusing on your personal performance will be one of the best things you can do for the growth of your business. Setting production standards for yourself that the whole team knows and can watch says clearly, "I am not above the rest of you. I expect the same from myself as I do from each of you." It allows the team to hold you accountable when you are not performing as well as you should. A slip in your personal performance can devastate your team.

> **Champion Team Rule:** *Your individual, personal productivity is the most valuable asset in your business.*

Even if you have 10 buyer's agents who bring in more gross revenue than you do, your productivity is still more important. The primary reason why that is true is that all 10 of those buyer's agents are watching you. If you allow your performance to slip, it gives them permission to let their performance slip as well. You now have 11 people who feel that it's acceptable to fail to meet the predetermined standard. It's not just you; it's all 11 people. When you have 100 percent of your sales staff feeling that it's OK to fail to achieve production results, disaster is right around the corner.

If you have one buyer's agent who is not meeting the performance standards, she won't infect the others as quickly as you would if you failed to meet them. You will have a little more time to respond. The other nine agents are not watching one another as closely as they are watching you. Many of the buyer's agents will never be affected by the failure of one of their colleagues to perform. Set and adhere to your own performance sales standards—always! Another reason to do this is that sales is the most profitable segment of your business. Your profit margin on the 10 buyer's agents, individually or collectively, is nowhere near the net profit that you can create for yourself and your team.

Important Team Positions

There are certain positions that carry more weight than others. These positions and how and whom you fill them with will lead to either increased sales or a plateau in sales. The quality of the people in these positions determines the attitude or altitude of the business. It will also determine the level of freedom that you as the business owner will experience. These important positions are your first assistant, your first buyer's agent, your lead manager, and your administrative office manager. These four positions hold the key to your success as a team business. I want to deal with them in order of hiring and implementation.

Your First Assistant. This person can make you or break you in the short run. Hiring the wrong person will never devastate you in the long run, but the havoc that can be created, both personally and professionally, can have consequences for some time. I have seen agents swear off assistants forever after one poor hire. I have seen others trudge down the road, determined to succeed at this "assistant thing," but making the same mistakes time and time again because they didn't pause to evaluate what they were doing wrong in the hiring and training process.

The first assistant you hire can shape your attitude toward building a team. Anything that has the potential to control your attitude has the opportunity to significantly influence your success. This person will be the cornerstone of the foundation for your team. If there are flaws in his character, cracks in his skills, and fissures in his attitude, you will have to replace him in the future in order to grow. Let me say that again—you will have to replace him in order to grow! There is no more important person than this first hire. Your investment in direct income-producing activities depends on it. You won't be able to increase your leads and your business if this first hire isn't outstanding. That means that you need to invest time, care, and diligence to guarantee that you hire the right person the first time.

Your First Buyer's Agent. The next most important hire will be your first buyer's agent. Selecting someone who has Champion growth capacity is essential. In small companies, because the work environment is closer and more intimate, greater importance is placed on tenure, and this can lead to a feeling of entitlement. Too often in small companies, length of service plays a greater role in advancement than performance does. If your long-term goal is to build a team with multiple buyer's agents, the first such agent that you hire will assume that, because of her tenure, she should lead, coach, and train the other buyer's agents, even if, in fact, she isn't best suited for that job.

In selecting your first buyer's agent with the future of your business in mind, choosing someone who has the capacity to lead will help you avoid the problem that arises when you bring in someone from the outside at a higher level. Too often, when we are forced to bring in a lead buyer's agent, we lose our first buyer's agent or even several buyer's agents because their egos won't allow someone who is new to the team to become their boss.

Your Lead Manager.   This is probably the most important position that no one else talks about. You need to have someone to manage, track, process, convert, and hold salespeople accountable for the leads they receive. The failure of real estate salespeople to convert leads is one of the largest losses of revenue in the business. The conversion rate on leads by real estate salespeople is really pathetic. Even Champion Teams convert at very low levels compared to the number of leads that are generated. The Champion Lead Agent has a higher conversion ratio, but the agents under him are frequently all over the map. This lack of effective categorization and conversion of leads means that the lead manager's position could be the most important position of all.

Teams that have implemented the concepts and systems of an effective lead manager have been very effective at using their lead manager to dramatically improve the categorization, tracking, management, and conversion of their leads. The teams I coach have seen conversion rates quadruple because of the lead manager and the strategies and systems we coached them to establish.

The lead manager's role could also be to track and administer the leads, to hold the buyer's agents and listing agents responsible for effective follow-up reporting, and to distribute the leads and information to the sales agents. He does this by monitoring the calls and activities in your CRM system. At least once a week, he should check all the different categories of leads and what follow-up is taking place. He is looking for which sales agents have hot leads, how hot those leads are, how committed the leads to doing business with the team, and what the time frame for a contract is. This person is on the team to wring out more revenue from the leads the team has created.

Sales-Oriented Lead Manager.   Some of the teams I coach have taken the step of hiring a sales-oriented lead manager. The reason for this is that the larger the team, the more training and turnover of buyer's agents it experiences.

> **Champion Team Rule:**   *The larger your team, the more training and turnover you will encounter.*

Every time you turn over a buyer's agent or a salesperson, your training time will increase. In addition, the lead conversion ratio for your team will drop. You will be turning over good leads to a new team member who won't be able to convince as high a percentage of the leads to buy or sell because that he isn't skilled enough. The amount of wasted leads and lost income is staggering.

Having a sales-oriented lead manager can ease some of that burden. The sales-oriented lead manager takes all the calls. He takes all the ad calls, sign calls, and Internet leads. His job is to remove the buyer's agents from the process of lead conversion and lead follow-up. The lead manager handles all the leads until the appointment is scheduled and conducted. He handles all the initial calls and follow-up and books the face-to-face presentation to secure the exclusive right to represent contract for someone else on the team. We have seen the conversion rate and the number of appointments to conduct buyer consultation interviews booked skyrocket when someone in this position is trained to the Champion level. The benefit is that you have to train only one person to the Champion level, not 10. You will be establishing more consistent and higher conversion ratios of leads to appointments because one person, your expert, is handling all of the inbound sales calls.

Obviously, this one person won't be able to handle the calls 24 hours a day/7 days a week, but he can handle them for a significant portion of the possible work hours in a five-day week. (The sales-focused lead manager position can be very seamlessly integrated with an interactive voice response (IVR) system or call capture system to increase your flow of leads and tracking of those leads.

Your Administrative Office Manager. The value of an administrative office manager will be felt mostly by you, the lead agent/CEO of the company. Having someone who can make the more routine decisions that arise in any business will free you up to be more productive.

A successful office manager will allow you to invest more of your time in direct income-producing activities. The person in this position will help collect the data, information, and research that will enable you to make better decisions on the major issues your business is facing. This allows you to deal only with evaluation and analysis, which lowers the amount of time you have to invest.

The office manager will also act as an intermediary between the staff and yourself. Many teams have an organizational structure in which the lead agent has everyone reporting to her. This approach creates a lack of focus, lack of intensity, and generally overwhelmed feeling for the lead agent. It's as if the lead agent is regularly being placed in a taffy-pulling machine every time she leaves her office. It's hard to get jazzed about securing more leads and more business when you are worn out from the demands of working "in" your business.

Having an office manager reduces the amount of time that you will be forced to work in your business. Working in your business is carrying out the servicing and administrative tasks. All of these functions are fundamentally things that an employee of your company should do. The owner of the company shouldn't engage in them. The goal of having good systems, checklists, and staff will lower the time you need to invest in your business.

The more time you can spend on growth activities and working "on" your business, the more income you will generate. Growth activities include prospecting, lead follow-up, and setting appointments with prospects. These activities create growth. Planning, strategizing, evaluating your business plan, determining sales ratios, setting performance standards for yourself and others, and making comparisons between actuals and goals are the functions of working on your business. Gathering and compiling numbers is working in the business. There is a key difference between the two. A terrific office manager will make sure that the one gets done, so that you can complete the other.

Step 2—Establishing the Correct Order

If you think success is a one-step process, think again. The objective in building a Champion Team is to identify the steps and take them in the proper order. You must have both the steps and the order correct. Taking the right steps in the wrong order will leave you well short of the success you desire.

As shown in Figure 4.1, there are eight stages of organizational growth for a real estate agent.

*Stage 1: **You.*** You are the sole employee of your business. You are the chief cook and bottle washer. If you don't do something, it doesn't get done.

You will have to focus on prospecting, lead follow-up, driving the leads to face-to-face appointments, securing listings, writing buyer's representative agreements, and doing all the administration before, during, and after the close.

*Stage 2: **You** and your first assistant.* The first step toward having a team is hiring your first administrative assistant. His purpose is to remove as much of the production-supporting activities as possible from your plate. Your job is to spend more time at the prospecting, lead generation, and lead follow-up activities.

*Stage 3: **You** and a closing coordinator and listing coordinator.* This is where the split in your business occurs. You now have two administrative assistants. The best division of responsibilities is to have one of these assistants handle everything before the contract offer, and the other handle the administration after a contract has been written. They both handle buyers and sellers.

Coach's Tip: *I really believe that your first two hires, if you really want a Champion Agent's Team, need to be administrative.*

Stages of Organizational Growth

There are seven stages to organizational growth for a real estate agent:

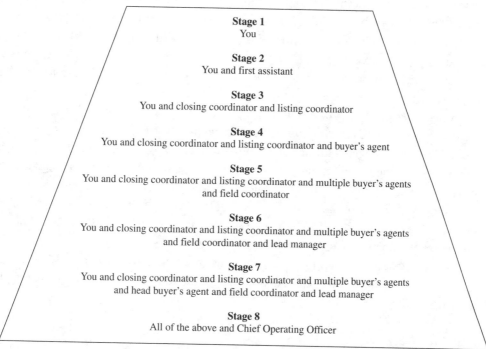

Stage 1
You

Stage 2
You and first assistant

Stage 3
You and closing coordinator and listing coordinator

Stage 4
You and closing coordinator and listing coordinator and buyer's agent

Stage 5
You and closing coordinator and listing coordinator and multiple buyer's agents
and field coordinator

Stage 6
You and closing coordinator and listing coordinator and multiple buyer's agents
and field coordinator and lead manager

Stage 7
You and closing coordinator and listing coordinator and multiple buyer's agents
and head buyer's agent and field coordinator and lead manager

Stage 8
All of the above and Chief Operating Officer

Figure 4.1 Stages of organizational growth.

*Stage 4: **You** and a closing coordinator, a listing coordinator, and buyer's agents.* Once you are solid in administration, you can branch out into revenue-producing assistants (buyer's agents). If you aren't solid administratively before you add your first buyer's agent, you will be pulled regularly into administration. You will work long hours trying to help the buyer's agent close deals where you are getting possibly 50 percent of the gross revenue while assuming 100 percent of the expenses.

*Stage 5: **You** and a closing coordinator, a listing coordinator, buyer's agents, and a field coordinator.* At this stage, you can have multiple buyer's agents working for you. Your two administrative team members are so valuable that turmoil is created whenever they are out of the office. By bringing on a field coordinator, you will be delegating the pictures, room measuring, lockbox reading, flyer delivery, directional sign straightening, delivery, and errands to the lowest-paid competent person. At this point in your business, your best administrative people need to be effectively chained to their desks and phones for maximum production. (The field coordinator can be a part-time position.)

*Stage 6: **You** and a closing coordinator, a listing coordinator, buyer's agents, a field coordinator, and a lead manager.* The addition of a lead manager to the team is essential if a team is to become a Champion Team. One of the largest problems large teams have is lead conversion. This includes the management and categorization of leads and accountability for how those leads are worked, called, contacted, and converted to face-to-face interview appointments. The number of leads that are lost, dropped, forgotten, miscategorized, wasted, and blown is staggering. It's the biggest expense or loss for most large teams.

*Stage 7: **You** and a closing coordinator, a listing coordinator, buyer's agents, a head buyer's agent, a field coordinator, and a lead manager.* The next stage is promoting one of the buyer's agents to manager. She will oversee the other buyer's agents. This person does all the initial training and ongoing training for all of the buyer's agents. She works in concert with the lead coordinator to hold the buyer's agents accountable.

*Stage 8: **You**, all of the above, and a CEO.* The CEO replaces you as the chief operator. He will oversee all the operations of your business. You then move into an advisory role in your business's day-to-day operations.

I really believe you can't deviate from this order until after you pass stage 5. You can add additional buyer's agents between stages 4 and 5, but you must not change the structure until you hit stage 5.

Don't Put the Cart Before the Horse

The biggest mistake most agents make is adding buyer's agents before they have administrative help. I guarantee that you will suffer significant consequences if you make that error. Your service to your clients will be substandard. You will need to invest your time in closing the buyer's agents' transactions, even if you hire experienced agents. The client's relationship will still be with the buyer's agent, not the team. When an agent decides to leave, the clients he has worked with will leave with him. The reason is that there really wasn't a team at all that serviced them.

If you reduced your production in the short run to help your buyer's agent and received only a fraction of the gross fee, and also didn't secure a long-term client, you put the cart in front of the horse. A great administrative assistant is the horse of your practice.

If You Build It, the Sales Will Come

I know that having that first extra mouth to feed is scary. To have another person or family to be responsible for, someone who is counting on your production for her livelihood, is an awesome burden. I understand how scary that position is as an agent and business owner. In more than 20 years of having an entrepreneurial sales business, I have never had to lay anyone off because of slow sales. I didn't want to do that to the people and families that were relying on me and my companies. I have certainly fired people for nonperformance, but I haven't ever had to lay anyone off.

The first time you hire someone and start paying her a base salary out of a 100 percent commission job, it will scare you to death. When you have to forgo your paycheck this pay period in order to pay that person, you will want to go back to the comfort of having no assistant. The best way to solve this problem is to increase the amount of time you spend on direct income-producing activities. Increase the time you spend on prospecting and especially on lead follow-up. When your cash flow is low, you need to respond quickly in this order.

1. *Aggressive action on price reductions.* You won't ever be able to keep a good listing a secret. Make sure you have good listings—get the price down. The shortest line between a commission check and you is a price reduction.
2. *Sell your committed buyer a home.* Anyone who is committed to you exclusively who hasn't bought yet and is reasonable in his expectations needs to have you to find him a house. Take him out more frequently and get him in a home now. If you take either step 1 or step 2, you could be cashing a commission check in 30 days.
3. *Go through all of your leads.* Call all of your leads (even older or longer-time-frame ones) and book appointments with them. One of the fastest ways to take care of short-term cash flow is to go to your leads. They are the third closest clients and prospects to a commission check. Be sure you have left no rock unturned in your desire to convert, commit, and build a high level of urgency in the leads in your database. Don't forget that there is a direct link between motivation and time frame.
4. *Increase your prospecting.* When you increase your number of contacts, you will increase your volume of leads. Some of the leads that you create will be immediate leads, and some will be long-term leads. The source you select to prospect will have a strong influence on the timeline and urgency of the leads. You are more likely to gain long-term leads from prospecting your sphere and your past clients. You will receive short-time-frame leads with a higher level of urgency when you prospect FSBOs s or expired listings, for example. This is due to the difference in the motivation level of these groups.

Avoid Building Your Team Out of Order

The most common out-of-order mistake that agents make is adding producing assistants like buyer's agents before they add support staff. When this happens, the lead agent is forced to train, manage, and coach someone to a reasonable level of productivity while still trying to carry out all of the aspects of her own production. When the buyer's agent makes a sale, it creates even more administrative tasks that the lead agent must take on as well. The problem is that administrative tasks are usually worth only half the money. They're worth only half the money because the other half is going to the buyer's agent. You will end up doing most of the administrative work to close the deal for only half the normal fee. Your efficiency model is blown up, your net profit is demolished, your hourly pay is reduced, and your prospecting ceases.

> **Champion Team Rule:** *If you are spending more than 30–40 percent of your time on administration, you probably don't have enough administrative help.*

Based on my years of experience, the tendency is for agents to run too lean on administrative staff rather than too heavy. Check your allocation of time. That will tell you if it's time to add staff.

Step 3—Just Do It!

I have met many agents who have been thinking of adding a staff member for years and have never done it. It's as if they are waiting for the perfect situation or the perfect person to walk up, bonk them on the head, and say, "Here I am!" You will never act on your desire or find someone outstanding if you have that philosophy.

If you have been evaluating the possibility of building a team or adding to your existing team for more than six months, it's time to act. A decision is in order—now. The biggest waste of time in life is the period between the moment you know that a decision needs to be made and the moment when you actually make it—when you move into action with that decision. The span of time that we waste in knowing and not acting kills too many people's success—don't let it kill yours.

Ready, Aim; Ready, Aim

Your systems, processes, procedures, checklists, and other support structures for your business will never be perfect. You will never get them to the point where there will be zero changes in the future. If you aren't changing, you aren't growing, improving, and staying ahead of the competition.

Establishing your business vision, organizational chart, hiring and monitoring practices, checklists, time schedules, task lists, and team communication systems is enough to create a solid foundation for starting the team-building process.

Control Risk Versus Reward

Too often, we examine the risk and interpret it as being too large. We view the hiring of a first administrative assistant as a $30,000-per-year expenditure. This is especially true with your very first hire. Your mind says, "Well, what if I don't increase sales; what if I have an off year; what if the assistant doesn't get it?" These are natural thoughts, but in many cases, people blow them out of proportion.

While you might invest $30,000 or $40,000 or even $50,000 in pay, taxes, and benefits for an assistant over the course of the year, you aren't taking that level of risk without a safety valve. If, six months after hiring your first or adding another administrative assistant, your production hasn't increased or shown signs of increasing, would you keep the employee? For most businesspeople, the answer would be *no*. A good business owner will not go much beyond a reasonable period of time in trying a new technique, a new staff member, or a new lead-generation system. I believe that six months is ample time to know whether something is working and producing a result. With a staff member, it could be closer to 90 days.

Your financial investment during that time period could be $7,500 to $15,000. For most agents, that expense is around two commission checks to test the waters. We invest two commission checks in harebrained marketing gimmicks almost at will. We are really trading the assistant's $10 to $20 per hour in pay for our potential earnings of $300 to $1,000 per hour. Can you invest more time in success-producing activities, even though you have to invest time in training?

With buyer's agents, you we have to evaluate things differently. The question is, if you don't work with some of these buyer leads, can you invest your time to secure more seller leads? Can you then convert those seller leads effectively enough to offset the reduction in income from buyers and turn a profit? Do you have a choice, since you might need to secure more listings to grow your business anyway?

I frequently coach agents to use the "old" Ben Franklin technique when evaluating risk and reward. Draw a line down the middle of a sheet of paper and write "risk" on one side and "reward" on the other (Figure 4.2). Then just brainstorm each side. I encourage people to write as much as they can as quickly as they can. When you do this, don't evaluate, score, or interpret what you put down—just write. The time to evaluate what you have written is not at hand yet. Once you have brainstormed it, then you should look at the difference in the number of items on each side. The sheer volume of the items is one factor to consider. The quality of the items must also be evaluated. Some of the risk items on your list will be small, but others will be more significant.

When I have personally done this exercise, there have been times when the reward side presented a tremendous opportunity and upside. There was a large difference in the volume of items on the reward side versus the risk side. The problem was that there was one item

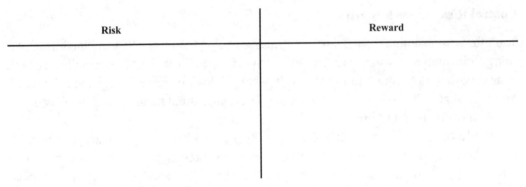

Risk	Reward

Figure 4.2 Ben Franklin balance sheet.

on the risk side that swayed my thinking. It killed the option of moving forward. Do this evaluation with the critical business decisions you are facing.

Benchmarks for Evaluating Your Business

I want to share with you a few benchmarks for evaluating your business. These are benchmarks that I have constructed through years of coaching agents to build teams.

The Rule of 30.   Most agents reach the point of diminishing return at around 30 units in production. They have difficulty increasing their production much more than that as a sole agent. They might be able to squeeze out another 5 or even 10 units, but they are bumping up against the ceiling of production for a sole agent. The mix of your business will also influence this Rule of 30. If you generate more transactions through buyer representation rather than listings taken, your maximum will be closer to 30.

Most sole agents who surpass the Rule of 30 by more than 10 units pay a high price in terms of their time and quality of life. They are simply willing to work more hours, and often too many hours, to grow their production. This 24/7 model isn't sustainable in the long term, and it leads to health problems, challenges with children, and relationship issues. It isn't the way to live and run a business.

Customer Survey Scores.   I believe that every agent should establish some type of customer survey system. You need to know how you are doing. If you survey your clients, you will be able to learn what's most important to them, what you did well, and what you didn't do well. You might find, through surveys, that your staffing levels are too low, and that your communication, reporting, feedback, and overall service were below what the client wanted or expected.

In order to achieve a high level of efficiency and a high return on your investment of time, your buyer's agents need to be doing more than 30 units of production a year. That would be at the bottom of the good scale on an efficiency model. If you had five buyer's agents who did 30 units each and you did 75 units on the listing side in your personal production, your total units for the year would be 225. You would have six people, including yourself, to handle those 225 units, or 37 units per person. That would put you in a solid efficiency category for effort and return on investment. The goal is to be north of 30 units, based on the producing members of the team. You also count in that group.

Using an efficiency model to see if change is needed is a wonderful way to check your progress (Figure 4.3). After coaching hundreds of teams personally in almost 10 years of coaching, it's clear to me that you need to understand the average production that should be done by each staff member. By calculating production per agent, you can apply a scale of performance to see if you are handling business efficiently and when to add more staff.

Efficiency Model in Units

	Personal Production	Sales Staff	Total Staff
Low	$0 - 50$	$15 - 25$	$0 - 20$
Medium	$50 - 80$	$25 - 35$	$20 - 30$
High	80+	35+	30+

To use the chart, divide total units by total staff to see where you fall in terms of your production efficiency. You can also evaluate your personal performance or your sales staff's (either buyer's agents or listing agents) performance.

Figure 4.3 Efficiency model.

A Champion Lead Agent will produce between 75 and 100 units a year in sales. These sales will result almost exclusively from listing activity. There will be few transactions on the buyer's side of the business. This Champion Lead Agent will have limited involvement in administration, so her listing coordinator and transaction coordinator must be stellar to achieve these levels of individual performance.

Got It! Now What?

One of the hardest moments in our road to success is when we learn something new that we know will help us progress toward our goals. Then the question becomes, how do we use it?

What are the next steps in the process? What do we need to do with our new knowledge? How can we apply it while maximizing our return and minimizing our risk?

My best advice at this stage is, if you think you've got it, pause and reread Chapter 3, "What Is a Champion Team?" If you didn't evaluate your organizational structure and take a long-term look at what your team's organizational chart would look like, do so now. If you didn't define your business vision with your core values and core purpose, invest the time to do that exercise now.

As I opened this chapter with clarifying your team on paper, I close the chapter with that reminder. You must plan, strategize, and clarify your vision, your team organization, and your actions before you can achieve the success you desire for your business.

PART II

A TEAM MUST WALK BEFORE IT CAN RUN

Designing the Positions and Hiring the Players

Far too often, even the most entrepreneurial business owners become reactive in their business. They react to an increase in sales by hiring people, then, when sales are slow, they quickly either lay off people or reduce their marketing to decrease costs. In this chapter, I coach you through establishing a structure and tactics for your team positions. I will focus on the support staff in an agent's business, rather than the sales staff—the staff that allows you to increase the amount of time you can spend on direct income-producing activities (DIPA) rather than production-supporting activities (PSA).

Do I Hire Generalists or Specialists?

Philosophically speaking, do you believe that people can do a lot of things well or only a few things well? There are huge differences in businesses that follow the philosophy of hiring generalists and those that hire specialists. Your vision for the size of your team a few years down the road will also determine whether you should take the generalist or the specialist approach.

Having a specialist business doesn't mean that people aren't doing things that they aren't so good at. In a specialist practice, your objective is to minimize the portion of your staff's day when this occurs. You must segment your business and the tasks and activities involved at a higher level than you would in a generalist practice. Obviously, if you are making your first hire, that person will have to wear many hats and be a generalist in the activities of your business. The most glaring mistake I see agents make in this area is lumping administrative functions with sales functions in one person's job description. The result is the creation of a hybrid position in which the skills and behavioral style of most individuals are incongruent with the position as designed.

I have made this mistake as well, so I speak from experience. I came back from an agent seminar where I got 1,001 new ideas. One of the speakers said, "Everyone on your team should prospect for at least one hour every day." He was a very credible trainer in the industry, so I came back and handed down the new edict to my two administrative assistants, Robin and Julie. In one day, I had turned two specialists into two generalists. I had created two hybrid positions with one statement. The results were disastrous. Not only did I spend time training two people who really didn't want to prospect, but I wasted my time doing it. My assistants obviously were not thrilled about doing something that clearly was against their behavioral style, which I didn't know at the time. The results were nil. I almost lost Julie because she got dissatisfied with her job because of that daily hour of forced pain. She played a major role in the growth of my real estate practice, and she is still a critical cog in the machine at Real Estate Champions some 15 years after that poor decision.

We, as lead agents, tend to create these hybrid positions or get talked into them by our staff. We combine sales and administration in one job description or position. We have administrative people who want to sell because they see the money in sales. We create the combo position buyer's agent/administrative assistant. This is a recipe for failure, both for the person and, especially, for your business. If the person fails at one part of the job, you will lose her. It will be hard for her to go back to her old position without losing face, so she will quit. The other possibility is that her performance will start slipping in the area she is skilled at because of her lack of focus, so you will have to let her go.

Coaching Tip: *Don't create hybrid positions combining sales and administration. In doing so, you are asking someone to serve two masters. They will eventually love one and hate the other.*

We have to recognize that more people today are doing fewer things, that most people's skills are in a very narrow range. Most of us could do about half a dozen things at world-class levels if we had the proper training, coaching, and encouragement. When you look at the world of business, especially in the accounting, legal, and medical fields, areas of specialization have exploded. In the medical field, we have specialists for every part of the human anatomy. We also have specialists for stages of our life and leading to our death. In the legal field, we have legal experts for contract law, trial law, business law, estate law, family law, environmental law, and personal injury law. I could write pages and pages of specific specializations for both the legal and medical professions.

In athletics, we also have specialization, especially in the team sports. On a basketball team of only 12 people, you have specialists: the guy who is on the team to stop and harass the opponent's best player; the guy who is the outside shooter who stretches the defense to the three-point line; the first guy off the bench, who is called the sixth man, whose job is to give the team a lift in scoring right away. In football, you have the designated pass rusher, the extra defensive back called the nickel back, and the third down running back who comes in on long-yardage third down plays. Even kickers and punters are on a football team for one purpose. We truly live in a world of specialists.

Look under the Hood before You Hire

Once you decide on the basic structure for your team, you will need to establish a few rules for the hiring process. I believe it's best if you create some ground rules before you start interviewing and deciding whom to hire. You can get so excited about the prospect of a new person or about a specific person that you want to hire that all logic goes out the window.

Establish to what extent you will work to verify information:

1. Do you want to talk with all previous employers?
2. How many references do you want to talk with?
3. What type of time gaps in employment history will be acceptable?
4. Will a few mistakes on the résumé immediately knock someone out of the running?
5. What if the person doesn't write a cover letter, which is standard professional practice?
6. Is there some test or assessment instrument that you want each serious candidate to take?
7. How many interviews will you use before the hiring decision is made?
8. Will you be the only one interviewing prospects?
9. Will you require a criminal background check?
10. Will you require a drug test?

All of these are things that you can legally do with any candidate for employment. (However, you must get permission from the applicant before conducting either a criminal background check or a drug test.) I would encourage you to consider doing most of these things, if not all of them, to ensure a good hire.

Be Sure to Date before You Get Married

I believe that establishing a probationary period or dating period is prudent. Telling the new hire right up front that you have a standard 90-day probationary period during which you will be evaluating him for permanent placement sets a strong standard. If you include some type of benefits package, don't extend it until that probationary period is over. In some

Coaching Tip: *Encourage the potential employee to work with you for a week in a contract labor relationship. At the end of the week, or any time during that week, you can decide to hire the person or determine that the relationship is not working. This trial period will help you feel confident that you are making the right decision. In addition, you are minimizing the risk of raising your unemployment insurance costs.*

states, doing this will help with legal liability and unemployment liability if you end up terminating the employee within the probationary period.

When the Honeymoon Is Over

When the honeymoon is over and it's not working out, it's time for the quick, no-fault divorce. The old adage of hire slow and fire fast is true. When you know someone is not going to work out, move on. It's not fair to the employee because he could be in a position where he fit better and where advancement was a possibility. For you, prolonging the agony causes the situation to gnaw at you and affects your attitude and activities. I guarantee that you will see a reduction in the DIPA time you invest. You will spend more time in PSA: checking, rechecking, and monitoring a poorly performing staff member. You could be investing all of that extra PSA time in training the right person, rather than trying to hold onto the wrong one.

After the honeymoon, the divorce proceedings need to begin quickly when there is an attitude issue. You can train anyone in almost any skill, but attitude is another story. Check to see if the person's home life or some other area of his life is causing the problem. Bring up the attitude problem and set corrective action goals for improvement. Coach and encourage positive progress. If the changes don't happen quickly or if the change is not sustained, you have only one choice left… do it now! Eventually, the person will start to influence and infect your attitude. When that happens, he has been there too long. The evaluation, coaching, and corrective action time has come and gone. You have now entered the damage containment and termination zone.

I have had personal experience in this area a few times when my attitude was influenced by an employee. When an employee starts having too much influence on your attitude, your activities won't be too far behind. That's why you have to act now and not delay… before the environment or your attitude turns south. Real estate is too tough a business to have people on your team who are dragging down your attitude. That will happen enough in just the normal course of business in an agent's practice.

The only caveat I would apply to this advice would be to consider the market timing. The real estate business, in most markets, has some seasonal elements. In many markets, the second and third quarters can be significantly busier than the first and fourth quarters. Where are you in terms of the seasonality of the marketplace? Can you make the transition at this time? You might find that waiting another 30 days would move you into October, when you will have more time to train the new staff member, so that she is ready for the spring season.

Hiring Family as Part of the Team

This is a very common practice in team building. It could be a spouse who is joining a successful practice or a growing practice. More and more, we are seeing two and three generations working together on real estate teams. The "family business" is a very challenging dynamic in real estate today. I have seen family teams that work wonderfully and others that implode because family members squabble to the point where they lose the business, and the family as well.

Champion Team Rule: *Nothing is worth losing your family over. When in doubt, don't do it.*

Joan, my wife, has worked with me in my business off and on over our 18 years of marriage. The first time was almost disastrous. It wasn't her fault; it was mine. The short story is, I treated her more like an employee than like my wife and equal partner. It's easy to get into that mindset when you have an established business and you are trying to integrate family members either for a season of growth or permanently. If we had talked more about how we would work together, if we had taken the time to establish boundaries for home and business and standards of performance, we would have been more successful that first time.

Fortunately for me, the experience wasn't so damaging that, when I really needed her again—when we established Real Estate Champions—she wasn't willing to jump in. Real Estate Champions would not be the company it is today without her involvement in those early years.

I can safely say that Joan was never passionate about any of the businesses that we have established together in our 18 years of marriage. She was and is passionate about helping me and her family be successful. The best arrangement for long-term success is to be sure that the family member is passionate about more than just you or the money. The person needs to be passionate about the business of real estate as well. I know that I can count on Joan to help anytime or anywhere. She will be right there by my side in the trenches when I need it most. However, when the crisis is over and the problem is solved or the project is completed, she will go back to doing the other valuable things she does and enjoys in life. Her passion is not real estate, training, education, coaching, speaking, or creating intellectual property.

Champion Team Rule: *Long-term success with family hires comes out of passion for the business of real estate.*

Generational hiring for a real estate team often comes about because of the money and the lifestyle. The child can see the money that her parent is making and the lifestyle the parent has, and she wants it for herself. The child will usually see all the good and little of the bad or the work. In many cases, she will see the finished product of years of business toil and not the path the parent had to tread to get there. The child will need to grasp this concept, even if she is an adult, to avoid problems.

Don't Remake *The Good, the Bad, and the Ugly*

Family businesses in any field have a chance of being either good, bad, or ugly. I have seen every combination in my years of training and coaching in real estate.

I have a client in Orlando who has three of her children in her business. Her son handles all the technology, Web sites, and computers for her practice. He does a masterful job. Her two daughters handle all the administration, marketing, accounting, scheduling, and client care. One of them is also the office manager and leads the team. I have another client in Long Island, New York, who has her daughter as an administrator in her practice. Her daughter is growing in strength as a young woman and really has made strong changes in the business. The loyalty and trust factor is the glue that holds these teams together in spite of the challenges that arise. The respect these children have for their parents as leaders of the family and leaders of the business makes these arrangements work.

I have another client in southern California who is an example of the bad and, at times, the ugly. Her son has been in her practice for a number of years. He has an entitlement mentality. His production as a salesperson is marginal. His wife now works in the business as well, and there is no solution to the situation except sending the kids out on their own to find out how the real world works. My client is struggling with that decision because she knows that her son and his wife won't make it on their own. It is truly an example of the bad and ugly that can happen.

Establish Boundaries

When it's your children, it's easy to be flexible when you wouldn't be with anyone else. Even as young as my children are (Wesley is 5 and Annabelle is 2 years), they are starting to learn how to pull my emotional strings. After 18 years of living with me, they will really know how to do it!

When one of your children who is a member of your team continually uses emotional arguments or maneuvers that no other team member would ever be allowed to use, or when you continually relax the standards of performance for your children beyond what you do or what you would let another member of the team do, you are in too deep.

When you have a family team, the boundaries and standards need to be discussed, defined, established in writing, and committed to in writing before the family member joins the team. You can't decide as you go along with family members. The stakes are just too high. Any time a promotion, advancement, or job change happens, these things must be determined all over again:

1. The boundaries between personal life and business life
2. Work hours, breaks, and time in and out
3. Work ethic and standards
4. The business vision, core values, core purpose, and envisioned future
5. Organizational structure
6. Adherence to checklists, systems, and procedures that are already in place

If you are hiring a family member for a sales position, there are additional standards that must be defined:

1. Sales expectations in terms of how much and how soon
2. Daily, weekly, and monthly prospecting expectations
3. Sales ratios that should be attained and in what time frame: contacts to leads, leads to appointments, appointments to closings
4. Adherence to your approved scripts and dialogues
5. Amount of time committed to role playing and practicing sales scripts
6. Personal education requirements: reading, listening to CDs, attending seminars, achieving designations

The more time you invest on the front end in establishing solid benchmarks and standards, the higher the probability the movie of your team will be *The Good, the Best, and the Champion.*

Hiring Your First Administrative Assistant

The decision to hire an assistant should be follow a long process of evaluation. For many agents, this is a turning point in their business. They begin to move from being focused only on the sales aspect of the business to being a manager as well. This transition may be difficult for an agent because agents often have trouble managing themselves, much less managing anyone else.

Many agents make critical mistakes before they begin the hiring process. This section is designed to help you with the entire process, from deciding whether you need an assistant through hiring, training, and, if necessary, terminating the assistant. I was able to develop this chapter based on my personal experience in hiring and training assistants during my years in real estate sales. My hope is that it will help you avoid the costly errors that I made.

We have a number of choices when it comes to how we learn in life. The most expensive way is trial and error. Obviously, you have personally experienced the pain of trial-and-error learning, or you would not have invested in and started reading this book. By reading this book, you are gaining access to other people's experience. You want to use other people's experience to build a better model. You want to use other people's energy to expand your business operations in real estate sales. This section will be helpful for agents who are hiring a first assistant, as well as those who have had difficulty in defining the assistant's role in their business.

Often, agents hire someone too quickly in the hope of "rescuing" themselves from the immediate pressure of administrative tasks. The truth is, until the assistant is fully trained, a new hire will usually put an agent in worse shape than he was before. Please read that sentence again. In part, this situation comes about because the agent does not have a well-defined picture of the qualities and job responsibilities of the assistant. Even after defining the position, the agent will need to discipline himself to spend time and energy training the assistant.

Coaching Tip: *Timing is essential. When developing a new assistant, you have to look beyond the tasks of today. You must look out a month or two, at the tenth time you will need to do those tasks. That's when the assistant will be able to do the tasks without your knowing about it.*

Everyone knows the old adage that says: give a person a fish, and you feed him for a day; teach him to fish, and you feed him for a lifetime. This adage is true of the members of your staff. If you always fish for them, they will never learn. Teach them what they need to know over time, forgoing the easy road of doing it yourself now. Things will get worse before they get better.

It's the "pay now, play later" concept of life. We are not wired this way. We want it now. It's as if we are all three-year-olds. Before you consider hiring, you must be prepared to spend the time to teach your staff the processes of your business.

In order to find the perfect assistant, there are three essential steps that you must take before you begin the hiring process. First, define the characteristics you are looking for in an assistant. Second, outline the assistant's job responsibilities. Third, evaluate the applicants based on their ability, their natural characteristics, and their behavioral style. The assistant's natural behavior needs to mirror the skills required for the particular job, not your skills. Before you interview applicants, you will also need to have created a compensation program.

The steps, once you have made the decision to hire an assistant, are

1. *Define what your perfect assistant would be like.*   Begin by asking yourself:

   - What am I looking for in an assistant?
   - What specific qualities and characteristics would this person possess?

   The CEO of a major corporation was once asked how he trained all his people to be so nice. He replied, "We hire nice people." The corporation's focus was on having friendly, helpful staff. Rather than trying to train someone to be friendly and nice, it hired people who were already friendly and nice. Before you begin looking for an assistant, you should know what characteristics are important to you, and then try to find applicants who already have these characteristics. This allows you to hire people who have the essential qualities naturally and do not have to be trained in those particular areas.

2. *Determine the attributes that define your perfect assistant.*   Your definition will be different from that of any other agent. You must spend the time to clearly define your perfect assistant, so that you will be fully prepared to find the "right" person for the job. You will also need to determine your own strengths and weaknesses, so that you can find a person who will strengthen your areas of weakness and allow you to invest your time in your strengths. (See Figure 5.1.)

Self-Evaluation Tool

1) What's the most frustrating thing about the real estate sales business?
2) Do I enjoy the administrative part of real estate sales?
3) What do I enjoy about it?
4) What parts of administration do I feel I am specifically skilled at?
5) What parts of administration would be easy to delegate?
6) What parts would be more difficult to delegate?
7) What would I do with my time if I delegated more administration to another?
8) What is one thing that, if I could perfect it, would make the biggest difference in my business?
9) Where and on what activities should I invest more time?

Figure 5.1 Self-evaluation tool.

3. *Outline the specific responsibilities of the job.*   At this stage, the outline may be brief. One way to outline an assistant's job is to first outline your own "new" job. Since you will be transferring some of your current functions to your assistant, you will need to determine what your new responsibilities will be as well as your assistant's responsibilities. One new job responsibility that you will have is managing your staff effectively by investing your time and energy in staff members' development. This is something you will need to do constantly, so that the members of your staff will continually improve and become more efficient. By investing your time, you will help your team become more self-sufficient and productive, which in turn will help your business become more profitable. Don't learn as you go.

It is important to understand that you are looking for people with different skills and behavioral styles for each of the jobs on the team. Each member of the team should complement the strengths and weaknesses of the other members. During the process of constructing your team, you will want to be sure that you are not selecting people who have strengths and weaknesses similar to yours. We all have a tendency to hire people like ourselves. The people we really need to hire probably will not interview well.

━━━━━━━━━━━━━━━━━━━━

I have been blessed to work with Julie Porfirio for many years. She is an integral part of my team at Real Estate Champions. She also was with me in my real estate sales career in the early 1990s. In both companies, she is the yin to my yang. She is the exact opposite of me. We couldn't be more different behaviorally, and it shows. There are many things that I am world-class poor at. The good news is that she is world-class outstanding at those same things. Her organizational and administrative skills are impeccable; mine are unbelievable... unbelievably poor, that is. She wants to get tasks done and serve; I want to accomplish goals and achieve benchmarks. She is hyperconcerned about the processes and systems; I am fixated on the result.

━━━━━━━━━━━━━━━━━━━━

It is easy to keep hiring the same type of people, but over time, those shared strengths and weaknesses will cause the team to function less efficiently. By constructing a team in which each member has different strengths and weaknesses, you will be able to develop a team whose members can use each other's strengths to accomplish tasks in the most efficient manner. Right now, you are probably faced with having to hire one person to do everything. Selecting the right person based on that person's future growth, behavioral style, skills, abilities, and attitude is essential. People usually hire based on skill and fire based on attitude. Make sure that your new hire has the right attitude. His attitude won't get better when he begins working. In fact, it will usually get worse. Don't make the mistake of focusing only on skill and experience. You can't train someone to have a good attitude.

The Hiring Process

Once you have made the commitment to hire an assistant, you will begin the process of hiring someone for the job.

Do not be in a hurry to fill your available positions. Staff turnover is a major money loser for your business. The lost productivity and time that result from rehiring and retraining are astounding. Make it your goal to hire the right person the first time. It is better to invest more time up front to get the right person than to hire a person who will then have to adapt to the situation. Efforts to make the person fit the job rarely yield good results. Again, the old adage of hire slow and fire fast is true.

The Compensation Package. Before you begin interviewing, clearly define the compensation package. Determine your policies on sick time, vacation time, insurance, and retirement plan. To some people, these other elements of compensation are at least as important as the hourly wage. My advice on compensation is to keep it simple. I find that most agents use complex systems of compensation, including hourly wages, bonuses, and pay-per-transaction bonuses like $100 per closing.

There are a number of problems with these models. The first is that they are usually designed to create performance incentives. That's how we think as salespeople, but it's not how good administrative assistants think. They want to have the security of knowing what they are going to be paid. They want to be able to budget and control their money. This is especially true if you hire someone with a high S/C behavioral style on the DISC profile (discussed later in the chapter). These people want security, and the monthly salary or hourly pay is that security.

By giving someone with this behavioral style a percentage of the gross or paying her based on a predetermined amount per closing, you are setting her and yourself up for failure if either of two things happens. These things are extreme success or failure. A month or two of low closing numbers can change this person's attitude, stress level, and performance.

Say, for example, that you are compensating this assistant with $100 per closing. Things go fine for a number of months. You are closing six transactions a month, so she is getting $600. In her mind, she has $600 a month in compensation, so she goes out and buys a new car and a few other items she has been putting off. Then you hit a rough patch in production. Those six closings a month drop to two for two months in a row. She is down $400 a month for two months. She can't make the payments on her new car, and (in her mind) it's your fault. It is in fact your fault—not because of the production drop, but because you created a losing compensation plan.

Pay your assistant the going rate in the marketplace without these transaction incentives. If you have a good quarter, give her a bonus for helping, based on how much you feel she contributed. Don't create any kind of bonus system that lets her begin to project what she might earn. That will get you into trouble. She will begin to expect that amount and plan to live on it. A bonus should be unexpected, not something that the receiver can plan on.

The frequency of bonuses should be determined by the amount you can afford. I wouldn't pay a bonus monthly, as some agents do. Why give someone a couple of hundred dollars a month? That amount is too little. Save the money up and give your assistant $500 at the end of the quarter or $1,000 at the six-month mark. Give her an amount that she can use to get something she will have longer than a dinner out. A bonus should allow her to buy that new TV, iPod, couch, or memorable trip. It should allow her to take a long week-end away with her significant other. With the monthly approach, the amount is probably not big enough for that.

You also can run into trouble when things go really well. Suppose you hire an assistant on a straight percentage of gross sales. He gets 10, 15, or even 20 percent of your gross. You make $200,000 a year and have done so for the last few years. You find someone who is willing to ride the ups and downs with you for 15 percent of the gross. I can guarantee that this person won't have a high-S/C behavioral style. This compensation plan is not a high-S/C person's definition of security. The assistant is doing a great job, and your production grows to $350,000 the first year. The assistant is really happy; he was expecting about $30,000, and he made $52,000. That's a 75 percent increase in his pay over what he expected. The next year is another great year; you are now at $500,000 in gross, and your assistant receives $75,000. That's a 150 percent increase in two years!

I had a client who started working with me who used exactly this structure. I begged her to change it because, given her talent, her business was going to explode. She didn't listen, and after the second year of explosive business growth, she paid her assistant (only administrative) about $150,000. She had to go back and try to renegotiate the compensation plan down, and she lost a good assistant. The truth is, she could have had three really top-notch people for the same $150,000. There is no way one person can do the same volume of work as three people in administration. Keep your compensation plan simple.

Determine Qualifications.   The first step in hiring an assistant is to determine what qualifications you are looking for. Write down five to ten qualifications that you want this person to have. Qualifications may include a computer background and a minimum amount of experience. Determining what you are looking for will make it much easier to find the right person.

ADMINISTRATIVE ASSISTANT

Opening for an administrative assistant to a real estate agent. Should be an organizer, a positive person, and be stable and predictable in work performance. Should have good written and verbal communication skills, computer experience, and word processing skills. Should also have a sense of humor, be a fast learner, and be willing to work hard. Will work in a fast-paced real estate office. We offer an exciting atmosphere in a people-oriented business. This is NOT an entry-level position. If interested, the first step is to send your resume to: **Name of agent, real estate office and address,** *OR* fax to **fax number.**

Figure 5.2 Listing for an administrative assistant position.

List Your Open Position.   The next step is to submit an ad to the local newspaper or find an Internet job-listing site. Most job hunters look in the Sunday paper or on the Internet for employment. It is important that you have an ad that will draw qualified candidates to apply for the position. You may want to run the ad for one or two weeks, depending on the response you receive. If you are set up with Internet service, you could also have your e-mail address listed as another way for job applicants to submit their résumés. Figure 5.2 could be used for an ad for an administrative assistant position. The items in bold type will need to be changed to reflect your information.

Another option is to use an employment agency. Sure, it costs money, but you receive prescreened candidates. You reduce the amount of time you would otherwise invest in weeding through résumés, references, and background checks. The time saved might be worth the cost, so that you can sell more homes.

After the ad has been published, you will start to receive résumés from candidates for the position. The next step is to go through these résumés to determine which applicants meet your qualifications and which you may want to interview for the position. Using a three-pile system for "Yes," "No," and "Maybe" will help you narrow your search down fast.

The Telephone Interview

When you begin the interview process (after you have determined what sort of person you feel would be qualified for the position), do the initial interviews over the phone to determine whether the person meets your criteria and whether she is still interested in the position after speaking to you. Phone interviews will help you reduce the number of personal interviews by one-half. It will save your time, as well as the applicants' time. It will save you the time that you would have spent interviewing candidates who do not truly meet your definition or qualifications for the position. You can spot the applicants whose financial requirements are much higher than you are willing to pay in a few minutes, rather than taking 30 minutes or an hour in a face-to-face interview. Figure 5.3 gives a list of questions that you can use during the phone interview.

Phone Interview

Name: _____ Phone Number:_____

Introduce yourself and give an overview of the job. Explain that this initial interview over the phone is being used to narrow down the field of candidates.

Ask any questions you may have regarding the specifics of the candidates resume (may want to use the space below to write down a few questions prior to the phone interview):

What kind of experience do you have?

What aspects of your work do you consider most crucial?

Of all the work you have done, where have you been most successful?

What would you say are the broad responsibilities of an executive assistant?

What would you say are the major qualities this job demands?

What aspects do you like best?

What are the most repetitive tasks in your job? And how do you handle them?

What are you looking for in your next job?

What bothers you most about your job?

How much money are you currently making?

How much money do you want?

What else should I know about your qualifications for the job?

This is the end of the questioning. If you feel that the candidate is appropriate for the job, then schedule an interview. Explain that you expect punctuality, you will want a list of references, and you will check those references.

Appointment Date:_____

Time:_____

Comments:

_____
_____
_____

Figure 5.3 Telephone interview questions.

Interview Questions

Name:_____ Phone Number:_____

Introduce yourself and make the candidate feel comfortable (offer coffee or water). Then proceed with the following statement:
"We are looking for an executive assistant, and I want to learn about your experience and the strengths you can bring to our team. You can give me the best picture by being completely open and, whenever possible, giving me specific examples from current or past jobs."

Describe a typical work day.

What skills can you bring to this position, other than the ones required in the job description?

What accomplishments are you most proud of?

What aspects of your job give you the most enjoyment?

What aspects of your job cause you the most problems?

©2006 Real Estate Champions, Inc.

Figure 5.4 Face-to-face interview questions

Once you have completed all the telephone interviews, the next step is to have face-to-face interviews with the remaining candidates. This will give you a further chance to determine whether their skills match the qualifications that you are looking for in an assistant. Figure 5.4 gives questions that can be used in face-to-face interviews.

After the interviews have been completed, you should have narrowed down the list of candidates to the top three to five. At this point, you may want another member of your team (or someone else) to interview them, to help you select the best candidate. Having someone else interview the candidates may be helpful because another person may see different qualities or traits that you missed when you interviewed someone. You also want to interview the candidates personally twice. Don't make the hire after one interview. It's too little time for such an important decision.

The DISC Profile.   At this point, you may also want the candidates to take the DISC profile. DISC is an acronym that stands for dominant, influence, steady, and compliant. DISC is a recognized and validated universal behavioral assessment system. We all have different patterns of behavior. There are many companies in the business world that talk about the DISC. There are a number of real estate companies that use the DISC profile as well.

There is no one who has done as much research, study, benchmarking, analysis, certification acquisition, and certification testing as I and my team at Real Estate Champions have done. There is a difference between playing with the DISC and being a certified expert in how it relates to achieving peak performance in your life. A DISC assessment measures the importance of those four factors (whether they are high or low) in one's behavioral style. Through our research, we have found that the best assistants, especially first assistants, have high scores in the steady and compliant categories.

People with high steadiness prefer an environment that is structured and predictable. Those with high compliance tend to follow the rules and procedures set by others. That's why I feel that high scores in these two categories are a good match for an assistant position.

The assessment indicates the types of traits or characteristics that people will generally show in a given work environment. This information is helpful in the hiring process because it allows you to see what type of work environment a candidate can excel in, and what type of environment will stifle her performance. It also helps you to avoid hiring someone whose behavioral style is the same as yours. People tend to want to be around people who are like themselves, but it is better to hire someone who strengthens your weaknesses and perpetuates your strengths. This choice allows the business to flourish.

The DISC profile is one of the most effective tools for assessing an assistant. It will help you map a person's general inclinations based on his natural and adaptive human behavior. Quite a few of our clients have joined me in using the DISC not only to help match a prospective assistant or employee to a certain job description, but to also see how well this person they will fit with the personalities already in the company.

You can test-drive this invaluable tool for free by visiting www.realestatechampions.com/FreeDISC. Once you see the power of even the free version, you'll want to invest a little more to get the full-blown results. The full version includes a more than 23-page report that tells you how to manage, motivate, and communicate with this person. It provides specific information on this person you are considering along with specific problems you will encounter and potential solutions. It's a peek into someone's personal brain space. It explains what a person's work environment ideally needs to be like and the areas that you, as his manager, will want to focus on for improvement. How many hours, weeks, and months would it take for you to find all this out through trial and error? How much time and money would it cost you in the interim?

The Live Interview

My recommendation is that you set aside a one-hour block of time for a live interview. You don't want to run out of time, and you want to encourage the applicant to ask questions about you, your company, and your business philosophy. By using the questions in

Figure 5.4, you will be better able to keep the information flowing. You may not want to ask all of these questions, but you should ask a good selection of them.

One question I used to always ask was, "Why should I hire you?" It really showed the assertiveness of the individual in stating her case. Applicants will share with you what they feel are their best characteristics and attributes. Make sure that what they believe is what you need from your staff members.

Because the decision is so important, I would suggest you operate on a minimum of two-live-interview system. You should tell applicants in advance that you operate this way. You want to interview them, and you want someone else to interview them: someone on your team, someone you trust, or someone who has a vested interest in your success. Your spouse or significant other is an excellent choice.

My wife, Joan, interviews many of the people we hire, even today. She has a keen sense of intuition about people. I will admit that there have been times in the past when I have plowed ahead with hires regardless of her suggestions, because someone's experience and résumé were "just what the company needs." Every time (read those words again) I have done this, the hire has turned out to be wrong, and in some cases, it has been disastrous. Joan always knew it at the time of hiring; it usually took me months to figure it out. My personal view is that God has given her this extra sense. I don't go contrary to her intuition anymore.

Your last step is a final interview to double-check. You should, by now, feel very comfortable with your decision. You have done all the testing, assessments, and reference checking. You should ask questions very similar to those you asked before to make sure the candidates are consistent in their responses.

Once you have completed the final interview, the next and final step is to decide which candidate you want to hire. By this point in the process, you should have narrowed your choices down to two or three top candidates. You may want to take a little time to review their résumés, their answers to the interview questions, and their assessment results prior to making a decision. You may also want to do a quick final interview, either over the phone or face to face, if you are having difficulty deciding between the final candidates.

It is important that you go through all the steps of the interview process. In general, people have a tendency to hire the first person who applies or interviews for a position. People do not want to take the time necessary to find the right person for the job. However, if you do not take the time at the beginning of the process, you may hire a person who is not right or not qualified for the position. This decision will lead to extra costs in training this person, as well as the cost of firing her if she does not work out. If you do have to fire someone, then you will have to begin the hiring process all over again. Take the time to do it right the first time. By taking the time, you will find someone who can enhance your team and help take your business to new heights. You might even bring the person in for a couple of days (paid) without a job commitment to see how she works with you.

Figure 5.5 gives some questions that will help you choose the right applicant for your position.

Interview Qualifying Questions

Ability, Suitability

1. What would you change about your current job?
2. How do you handle repetitive tasks?
3. What are you looking for in your next job?
4. What aspects of your job do you consider to be the most crucial?
5. Tell me about your role in a crisis situation.
6. How does your job relate to the overall success of your department and your company?
7. Describe what you think a typical day would be like on this job.
8. Tell me about a time when your performance did not live up to your expectations.
9. Where do you see yourself six months from now?
10. What kind of work interests you most?
11. How would that job help you reach your long-term personal and career goals?
12. How do you define a successful career?

Willingness

1. What role do you play in ensuring a smooth working environment when your boss is away?
2. What have you done to become more effective in your career?

Flexibility, Stress

1. What type of people do you get along with best?
2. How would you get along with people you don't like?
3. Describe the toughest situation you have ever faced.
4. How do you prioritize your projects?
5. When have you rescheduled your time to accommodate an unexpected work load?
6. Have you ever dealt with the general public?
7. When was the last time something or someone got you really upset at work? How did you handle it?

Planning, Organizing

1. Describe your method for keeping track of important matters.
2. How do you plan your day?
3. Tell me about a time when, despite careful planning, things got out of hand.

Teamwork

1. How do you establish a working relationship with new people?
2. What kind of people do you like to work with?
3. How do you define a conducive work atmosphere?

Manageability

1. How does your boss get the best out of you?
2. How do you get the best out of your boss?
3. What do you think of your current boss?
4. Describe the best manager you've ever had.
5. Describe the worst manager you've ever had.
6. What made them stand out?
7. How do you react to criticism?
8. How do you take direction?
9. Describe the toughest manager you've ever worked for.
10. Tell me about the kind of rewards that make you feel adequately recognized for your contributions.
11. How could your boss do a better job?
12. In what ways has your boss contributed to your reason for leaving your job?

©2006 Real Estate Champions, Inc.

Figure 5.5 Qualifying questions.

You can design the best training and monitoring system possible (which we will discuss in Chapter 6), but without the right hiring practices, your training and monitoring are worthless. You must hire the right people first. Don't shortcut the process of hiring, or you will never build a Champion Team.

6

I Hired Him—Now What?

Once you have the right people on your team, you need to set your sights on training them and monitoring their performance. Too many lead agents feel that they are too busy to invest their time in training. If you have this view, my best advice is, don't hire anyone. Wait until you are prepared to invest your time in allowing them to succeed.

Training and Monitoring Performance

Many agents fall short in the areas of training and monitoring performance. Once an agent has hired an assistant, he throws that assistant into the fire and provides little or no training. I think one reason agents do this is that it is what their brokers did to them. "Here is your desk and the phone," the broker said. "Now go make money." Most agents were never shown the value of training by their brokers. Therefore, they do not understand the importance of providing training to their assistants. Also, many agents' idea of monitoring is simply to tell their assistant when he does something wrong, instead of offering praise for a job well done and helping him learn from his mistakes.

Training starts by giving the assistant a clear overall picture of your business. This involves explaining to him what it is you do, where you want to go, what success means to you, and your definition of customer service. Explaining your business vision, core values, core purpose, envisioned future, and business plan and philosophy will help define both your job and your assistant's job.

There are four steps in training your assistant for success. Step 1 is to train him to do the job. This is where you show him how to perform each function so that it meets and exceeds your expectations. Show him how to fill out the listing form or how to input the form into the computer. It is important that you spend time each day coaching your assistant through the new processes or functions of the job. You should start at the beginning even with assistants that you know are experienced. The way you conduct your business is different from that of any other agent. Your philosophy of real estate is uniquely yours. You must share your business and the reasons that you conduct business the way you do with your assistant.

Step 2 is to train your the assistant to become responsible for all aspects of the job. Work with him diligently to make sure that he understands that he can perform his functions without your specific involvement. You must empower your assistant to take over the responsibilities of the job, which will help him feel pride in his work. He needs to take ownership of the job because what gets owned gets done. The better you train and delegate to your assistant, the more freedom you will have, and the more business you can do.

Step 3 is to allow your assistant to carry out his job responsibilities without interference from you, the agent. For many agents, this is the hardest step in the training process. Agents are used to having control over their businesses, and it is difficult to relinquish control. However, for the growth of your business, your team, and yourself, you will need to let your assistant do his job. He is going to make mistakes; we all do. You cannot be afraid of letting him make mistakes because that is how learning occurs. How would you feel if your child were still crawling at six years old because you were afraid that she would hurt herself in the process of learning how to walk? Your child has to risk falling down and bumping her head if she is to learn to walk, and you have to risk allowing that to happen. In the same way, you cannot move forward in your business without changes or mistakes. Accept that mistakes are a part of life, and let your assistant learn from his mistakes.

The last step is monitoring your assistant effectively. In monitoring, you give your assistant continued praise for all the good things he does for your business. Most of us do not praise our staff members enough for the things they do. Monitoring means giving them praise when they do something right more often than reprimanding them for doing something wrong. You need to set up monitoring systems that are fast and efficient, so that you can spend your time selling. If you do not monitor your staff members regularly, they will get off track quickly and will not be as productive.

Coaching Tip: *While you may be uncomfortable turning over responsibility and ownership of an area of your business, you must do so in order for your business to grow. Monitor your team members regularly in order to ensure they stay on YOUR track.*

Assistant Training Checklist

Figure 6.1 is a checklist that you can use on your assistant's first day. It includes such things as showing him where the supplies are, explaining phone protocol to him, and letting him know your expectations as the lead agent and business owner.

Assistant Training Checklist

Name:_____   Date:_____

____ Office tour (show locations of office equipment, break room, restroom, and time clock).

____ Introduction to other team members.

____ Explain work hours, lunch hour, and breaks.

____ Explain pay periods and pay day. Also, if applicable, explain raises, overtime, vacation pay, and holiday pay.

____ If hired under a probationary period, explain when it ends and what could happen if s/he is not fulfilling expectations.

____ Provide a job description. Explain that there may be additional tasks that the assistant will be expected to complete that may not be on the list.

____ Have him/her read assistant manual and procedural manual.

____ Show location of supplies and how to use equipment.

____ Explain parking.

____ Explain phone protocol and how to handle clients.

____ Explain your expectations (being on time, completion of work, etc.)

Date Completed: _____

Agent: _____

Assistant: _____

©2006 Real Estate Champions, Inc.

Figure 6.1 Assistant training checklist.

This checklist is a tool that you can use to help you make sure that you have covered the necessary items and to help the assistant become comfortable in his new job.

To-Do Lists and Weekly Meetings

There are a few basic things that an assistant can do to organize his day. These include creating daily and weekly to-do lists, using prioritizing folders and request forms, and time blocking his schedule. These items will be explained in further detail in the following sections.

To-Do Lists.   In order to plan his day effectively, your assistant should have a to-do list of the projects that need to be completed each day. This list can be created manually (for example, by writing the list in a notebook), or a computer-scheduling program can be used. Once your new assistant has decided how to set up his to-do list, it is important that he prioritize the tasks on that list by determining which ones need to be completed today or by the end of the week. Once the tasks have been organized, the assistant should give today's tasks priorities such as A, B, C, and so on, where tasks labeled A are critical (need to be completed as soon as possible), those labeled B are important but not as critical, and so on (see Figure 6.2). This technique allows your assistant to keep track of the order in which the tasks need to be completed.

**Real Estate Champions
Daily Priorities Tool**

Priorities	Category	Activities
A-1		1.
A-2		2.
A-3		3.
A-4		4.
A-5		5.
		6.
B-1		7.
B-2		8.
B-3		9.
B-4		10.
B-5		11.
		12.
C-1		13.
C-2		14.
C-3		15.
C-4		16.
C-5		17.
		18.
D-1		19.
D-2		20.
D-3		21.
D-4		22.
D-5		23.
		24.
E-1		25.
E-2		
E-3		
E-4		
E-5		

Figure 6.2 Daily priorities tool.

At the end of each day, your assistant should update the list to reflect the items that were completed that day. If your assistant writes his list on a notepad, he should rewrite it at the end of each day. Similarly, if he uses a scheduling program, he should update it daily, using the same techniques as when using a notepad. When updating the list, the assistant will remove any items that were completed, change the priorities of items, and add new items to the list. By updating the list before leaving for the day, your assistant creates his list for the next day. You should ask your assistant to give you a copy of the list before he leaves the office. This allows you to see what your assistant has completed during the day and what still needs to be done. You need to know his progress and what he views as priorities. He might have the wrong priorities.

A second to-do list can be used for weekly and monthly tasks. This list should be continually updated, with monthly tasks becoming daily or weekly tasks as the completion deadline comes closer. By continually updating these lists, your assistant ensures that items will be completed on time.

Daily Meetings.   Another important thing to do in conjunction with the to-do lists is to go over them in your daily meeting with your assistant. By going over the list with your assistant, you are able to organize his day so that he can complete the tasks you deem most important. You may add, remove, or change items on the list to reflect your priorities. This process helps you to keep both your priorities for the day and your priorities for the business on track. These daily meetings should be short—15 minutes or less.

Weekly Meetings.   The to-do lists can also be used as a tool during the weekly meetings with all staff members. By going through the priorities for the business, you and your team can establish priorities for the week and the month. Once these are established, each team member can develop her own to-do lists to reflect the priorities of the business.

Prior to the meeting, each team member should make a list of what she thinks the tasks and priorities for the week are. During the meeting, the team will go over everyone's priority list for the week and determine the top five or ten things that need to be completed that day, week, or month. This meeting helps the members of the team understand the priorities of the business as a whole, instead of only their own area of it. The weekly meetings are a little longer than the daily ones. However, they should not be longer than one hour.

Being a Self-Starter.   Once the priorities have been established, the assistant needs to be a self-starter. He needs to understand what the Champion Agent expects him to have completed and how she wants it to have been done. The Champion Agent and other team members do not have time to organize each aspect of the assistant's day. They need to focus on the tasks that will bring in more money, which are listing and selling homes.

Time Blocking for Success

Many of the tasks that an assistant does are routine and have to be completed daily or weekly. Daily tasks may include opening new pending sales, completing mailings, and preparing listing packets. Weekly tasks may include ads, promotional mailings, and following up with agents about showings and with sellers about listing activity. Given the many tasks that an assistant has to complete daily and weekly, he should have his schedule time blocked, so that he performs a specified task at the same time every day or every week. This helps the assistant stay focused on a particular task during the scheduled time. It also increases productivity and efficiency. Instead of switching from closings to listings to mailings every 15 minutes, the assistant can block an hour a day to do listings, an hour to do closings, and a half-hour in the morning and a half-hour in the afternoon to do mailings.

To begin the process of time blocking your assistant's schedule, first have him list all the activities that he needs to complete during the day and during the week. Some activities, such as preparing ads, are done weekly; others, such as dealing with listings and escrows, should have time blocked out for them every day. Once you and your assistant have listed the tasks, determine the time during the day when your assistant is the most productive and the time when he is least productive. Is his most productive time in the morning or in the afternoon? When is his downtime? Tasks that require more focus should be scheduled during high-energy times, while tasks that do not require as much focus should be done during low-energy times.

Once you and your assistant have determined the tasks and your assistant's productivity levels, you are ready to begin developing the schedule. Figure 6.3 can be used as an example. Remember to schedule specific closing or listing functions that need to be done weekly, such as following up with the title company, the escrow company, attorneys, and lenders. These follow-up activities may need to be included both at the beginning of the week and at the end to make sure they are completed. Include flextime in the schedule to complete miscellaneous tasks. During the day, there may be some activities that do not fit into a particular category. Flextime gives the assistant time to complete those activities.

When I implemented a time blocking schedule for my assistants over 15 years ago, I saw an immediate spike in productivity. One of the time blocks was a break from answering the phone for 90 minutes each day. I found that my staff got more done in those 90 minutes than they did the rest of the day. They were also happier with their jobs and performed better. They looked forward to those 90 minutes as the best time of their day. Even if you have only one assistant and the phones need to go to voice mail... do it!

Assistant's Time Blocking Schedule

	Monday	Tuesday	Wednesday	Thursday	Friday
8:00	Develop to-do list for today	Develop to-do list for today	Develop to-do list for today	Develop to-do list for today	Develop to-do list for today
8:30 9:00 9:30	Closings	Closings	Closings	Closings	Closings
10:00 10:30	Listings (Pre-listing packets, process new listings)	Listings (Pre listing packets, process new listings)	Listings (Pre listing packets, process new listings)	Listings (Pre listing packets, process new listings)	Listings (Pre listing packets, process new listings)
11:00	Return phone calls	Return phone calls	Return phone calls	Return phone calls	Return phone calls
11:30	Prepare any mailings & list for…	Prepare any mailings & list for…	Prepare any mailings & list for…	Prepare any mailings & list for…	Prepare any mailings & list for…
12:00 12:30	Lunch	Lunch	Lunch	Lunch	Lunch
1:00 1:30	Projects	Projects	Projects	Projects	Projects
2:00 2:30	Complete to-do from request forms	Complete to-do from request forms	Complete to-do from request forms	Complete to-do from request forms	Complete to-do from request forms
3:00	Return phone calls	Return phone calls	Return phone calls	Return phone calls	Return phone calls
3:30 4:00	Miscellaneous closing or listing projects	Miscellaneous closing or listing projects	Miscellaneous closing or listing projects	Miscellaneous closing or listing projects	Miscellaneous closing or listing projects
4:30	Get to-do list ready for next day	Get to-do list ready for next day	Get to-do list ready for next day	Get to-do list ready for next day	Get to-do list ready for next day
Other:					

Figure 6.3 Assistant's time-blocking schedule.

The schedule should be set up in half-hour increments. All of the time in the course of a day should be accounted for. There should not be any time during the day that does not have a task assigned to it.

Once the schedule has been set up, let your assistant know that he should try to stick to it as closely as possible. As in any job, projects and tasks that need to be completed as soon as possible will arise without notice. But the more closely your assistant is able to stick to the schedule, the more efficient he will be in his use of time. It will allow him to complete more tasks in less time. However, do not get frustrated if the schedule does not work as well initially as your assistant thought it would. Schedules are meant to be changed and adapted when tasks and responsibilities change. A schedule will continue to evolve. If your assistant's first schedule does not work as well as you wanted it to, adjust it and see how it works then. Most likely, you and your assistant will do half a dozen major edits before the schedule is right. Continually adjust the schedule until it meets your and your assistant's their needs.

Philosophy of the Gatekeeper

Your administrative staff needs to adopt the gatekeeper philosophy. The first step is to set up your business as a fortress, making it hard to get in to see the royalty—which means you. The fortress should be similar to the old castles in Europe. A castle has very high stone walls that are difficult to climb over. It has a large moat around it to prevent people from reaching the stone walls. There is also a large drawbridge that can be lowered to allow the people whom you choose to have admitted to come in. The walls are impenetrable and unyielding. You set the standard for access to the castle inside of the walls. Then you grant access only to those who meet that standard.

There is one person who truly controls who gets into or out of any fortress. That person is the gatekeeper. The gatekeeper has total control of the drawbridge that grants access to the fortress. You need to train the members of your staff to become strong gatekeepers. They should have a militant approach to allowing people access to you. There will be many people who want to enter the fortress, but only a few of them should be let in. You need to clearly identify to your staff who is to be granted access to you and who is not. There should be only a few people who pass easily through the gate to you. Certainly, an inbound prospect call or a prospect who is returning your call needs to be routed to you quickly. The rest of the calls should be screened thoroughly to see if another team member could assist the person first.

A highly trained assistant is able to answer the most caller's questions. If your assistant asks who is calling and determines what the caller needs, he will be able to answer 90 percent of the calls without your having to invest any time at all. Too often, callers who want to speak to the agent are other agents checking for availability, appraisers verifying information, or Realtors checking on showings—all of whom the assistant can easily help. If, for some reason, the assistant cannot answer a particular question, he can take a message. Taking a message involves more than just noting the caller's name, her phone number, and the date and time of the call. A highly trained assistant will find out the specific reason for the call and try to handle the question right there on the spot. This is one of the biggest time-saving techniques of all.

If he is unable to handle the situation on the initial call, a highly trained assistant will find out the answer and then return the call himself. Finally, if it is absolutely necessary for the Champion Agent to speak to the caller, the assistant should set a specific time for the Champion Agent to return the call, effectively making a mini-appointment for the return telephone call by the Champion Agent. These steps will create a highly controlled and highly productive environment for the whole team.

Five-Minute Rule. It is important that you understand the five-minute rule of telephone calls. This rule states that completing any telephone call and refocusing on the activity you were engaged in prior to the call will take at least five minutes. When changing from one activity to another, it takes most people at least five minutes to refocus on the new activity. Even if the telephone call is only 30 seconds long, by the time your mental juices start flowing again, you or a member of your staff will have lost at least five minutes of productive time.

I was recently interviewed by the staff of the National Association of Realtors (NAR) for an article. The interviewers asked me this question: "What's the best sales tool today in real estate?" My response shocked them. The reason it shocked them was that they were expecting some type of technology tool like a Web site or personal digital assistant or calculator or Web-lead service generator. I said, without hesitation, that the best sales tool is still the telephone. My friends, the Internet isn't even a close second. It's a great tool, but it's not the best yet, and it may never be for the simple reason that the written word doesn't have the power that the spoken word does.

While this book is valuable, the truth is that this material and I are much better "live" than on the printed page. You and I both know that when we are talking to a customer, client, or prospect, the phone is a more effective form of communication, as it will achieve higher sales results than sending out an e-mail with the same material in it. (This goes back to the method of contact that I talked about in Chapter 2.)

The phone also has a negative side. It makes you more accessible, especially in the age of cell phones. The telephone is your most valuable business tool, but it is also the most distracting if it is not controlled. Gain control of the telephone and you will have gained control of your time. That's truly the battle for most agents and teams in real estate.

Telephone Procedures

The telephone is the most distracting device in the office. It is constantly interrupting throughout the day. It will repeatedly take your assistant away from the project she is currently working on and will try to move her to another task or problem that needs to be solved. It is important for your assistant to have control over the telephone, not the other way around.

Here are a few suggestions for controlling the phone:

1. Establish a time when the phone will not be answered (for example, from 9 to 11 a.m.).
2. Return all calls at a specific time (for example, between 11 a.m. and 12 p.m. and between 3 and 4 p.m.).
3. Have a message on the answering machine stating that calls are returned at specific times and that, if the caller will leave a message, the call will be returned at those times.

Whenever your assistant is answering calls, she should let the caller know that either the Champion Agent or someone else will take care of the matter and will call back at a specific time. The assistant needs to get a number where the caller can be reached during that time. This way, the caller knows that the request will be handled and that he will be called back.

Another problem that most assistants and agents will encounter is ending a telephone conversation with a client or potential client who wants to chat. It is sometimes difficult to gracefully end a conversation with someone who wants to keep on talking. Given the number of tasks that need to be completed during the day, no assistant or Champion Agent has unlimited time to waste talking to someone regarding matters that don't relate to the business. Here are a few suggestions of how to end the conversation quickly, yet in a positive manner.

If you are speaking with a client who wants to continue to chat after all the business-related issues have been discussed, you might say: "I have one more quick question before I let you go…"

When returning a phone call to a client who enjoys talking to you, try using the following:

> *"I just have two quick questions for you, and then I will let you go."*
>
> *"I have another scheduled call in a few minutes, but I wanted to get back to you right away."*
>
> *"If we can't resolve this in a few minutes, I can call you back later."*

The truth is, more than 90 percent of the time, if you establish a time parameter, you have shrunk the call time to a few minutes, and a follow-up call is unnecessary.

If your assistant says these things politely and up front, the client will understand that she is calling on business-related issues and that she will end the call as soon as those issues are resolved. This sets a tone that says that your team values the clients' time, that your team is focused on helping them with their business-related questions or problems, and that the team's job is to get those questions and problems answered and resolved as soon as possible.

Telephone Etiquette.   When answering the phone, anyone who is on your team should be professional and pleasant. It reflects poorly on the Champion Agent if members of her support staff are rude and abrupt with potential clients or with other agents who are calling the office.

Here are suggested scripts for answering the phone and taking messages. It is always more pleasant for the person on the other end if the assistant remains upbeat and pleasant.

> *"Hi, **Agent's Name** office. This is **Your Name**. How may I help you?"*
>
> *or*
>
> *"Good morning (or afternoon), **Agent's Name** office. This is **Your Name**. How may I help you?"*

Taking a Message:

> *"I am sorry; **Agent's Name** is currently not available (on an appointment, at a meeting, on the phone, etc.). May I take a message and have him return your call this morning (or afternoon)? Can I get a number where you can be reached this morning (or afternoon)? I will have him give you a call back then. May I tell him what this is regarding?"* (This is where the assistant needs to probe, so that he can handle the question now.)
>
> *or*
>
> *"I am sorry; **Agent's Name** is currently not available (on an appointment, at a meeting, on the phone, etc.). May I take a message and have him return your call? He will be returning calls at **specific time**. Can I get a number where you can be reached at **specific time**? I will have him give you a call back. May I tell him what this is regarding? I would like him to be well prepared to serve you."*

When taking a message, your assistant should be sure to get the following information:

- *Name of the caller.*   Make sure your assistant gets the caller's first and last name.
- *Phone number where the caller can be reached.*   It may be helpful to get two numbers and find out when the caller will be available at a particular number. The assistant should then repeat the number back to the caller to ensure accuracy.

- *Message.*   Your assistant should ask the caller what the call is regarding. It is helpful for the agent to understand, when returning the call, why the caller called. Knowing what the call is about may also help the assistant to prepare information that the agent needs prior to returning the phone call. He also might be able to handle the return call himself.

There are phrases that the assistant must avoid using when answering the phones. These phrases cause callers to question the assistant's knowledge and interest in answering their questions or solving their problems.

Here are a few examples of phrases to avoid. Included are examples of what would be more appropriate to say instead.

Avoid	Instead, say
"I don't know"	**Say**: *"That is a good question. Let me check on that information for you and call you back. What number should I call to reach you?"*
"Just hang on a second, I'll be right back."	**Say**: *"It may take a few minutes for me to find that information. Would you like to hold, or would you like me to call you back with the information?"*
"We can't do that."	**Say**: *"Let's see what we can do for you to solve the problem."*

When the assistant answers in a positive manner, the caller will be more receptive to the response even if it is not the answer she wanted. Your assistant should try to help the caller as much as possible. This will leave the caller with a positive impression of you, your assistant, and your business.

Job Responsibilities of the Team

It is important to determine the job responsibilities of each member of the team. The Champion Agent's focus should be on direct income-producing activities (DIPA) (see Figure 6.4). The administrative functions or production-supporting activities should be delegated to the assistant. The Champion Agent still needs to coach the administrative process but does not participate in the process daily.

There are only a few activities that you can do each day that will earn you the amount of money per hour that you desire. These DIPA are the only activities that will pay you your true value per hour.

Champion Agent
Job Description

- Goes on listing appointments set by the prospecting agent and lead agent.

- Prospects daily for new business (i.e., past client, expired's, FSBO's)

- Qualifies appointments to ensure quality.

- Negotiates contracts with buyers, sellers, and other agents.

- Follows up on leads generated by lead agent and prospecting agent.

- Plans business daily.

- Evaluates production and profit.

- Coaches and manages all staff members.

- Practices sales skills.

- Conducts listing presentations to get new listings.

- Conduct buyer interviews to secure buyer exclusive right to represent contracts

- Overall responsibility for the business.

©2006 Real Estate Champions, Inc.

Figure 6.4 Champion Agent job description.

Your staff should take on all the other responsibilities, so that you can focus on those activities that provide the highest return. The more you are able to delegate efficiently, the more productive your business will be in both the short and the long term. Efficient delegation will also give you more freedom and allow you to spend more time with your family.

Coach's Tip: *Always remember that you are a leader, not a manager—there is a difference.*

Figures 6.5 to 6.7 give suggested job responsibilities for the listing coordinator, the closing coordinator, and the field coordinator or runner. In some offices, there may not be a separate person for each of these positions. For example, there may be only one assistant who carries out the receptionist, listing coordinator, and closing coordinator functions.

Use these lists of responsibilities as a guide. Adjust them as needed to fit the needs of your particular business.

Listing Coordinator Job Description

- Prepare listing packets.

- Send "Thank you" letter to listing appointments (same day as appointment).

- Keep an update of expired listings, notifying agent when expiration date is near.

- Type letter to the seller requesting an extension, and send the MLS addendum with the new expiration date.

- Handle all MLS changes and follow-up to make sure change was completed and accurate.

- Process all listing contracts. Submit listing for MLS input.

- Set-up showing appointments, as necessary.

- Call agents regarding showings on listings.

- Call sellers once per week, usually same day every week, with update on showings, inquiries, etc.

- Update the agent daily on all showings and activities.

- Keep track of listing inventory. Discuss any important changes with agent.

- Complete any follow-up paperwork regarding listings, make sure that it is completed correctly and in a timely manner.

- Write and place newspaper and home magazine ads.

- Send clients a letter and copy of the ad we ran of their listing.

- Design flyers.

- Install or order "For Sale" signs, and follow-up with sign company to make sure sign is installed -- and installed at the proper location.

- Install lock box and make duplicate of key for office in case it is misplaced.

- Install directionals and flyers. Follow-up to make sure that the directionals are up and that the flyer box is full.

- Have a schedule for the lock boxes to be read at vacant listings weekly. Try to read them the same day every week, so that you have an accurate read of how many showings there were in the past week.

- Schedule Open Houses with sellers.

- Any additional tasks that fall between the generation of the listing lead and the time of a sales agreement.

©2006 Real Estate Champions, Inc.

Figure 6.5 Listing coordinator job description.

Closing Coordinator Job Description

- Take care of all title company communications for closings. Make sure title company or attorney has all necessary paperwork. Follow-up to see when people are going in to sign, and when it will be recording.

- Process all sales agreements. Make sure the Admin has all the necessary paperwork to open escrow.

- Follow-up weekly with agents, lenders, attorneys, and title company who are involved with the sale. Make sure that everything is completed in a timely manner and that we will be closing on time.

- Document all conversations with the other agent, lender, attorneys, and title company, and keep on file for future reference.

- Coordinate all home inspections and appraisals.

- Review files weekly to make sure that all contingencies are completed, and that any missing paperwork is completed and in the file.

- Keep track of all upcoming sales. List the close date, Seller/Buyer, address, price, total commission, and our commission.

- Finalize sold files of the past closings. Make sure everything is complete.

- Complete any follow-up paperwork regarding sales, making sure that it is completed correctly and in a timely manner.

- Track and maintain commission status reports.

- Order sign down, remove lock box and directionals once property has closed.

- Update and maintain current mailing lists. Once a transaction closes, make sure that the addresses and phone numbers are updated.

- Any additional tasks that occur from the time the contract is presented through the close of escrow.

©2006 Real Estate Champions, Inc.

Figure 6.6 Closing coordinator job description.

Assistant's Responsibilities

The following sections are included the benefit of both the agent and the assistant. They outline the basics of the assistant's job. Since each office is set up differently, the job responsibilities may differ. However, the information outlined here will be helpful to any team.

Field Coordinator or Runner Job Description

- Deliver packages.

- Set up new listings: Put up directionals, take photo, make duplicate key for office.

- Keep track of lock boxes and their locations.

- Makes sure the listing is maintained: Directionals are up, yard sign installed properly, flyer box full, etc.

- Take out garbage weekly. Separate items for recycling, if necessary.

- Perform miscellaneous office tasks, such as filing and photocopying.

- Put together listing packets.

- Put together marketing packets.

- Notify assistant when low on sign supplies (stickers, signs, stakes, etc.)

- Once listing is sold or expired: Remove directionals, lock box, etc.

- Take photos to lab to develop for ads.

- Assist with any mailings.

- Any additional field activities that could be delegated to the field coordinator.

©2006 Real Estate Champions, Inc.

Figure 6.7 Field coordinator job description.

Communication

A well-functioning team must have strong and constant communication. Communication comes in many forms, including written, oral, and both inter- and intraoffice e-mail. In order for the team to be highly efficient, communication among the team members needs to be tracked to ensure that the team members are accountable for their assigned tasks. In the tracking process, both the receiver and the sender create a record of the task.

There are four keys that you and your office can use to help the flow of information throughout the office: regular staff meetings, request forms, listing out questions, and being aggressive.

Regular Staff Meetings.   Daily and weekly meetings strengthen communication with your team. The focus of the daily meeting is on setting priorities for the staff for that day. This meeting is an opportunity for you to coach and direct the members of your team. If you do not have daily meetings, you are allowing your assistant and the other members of your team to set their own priorities, which may be different from yours. To be able to set your daily priorities with your team, you need to schedule 15 minutes daily for a meeting between you, your assistant, and the other members of the team.

One of the things that frustrates assistants is being overwhelmed with work. An assistant who does not understand what the agent's priorities are will feel even more overwhelmed by all the tasks that need to be completed. As the lead agent, you need to help your assistant define and determine what tasks need to be completed today and during the week. If you take 10 minutes a day to walk through the priorities for the day with your team, your assistant will be able to complete the tasks in the order in which you want them done and will complete the most important tasks for the day and for the week. Daily meetings can make the difference between business success and failure.

Weekly meetings with your assistant should focus on the overall goals and functions of the office. Use this meeting to look at and evaluate all of the activities scheduled during the week. You should also use this time to review the activities of the last month and to set new priorities for the month ahead.

There should also be weekly team meetings that all members of the team are required to attend. These weekly meetings will allow all members to explain their activities for the week and determine their priorities for next week. This is vital for a strong team. It allows evaluation of the completed week and an investment in the new week. It provides a time for brainstorming to determine solutions for ongoing problems. It will also enhance the team-building spirit. This meeting will give the team an opportunity to put an exclamation point at the end of a great week.

Request Forms.   Written request forms are crucial for an effective flow of tasks in the office. The requests are passed from one person to the next person in the team. We have included examples of these forms and directions on how to use them. These forms will enable you and your staff to set deadlines for you and for other members of your team. This information helps to avoid the occurrence of a "cold sweat night"—a mental wake-up call at 2 a.m. that finds you sitting straight up in bed, wide awake, wondering whether a particular task was completed or not. Once this happens, it becomes very hard for you to get back to sleep, since you cannot get that worrisome question out of your head.

Many agents use e-mail to direct their assistants. I think that is a mistake in the short run for new assistants. If you have a new assistant, use paper request forms. The tangible, physical piece of paper carries a greater impact. It doesn't get lost in all the spam e-mail we get. It also gives you a

Coaching Tip: *The use of request forms will instantly raise your productivity by at least 25%. It will also decrease mistakes made by you and your staff.*

chance to check the assistant's progress on a regular basis. You can switch to the more efficient e-mail in a few months, once you are confident of your new assistant's their execution.

Lists of Questions.   The assistant should have her questions well organized, so that she can ask the agent all the questions she has at the same time. She should save up the questions and ask them once or twice a day. This allows her to stay focused on the tasks that she is completing. It also helps the agent stay focused on sales without constant interruption. One appropriate time for the assistant to ask questions is during the daily meeting.

While the assistant is compiling her questions, she should also determine one or two answers to each of the questions. This step gives the agent an understanding that the assistant is attempting to solve the problems on her own, but that she needs to be sure what the correct solution is. It also gives the agent an idea of possible solutions. Even if the agent then has to reject both of the assistant's solutions, the process of working out possible solutions and receiving the agent's response to them will help the assistant understand why a particular solution will or will not work and why the task should be done in a particular way. This procedure gives the assistant an opportunity to learn how to solve the problem, so that if it arises in the future, she will be able to handle it. It also reduces the chance that the agent will get involved in or take ownership of the situation. A good assistant will not allow their Champion Agent to engage emotionally with a problem. It hampers the agent's performance, and sales will drop.

Be Assertive.   Another part of communication is being assertive. The assistant should be up front and direct with the agent and other team members if she needs to have something explained further or if she is missing paperwork for the file. The assistant must be able to say, "I need this" and not feel shy about it. Agents will sometimes be focused only on the sales aspect of the business and will not be aware of the work being done behind the scenes. The assistant must be able to let the agent and other team members know what is needed.

Request Forms

In a busy office, it is important to communicate clearly what tasks need to be completed, how to complete them, and the deadline for completing them. Sometimes telling the person what the task is and then giving him a deadline is difficult and time-consuming. A request form allows the person who is assigning the task to quickly write out what needs to be done and when she wants the task completed. Then the person who will complete the task can organize his day, knowing what tasks need to be completed and the deadline for each one. Once each task is completed, the person performing it signs at the bottom of the form, indicating that he has completed the task and the day it was completed.

Request forms help the operation of the office in many ways. First, they help team members stay focused on the tasks they are currently trying to complete. When there are constant interruptions, it takes twice or even three times as long to complete a task as it would take if the person performing the task were able to stay focused on the task without interruption. Each time someone is interrupted, it takes that person at least five minutes to refocus on the task he was working on prior to being interrupted. Request forms allow a clear way to communicate without interruption. The task is assigned without a word being said. This allows the members of the team to be more productive—able to stay focused on one task before moving to the next.

Second, it provides a way to track tasks and their completion. When the task is written down and assigned to a particular team member, there is documentation showing the request. If there are multiple people in the office, the request forms can use a different paper color for each member of the team. This allows the assistant or other team members to know, at a glance, who is requesting the task.

The use of request forms is not limited to requests made by the Champion Agent to other members of the team. They can also by the assistant or other members of the team to make requests of the Champion Agent, other assistants, or other members of the team.

Figure 6.8 is a copy of the request form. To use the form:

1. Fill in the date of the request.
2. Write out the request.

Request Form

Date: _____

Request:

_____
_____
_____
_____
_____
_____
_____
_____
_____

Requested By: _____

Date To Be Completed By: _____

Completed By: _____

Date Completed: _____

©2006 Real Estate Champions, Inc.

Figure 6.8 Request form.

3. Fill in the name of the person requesting the task.
4. Fill in the completion date.

   After the task is completed:

5. Write in who completed the task.
6. Fill in the date on which the task was completed.

Once the task has been completed, the request form goes back to the person who submitted it, so that that person knows that the task was completed and when.

Hiring, training, and monitoring the administrative staff is a challenge for any agent, whether that agent has one assistant or ten assistants. The right selection and preparation can help you avoid the turnover in staff that most agents experience. We all want to increase our production and delegate the things we don't like to do to others. An assistant can be a great asset or a significant liability. Your actions will ultimately decide which one it will be.

Expanding Your Sales Team

Many lead agents have as their goal expanding their sales team. Many even make this their primary objective soon after they start their real estate practice. The allure of having other people create your revenue can be powerful.

Agents' desire to expand their sales team has really picked up momentum in the last few years. Increased recognition of agents with large sales staffs at sales rallies and year-end awards ceremonies has increased the profile of sales teams. For many years, the national real estate brands failed to separate team production from individual sales agent production. This policy led those agents who wanted the spotlight of recognition to form teams. They couldn't win awards otherwise. Now, most of the national and regional brands are creating separate recognition tracks for individual agents and for teams.

The expansion of your sales team is an effective strategy to

1. Increase gross income.
2. Increase units sold.
3. Increase referrals.
4. Expand your database of sphere of influence members and past clients.
5. Increase your prospecting and lead generation.
6. Improve your personal sales skills (most agents will be forced to improve here if they are to teach effectively).
7. Decrease your cost per transaction.
8. Improve your quality of life.
9. Increase your time off.
10. Create more regular revenue and cash flow.

Evaluate Your Options

There are really only four options for increasing your sales team. You can select any one of these options or try to use all four at once. (I do not recommend using them all at once. If you do, it is likely that you will use all of them poorly. The result will be heavy losses in terms of your time and your personal production. Your cash flow from commissions will take a significant hit as well.)

Your options for expanding your sales team are to add

1. Buyer's agents
2. Showing agents
3. Listing agents
4. Telemarketers or prospecting agents

Each of these four options has its own unique challenges. Some also carry greater risk in the beginning. Some require larger amounts of training, monitoring, and coaching than others. For example, it's easier to train a buyer's agent than to train a listing agent. The listing agent is a more skilled position where fixing mistakes costs the lead agent more money and time. The loss of a listing that the listing agent should have secured or secured at the right price is a heavier burden than the loss of a buyer to represent.

Buyer's Agent

A buyer's agent is a lead agent's most common first sales hire. Agents are trying to rid themselves of the more time-consuming prospect—the buyer. The ongoing maintenance of a seller is less and can be carried out in a normal nine to five weekday. When you compare the average amount of time invested with a buyer prospect to contract to that invested with a seller prospect to contract, the amount of time required for the buyer is at least three times greater, on average. Thus, a buyer's agent is the first hire for over 95 percent of agents who are seeking to build a team.

Showing Agent

Showing agents merely assume the time-consuming task of showing property to buyers. Their duties could be expanded to include the writing of the contract, depending on their competence level. A showing agent could eventually expand into the role of buyer's agent. You are, however, limiting this agent's involvement to the most time-consuming activities of showing homes.

Many agents who are expanding their sales teams hire buyer's agents and turn over the leads and handling of ad calls and sign calls to these agents when they join the team.

My advice to my clients is to start new hires at the showing agent level and then elevate them based on performance.

With a showing agent, you are not turning over the lead at an early stage in the relationship, hoping that the agent will be skilled enough to compel the prospect to come into your office for the buyer presentation. A showing agent is not handling ad calls and sign calls, as a buyer's agent might do. With a showing agent, you still control the buyer consultation interview and the contract writing and negotiation. This allows you to achieve better conversion of the ad calls and sign calls, and better conversion ratios at the buyer interview with the prospect.

Listing Agent

From many years of experience in coaching agents to build teams, I have found that this is one of the hardest positions to fill with a talented person. It's a rare individual who has the discipline and sales skills necessary to be a Champion Listing Agent, but still wants to work in a team environment when it's not his team. You can find "wannabe" and "never be" Champion Listing Agents to place in this position, but the net result will be much less than desired.

Most lead agents don't have the discipline necessary to achieve Champion Listing Agent status. They don't prospect consistently enough. They don't practice the scripts and dialogues for their presentation until they are perfect. They fail to invest the time to be an incredible objection handler and closer. They fall short of having the discipline to craft the powerful benefits, competitive points of difference, value counseling, and price counseling segments of their presentation. Champion Agents do this to take out the competition, reduce the time required for their presentation, and ensure that they secure the listings at the right terms and under the right conditions every time.

A true Champion Listing Agent will be willing to do whatever is necessary in terms of training, practice, and correction to be a sales master in his mindset and in the preparation and delivery of his presentation. He will have the focus and mental strength to apply the four rules of real estate effectively to all prospects.

The Four Rules of Real Estate.
1. *Be there.*   This rule means that you show up on time. Being on time for a listing appointment can often mean the difference between getting the listing and not getting the listing. It means preparing before you go on an appointment, so that you are ready. Being there also means treating your real estate career like a real job. Show up at work at the same time every day. My day started at 7 a.m. during my sales career. It was very rare for me not to be in the office at that time.

2. *Focus mentally.*   Focusing mentally means being in the moment with intense concentration. The better you focus mentally, the more results you will get from the time you invest. If you need to listen to the client, focus on what the client is saying. If you are formulating your answer or response while the client is speaking, you are not listening to the client. Learning to focus is one of the most valuable skills you can acquire. Focus always comes before success. Focus means paying attention to what is happening around you and paying attention to the details of success. It is usually a small thing that separates success from failure. Just ask the U.S. women's soccer team—or, better yet, ask the Chinese team. In the World Cup a few years ago, one penalty kick made the difference between first and second place. The difference between the number 1 PGA tour player and the number 150 is about one stroke per 18 holes and more than $9 million in earnings. Focus mentally in the moment you are in.

3. *Tell the truth.*   In every situation, tell the truth. Agents are often given the opportunity to tell people something they don't want to hear. For example, suppose a seller's home is worth $150,000, but she wants $165,000. What do you do? Many agents will take the listing at $165,000 and deal with the $15,000 price reduction later. My belief is that you should tell the truth. You may not get the listing, but at least you will know that you were honest. Too many of us hedge or shade the truth. You need to understand that if you do this, a time of reckoning will come. It may not be now, but it will come. It may be when the market slows and you have a bunch of listings that will not sell. Remember, the truth will set you free.

4. *Accept the results and move on.*   Too often, agents let the highs get too high and the lows get too low. We need to accept the results we get. Work to understand your results and the reasons for them, and then move on to make any necessary changes.

   Babe Ruth realized that striking out is part of playing baseball. He knew he would have other opportunities. He would have other times at bat—some today and some tomorrow. If a pitch fooled him, he learned from it, so that he wouldn't be fooled again. We are all going to strike out. We are going to strike out with buyers and sellers, with other agents, and with our broker. It is just part of life. We must learn from our mistakes and move on.

   If you continue to worry about the lost deal, you won't be able to focus on the deal that is currently in front of you. The process of your daily disciplines and the improvement of your skills are what you can control.

My advice is to evolve into having a listing agent. Don't try to acquire listing agents right away. Focus on building good buyer's agents. The time you will save by removing the buyers from your car for good is huge. After my second full year in the business, I never had a buyer in my car again. However, I never managed to find the right person to take on the listing agent position permanently. When I was unavailable, someone else on the team completed the task of listing clients' homes. I would not have wanted to rely on someone else full time.

Telemarketer or Prospecting Agent

The focus of this member of the sales team is on lead generation, prospecting, lead follow-up, and appointment setting. She is on the team to increase the number of appointments you go on. As a general rule, her prospecting and lead generation involves calling new listings or new sales using a just listed or just sold script to secure appointments where you can make listing presentations. She can also help you as a lead agent expand your business into higher-impact areas of sales, such as FSBOs and expired listings. A prospecting agent could also use an "I have a buyer" calling strategy to secure listings and sales.

An effective prospecting agent or telemarketer will increase the lead agent's listing inventory. She will also effectively support the buyer's agents by increasing the inventory of listings, which will increase ad calls, sign calls, open house appointments, and interactive voice response (IVR) calls as well.

Should I Hire a Buyer's Agent?

When you are expanding your team by adding buyer's agents, there are a couple of key questions you need to ask yourself before you embark on this path.

1. *Do I have enough leads to support a buyer's agent?* You will need to have enough leads to support and feed the production for your new buyer's agent. The more inexperienced the buyer's agent is, the greater the burn rate on your leads will be. The burn rate is the number of blown opportunities with viable leads that the buyer's agent has in the learning process. An inexperienced buyer's agent's sales and conversion ratios on leads will be significantly lower than those of a fully trained, successful agent.

   Coach's Tip: *If you are generating 30 to 40 buyer leads per month per buyer's agent, or if you could increase your marketing to create that number, you have enough leads to adequately support a buyer's agent.*

   If you have a reasonable inventory of listings that the buyer's agent can hold open (somewhere in the high single digits), you should be willing to consider increasing your marketing efforts to increase the number of leads. Adding an IVR system will increase the number of leads dramatically in most markets. I have seen a few markets that are the exception, but there aren't many.

2. *If not, how am I going to increase the lead sources or the lead volume?* You must pause and create a specific plan. You also must be willing to carry out this plan for around six months until you have collected enough data to indicate that the plan needs to be changed. Agents are famous for trying a new lead-generation strategy for 30 days,

then scrapping it and replacing it by the latest gimmick they heard about. In fact, 30 days (or even 90 days) is usually not long enough to determine the sales ratios from a marketing strategy.

You can also create a plan for increasing your number of sources, meaning where the leads come from. A new source might be a new IVR system or home buyer seminars. An increase in lead volume could also come from investing in your current sources. You could increase the frequency, quantity, or quality of your marketing to drive up the leads from your existing sources.

3. *What percentage of his income should I expect the buyer's agent to produce on his own?* You must establish production goals or expectations for a new buyer's agent. He needs to be hired with the expectation that he will be responsible for producing some leads himself from his own contacts and some from working your inventory. Most lead agents are not clear about their expectations for the buyer's agent.

4. *Do I have the sales skills of this business down, so that I can teach them to others?* You really need to evaluate this question honestly by taking off the rose-colored glasses. Do you really have your sales skills down well enough to be able to teach them to someone else? Would your broker hire you to teach the sales team in your company? Would I hire you to represent me and Real Estate Champions in teaching sales training to other agents? If you can't say yes, there is work to be done.

5. *How much time am I willing to invest personally?* Making a buyer's agent a success will take you some time. One of the biggest mistakes I made early in my career as an agent and even early in building my company, Real Estate Champions, was assuming that because a real estate agent or salesperson had experience and documented sales success, she had sales skills. I never make that assumption anymore, even when someone comes with impeccable records of success in sales—that doesn't always mean that she knows how to sell. You need to know how much time you are willing to invest to make your new buyer's agent a Champion.

6. *How much time will this take each week?* You have only a finite amount of time to invest each week. Working with a buyer's agent for an hour a day should be enough to help him become successful in less than four months.

7. *What is my expected return in these areas?*
   A. Quality of life
   B. Income
   You need some goals in terms of money, time off, reduced stress, and consistency of income. What reasons or factors are leading you to consider hiring a buyer's agent at this time? The more clearly you have crystallized your expectations, the higher your the probability of success. You can't hit a target that you can't see, and neither can your buyer's agent.

8. *Is the timing right now for me to do this?*   Timing in adding staff is everything. All the other factors can be perfect, but if your timing is wrong, you will fail. Even if you hire a future Champion Agent as a buyer's agent for your team, if the timing is not right, the whole thing will implode.

Develop the Parameters

Too many agents leap into the mega-agent game of having buyer's agents too quickly or without forethought. Buyer's agents can be extremely valuable and productive, but they can also cripple a lead agent's business because the agent is not prepared to handle them. You really need to evaluate each additional buyer's agent in terms of the short-term costs versus the short-term and long-term gain.

Staff turnover is one of the most costly aspects of any business. When I turn over a salesperson in my company, it costs me no less than about $21,500. That cost includes salary, taxes, sales manager time, training, prorated share of space rental, computers, phones, long distance, and blown leads not converted. (The figure for blown leads could be much higher than the number I factored in. I just don't want to make myself ill thinking about it.) Your figures might be even higher when you take your time and your value into account. Before you hire someone, you have to be able to minimize the risk to you as much as possible. There are a couple of rules to follow with regard to minimizing the risk.

Many agents who are entering the business want to work for a successful agent before venturing out on their own. These are not the people you are looking for. You are not in the business of training your own competition. Because the cost of training is so high, in terms of both money spent and training time invested, you can't afford to have a buyer's agent leave inside of a year. If someone is not willing to give you a two- to three-year commitment, pass on that person. If her secret ambition is to own her own real estate sales business or if her ego will not allow her to work for you, move on.

You will often see the ego part demonstrated by the person's wanting a more prominent position in your advertising, marketing, or signs. It may come up in how she wants her title to appear on her business card. She may want to be on the periphery of your team while trying to create a name just for herself. If a candidate says anything about building her own brand, you should have warning lights flashing in your head. The odds are that she will be using your business and skills to build her own business and will leave before you turn a profit on her. Once people of this type feel that they have "learned" enough, they will be gone. They will constantly be looking at their side of the equation, and they will be focused on how much money you are making from them.

I firmly believe that you need to have any agent you employ sign a very strict non-compete agreement. I realize that this is a very tough stance to take with a new buyer's agent. But I also believe that to do it right, you will invest too much of your time, energy, emotion, money, and leads to not guarantee a return on your investment. Someone who wants to be part of your team for a long time will sign such an agreement. Someone who wants to learn and leave will not.

The strict noncompete agreement that I used prohibited agents from contacting the clients they worked with while they were on my team. It prohibited them from taking leads with them if they left. It also prohibited them from working in my predetermined geographic area for a period of two years after they left. You might be thinking, are these agreements enforceable? The answer is, that depends on the state. The question isn't enforcement but perception. I am not saying that you should sue someone over a noncompete contract. You want to use the agreement as a deterrent to an agent's using you as a training company. On average, based on the investment you make in training a new buyer's agent, I believe that it takes about 12 months for the agent to achieve a net profit level with you. A buyer's agent who leaves in six months will cost you money—guaranteed. The noncompete agreement tests the agent's commitment level.

You could put a repayment provision in there if people want out early. They can repay you $25,000 for the training and education they received. There are a lot of options with the noncompete agreement. However, you must have an agreement with regard to the clients they work with. This agreement needs to be final before someone comes to work for you. I believe the clients are yours, and that you should retain ownership. An agent can take her sphere of influence with her when she leaves, but the clients she represented in a transaction are your property.

The reason that this is a nonnegotiable point is that the real profit for you as a Champion Agent doesn't come from the first transaction; it comes from the second. The first transaction is more like a loss leader. It's like milk in the grocery store. Milk is usually on sale to get you to shop at one particular store rather than another. The grocery store expects to lose money or make only a small profit on the milk. It's the other items that you put into your basket that give the store a profit. The buyer's agent's initial sale is really a short-term, small profit at best.

How Much Is a Buyer's Agent Worth?

We have done extensive studies with our clients to arrive at a compensation range that we feel accurately takes into account the profit from buyer's agent sales, as well as a formula for calculating your net profit from buyer's agent transactions. The calculation of the net profit you generate from a buyer's agent must factor in the time that you spent in training, transaction involvement, management, and coaching. When calculating expenses, lead agents often overlook this personal investment of their time. If you were not working to train the buyer's agent or help her with her transactions, you could do more transactions of your own.

There are other expenses that can be calculated on a per-unit basis. There are legitimate costs that you incur that can be assigned to each transaction. We call these the cost per transaction. We all have an average cost per transaction that can be assigned each time we do a transaction. The increase in units created by the buyer's agent does helps lower the cost per transaction overall.

Champion Calculation

Let's look at a typical net profit for a lead agent.

The total commission is $6,000, and you split the commission 50/50 with your buyer's agent:

Lead agent	$3,000	Buyer's agent	$3,000
Cost/transaction	$1,200	Cost/transaction	$ 0
Lead agent time		Buyer's agent has	
(4 h/unit at $200/h)	$ 800	limited expenses	$ 500
Net Profit	$1,000	Net Profit	$2,500

All of these calculations are based on net profit without considering your payments to your brokerage company. You will need to factor your split into the equation if you have a split arrangement.

When the commission check and the sale price are within the average range of $5,000 to $7,000 and $200,000 to $275,000, we tend to see a net profit from a buyer's agent transaction. The amount of this profit tends to be between $500 and $1,500 per unit, when all legitimate costs, including your time, are factored in.

Too many agents falsely believe that they are getting rich through buyer's agents. The real profit from the buyer's agent comes on the second transaction with a past client or a referral. It is when you list a home for sale in the future and that buyer makes another purchase that the true value of the buyer's agent is realized.

Champion Team Rule: *The real monetary value of a buyer's agent is a short-term, small net profit with a much larger future profit on the next sale.*

If you are blessed to sell in an area where the average commission check is $10,000 or greater, you will find the short-term net profit from the first transaction to be closer to the $3,500 and up range. Don't be fooled, as most are, into thinking that the net profit from buyer's agent sales is a windfall profit for you and your business. The lower than expected net profit is why I caution lead agents not to sacrifice their personal production for others.

Design a Compensation Plan

Most agents have never really looked at the profit numbers on buyer's agents. Many of them think that they are making a large income from buyer's agents when that's not really true. It's really a small profit per deal.

Champion Calculation

Let's say your average commission check through your buyer's agent is $6,000. You operate on an 80/20 split with your company because you are a very good agent. Thus, the gross fee that you split with your buyer's agent is $4,800. That amount is split 50/50 between the two of you. You each receive $2,400. Out of your $2,400 portion, you have to pay your advertising, marketing, overhead, other assistants, and all the expenses of running your business. Most agents' initial cost per transaction (what it costs them to do a deal) is between $1,500 and $3,000. This includes advertising, marketing, staff, expenses, car, and cell phone costs. Everything you spend to run your business is divided by the number of transactions you do. Obviously, as the number of units you do goes up, your cost per unit will come down. The buyer's agent will help your cost per unit come down. If you are at the lower end of the cost per transaction, or $1,500, your net profit from this transaction will be $900. That is before you factor in the personal time you invested in the transaction. (That is not a lot of money.)

Let's say you are worth $200 an hour and you work with a buyer's agent for two hours per transaction, which would be easy to do when you consider training, monitoring, managing, helping with the clients, and closing the deal. The truth is, two hours is nothing. You would then net, after factoring in your time, $500 for a transaction.

Having buyer's agents isn't highly profitable for an individual transaction. I always tell agents that they will net somewhere between $500 and $1,500 before they factor in their time. The exception would be if your average commission check is substantially higher than $6,000. If the average commission in your market is $15,000, you have more profit and more options. The vast majority of the buyer's agents will help you generate a small, short-term profit.

Buyer's agents will also provide you with a higher quality of life. You will be able to take most weekends off (or maybe even all of them). This will improve your quality of life with your family, who would like to spend more weekends with you. You won't be fielding ad calls or sign calls or conducting open houses over the weekend. You really will be able to turn off your cell phone over the weekend and be free. My buyer's agents were responsible for the weekends. They responded to other agents' inquiries about my listings. They handled the ad calls, sign calls, and open houses. Their job was also to respond to agents who had made written offers when I was out of town, which was every weekend, and to instruct those agents to fax the offers to my office to be presented on Monday when I returned. I did not work on weekends.

When you have a buyer's agent, you are able to focus more on securing listings. My buyer's agents wanted me to focus on listings. They thought that if I got more listings, they would have more leads, which was true. (I wonder where they heard that.) What was good for them was also good for the team. With a buyer's agent, you end up utilizing your time better because it takes less time to work a listing than it does to work a buyer, even when you factor prospecting time into the equation.

There are as many variations on compensation plans as there are stars in the sky. I will try to explain the guidelines that I think all agents must apply to arrive at a fair and equitable compensation plan. I am sure some agents will disagree with my results, beliefs, and guidelines, and that's fine. I know there will be a large number of buyer's agents who will take issue as well.

A number of years ago, I was speaking in Eugene, Oregon, to a large group of agents. A buyer's agent asked me how a buyer's agent's compensation should be structured. I tried to deflect the question because I sensed from her attitude that my views and hers were vastly different. She explained that she was on a 70/30 split where she got 70 percent, and she felt that her agent was getting a great deal in getting 30 percent of what she generated. I finally could not hold back any longer and told her and all the other agents that her agent was losing money every time she did a transaction. She proceeded to get angry and tell me that I was wrong. That 30 percent was a lot of money for her agent because it was "money she wouldn't have had otherwise." I can tell you that this is the argument a buyer's agent will make every time when asking for more money. Be ready for it. My job is to give you the truth about compensation.

The true way to determine what you can pay a buyer's agent is to base it on your average cost per transaction. Whatever it costs you to do a transaction, on average, must be applied to your side of the ledger. There are expenses for each and every transaction you engage in. Each transaction needs to pay for a portion of the overhead, marketing, advertising, your time, staff time, gas for your car, MLS dues, and all the other costs that you have as a real estate agent. The buyer's agent is really receiving a (predominantly) net dollar check with limited expenses. You still have to run the transaction through your system and incur costs that the buyer's agent doesn't.

Champion Calculation

Let's say that you and a buyer's agent have a 70/30 split arrangement like this lady in Eugene. The gross commission that she just generated was $6,000. You are on an 80/20 split with your company. You now have $4,800 to split between the two of you. She gets $3,360 of that commission; you receive $960. You pay all the expenses of your business, and your cost per transaction is an average of $1,500. You have just lost $540 for the joy of conducting that transaction. You still have the legal liability for the transaction in our suit-happy world, even though you didn't make a dime. Make sure you balance your compensation package using your cost per transaction. Your average commission check will also play a role as well. If your average commission check was $15,000 instead, your broker would get $3,000. The buyer's agent would get $9,600, and you would receive $2,400. After the cost per transaction, you would net a whopping $900 out of a $15,000 check. That's hardly worth the effort, in my view. If you use a 50/50 split with buyer's agents, you are usually in the ballpark. But in some cases, 60/40 to you would be better. You have to do the calculating to find out if you will be profitable.

Remember that in all these computations, I did not factor in the value of your time yet. Let the buyer's agent know how you arrived at your commission split numbers. Share your cost per transaction with him; he knows that you have expenses. You will often hear, "So-and-so will pay me more." Tell him it's not your problem that so-and-so doesn't understand his business. Does he want to work with someone who, when the market changes, might be out of business?

Single-Tier Compensation Versus Two-Tier Compensation. Another mistake that agents make is using a compensation system with two or more tiers. They give the buyer's agent a higher split for sphere, past clients, or referrals from those sources. This approach creates a tracking and monitoring nightmare. How do you really know that this lead didn't come from an open house, an ad call, or a sign call—basically from the agent's working your lead-generation success? The truth is, you don't know. Too many people's ethics and integrity get clouded when they are behind on their bills or having a bad month. Logistically, a multitiered structure is also a hassle to operate.

If you follow the 1/3, 1/3, 1/3 Rule, the buyer's agent will get some really easy deals from your referral sources and from current sellers that you can't work with. He will probably have about as many of those deals as referrals that he himself generates. These sources cancel themselves out. A buyer's agent needs to know that you have an understanding of your success and why you are making the financial compensation decisions you are making. He also needs to know and believe that you are fundamentally a fair person.

Listings generated by the buyer's agent need to be compensated at a lower level than buyers. If you are on a 50/50 split with your buyer's agent for buyers, that level is too high for listings. The reason is that your involvement and risk are greater on a listing than on a buyer lead. If the buyer's agent is a solid producer, you get involved in overseeing and managing the process, and your staff closes the transaction.

On the listing side of the transaction, you must secure the listing, position and market it, and take the risk that it might not sell. You will invest more of your dollars and time into a listing than into just closing a transaction for a buyer. The seller and the buyer are in two different stages in the life of a transaction. You are farther away from getting a commission check with a seller than with a buyer, and you are carrying a greater risk. You can't afford to pay at the same level. Nor can you afford to allow the buyer's agent to take listings until he is fully trained in the listing process and has a solid presentation. If you allow him to take listings before this, I guarantee that you will end up with listings you don't want, at prices you don't want, with increased marketing obligations you don't want, with shorter listing terms than you need. It's not the buyer's agent's money that carries and pays for the expenses of the listing. Often, either he is hoping that something good will come out of a bad situation, or he simply doesn't know enough yet—he knows just enough to be dangerous.

Setting the Standard—The 1/3, 1/3, 1/3 Rule.   As Champion Agents, we must set standards for our buyer's agents to follow. The most important performance standard should be the number of daily contacts. How many contacts does the buyer's agent need to make each day? How will you monitor that number of contacts? How will the buyer's agent report them to you? Remember the Champion Rule that states, "When performance is measured and reported, performance improves faster." There must be a method for measuring and reporting the performance of buyer's agents. What are the daily, weekly, and monthly standards for contacts, leads, buyer interview appointments, exclusive right to represent contracts written, offers, and closed transactions that the buyer's agent must meet? What's the standard for open houses conducted monthly? What's the standard for percentage of contacts from the call capture numbers you secure? What are the conversion ratio standards for contacts to leads, leads to appointments, appointments to exclusive agency agreements, and exclusive agency agreements to closed transactions? How will you monitor and report the buyer's agent's asking for and receiving referrals? Setting all these standards and monitoring performance will dramatically improve a buyer's agent's success rate. You are doing this for his benefit as well as yours.

In establishing standards for buyer's agents, I believe it is essential that you focus them on the creation of business. There are far too many buyer's agents who expect the Champion Agent to provide all the leads and deals for them. They think that all they should have to do is wait for the best opportunities to come in; they want the easiest ones and nothing else. We usually attract buyer's agents by telling them that we have more leads than we can work. This entices them to work for us just as a late night infomercial entices us with the easy, no-money-down way to buy real estate. We must establish a standard of truth and a standard of work before someone joins our team. Too many buyer's agents act like baby birds in the nest waiting for mommy bird to come back with a worm for them to eat. The 1/3, 1/3, 1/3 Rule helps paint a realistic picture and set a performance standard for achieving success.

First 1/3.   You will provide solid, high-quality leads from your past clients, current clients, sphere of influence, and other sources. You will expect that 1/3 of the buyer's agent's production for the year will come from these sources. These are really easy transactions because the agent will not be competing with anyone to secure the buyer. In fact, the trust has already been built through your credibility. These leads are "just don't blow it, and you will have a transaction and a commission check."

Second 1/3.   This third of the buyer's agent's production comes from his own past clients, sphere of influence, and current client referrals. You expect him to ask everyone he talks with, knows, and hangs out with for referrals well enough and frequently enough to ensure that 1/3 of his total income for the year comes from this source. This allows you, as the Champion Agent, to increase the number of transactions and net profit by engaging in transactions that you might not otherwise have gained access to. It also enables the buyer's agent to establish the habits of referral discussion and dialogue quickly.

Third 1/3.   This is the area that the buyer's agent really has to work for. He needs to get out of the nest and find transactions through his own actions. This 1/3 should come from open houses, ad calls, sign calls, Internet leads, IVR systems, magazines, floor time, or any other form of active prospecting and lead follow-up. If all a buyer's agent is doing is the first 2/3 of his production, you can get anyone to do that. You want a buyer's agent who will create some of his own business. This reduces his dependence on your other lead sources and should allow you to increase sales and potentially add additional buyer's agents to your mix.

Managing, Monitoring, and Coaching

Most lead agents have challenges with all three of these activities. All of them are important in building the sales production of your buyer's agents. When you are building your team, you will not be able to do all three well right away. You need to evaluate which of them is the first priority, then the second, and then the third. Taking the right steps in the wrong order still leads to failure.

Rank the importance from one to three in your view:

Managing   _____
Monitoring   _____
Coaching   _____

I have asked this ranking question numerous times, and I rarely get the right order from lead agents. Most of them feel that management is the number one priority. They believe that they need to manage people well so that those people are more productive. I view management as the least valuable of the three activities. If you have hired properly and you have a high-capacity individual or a future Champion, management is the easiest of the three.

The most important activity initially is monitoring: establishing a set of monitoring benchmarks in terms of the activities your buyer's agents need to do, creating a daily and weekly reporting system, and setting standards so that you can compare activities to results. Identifying minimum standards that the buyer's agents must maintain if they are to remain with the team is vital. These standards for sales activities—prospecting, lead generation, lead conversion, presentations, showings, closing the prospect to a contract, and service to closing—must be monitored if improvement is to happen.

Creating and using monitoring systems will enable you to compare, evaluate, and improve performance faster if you have more than one buyer's agent or showing agent. The truth is, you won't know how to manage or what to coach your buyer's agents in without a well-implemented and well-executed monitoring system. (That's why monitoring comes first.)

Coaching is the second priority. It links with monitoring to build constructive accountability. We all need coaching; the only question is who will provide it. Being able to evaluate your buyer's agents' performance ratios and to design strategies and action plans for them to carry out individually and jointly with you or another team member improves their performance more quickly. Remember, if they knew what they were doing wrong in real estate sales, they probably would not be members of your team working for you.

Managing is the least important of the three activities. When you have selected people with strong character and self-discipline, the job of managing them becomes almost routine.

The Listing Agent

I clearly stated earlier that I think the hardest position to fill is that of a great listing agent. The listing agent needs to have the same philosophy, temperament, mindset, behavioral style, and sales skills that you do. She needs to have the potential to be a carbon copy of you. I know successful listing agents who are not a "mini-Me" version of the lead agent, but work still gets done. However, the road is fraught with challenges, frustrations, and setbacks until a successful track record and trust are built. In that model, the lead agent will be Monday morning quarterbacking a lot of what the listing agent contributes and how she operates.

When they are considering adding a listing agent, the two areas that most agents fail to evaluate well are sales skills and behavioral style. Does the candidate currently possess or can you train and coach her to have the sales skills that the position demands? Does she score well on the sales skills assessments we asked you to take in Chapter 2? Does she have her highest scores in the areas of qualifying the prospect, presentations, objection handling, and closing? Is she capable of going head to head with other lead agents and winning? If not, is she willing to work at these skills until she can do this?

The truth is, a listing agent probably has to have better sales skills than you do because she isn't the lead agent. If you are the lead agent for a successful team that has built your career to a solid level, you have the credibility of having done it. The listing agent doesn't carry that when she walks in the door—you do. The listing agent is presenting your credibility for you in your absence. She is working to convey the competitive points of difference, track record of results, and conviction of the team's beliefs while playing only a minor role compared with your role in achieving that level of success.

New listing agents haven't had a hand in any of your team's success thus far. Their sales skills carry tremendous weight in securing a listing in spite of the other agents competing for it. They must get all of their listing contracts ratified at the listing presentation and finally secure the listing with the right terms and conditions to ensure that the commission will be earned. The right terms and conditions include the correct price, a long enough term, and realistic expectations on the part of the sellers concerning marketing, advertising, showings, open house frequency, communication frequency, type of communication, how the team works, negotiation of the contract, and overall results. Anyone can easily take more listings if he takes them without the right terms and conditions.

Coach's Tip: *The listing agent you hire must have the same behavioral style as you, or at least one that is very similar. (I talk about behavioral style and using the a behavioral assessment extensively in Chapter 8.)*

A good behavioral style assessment will help you determine how someone will react in certain situations. If a person views the world the same way you do because of having similar behavioral style, that person will be more likely to replicate you in the field in terms of communication to the prospects, and in sales presentations in terms of sales skills, sales processes, and sales structure. Your training will be more effective with such people because you, in effect, speak their language. For example, it will be easier for such a person to replicate your listing presentation. You will experience fewer new challenges and problems, and you won't be investing your time in new solutions based on behavioral makeup.

Through our years of validated research on behavioral styles at Real Estate Champions, we can tell you the exact problems a salesperson will have in his sales business before they occur, based on his behavioral style. I discuss this topic extensively in Chapter 19, "Building Your Ideal Business," of my previous book, *The Champion Real Estate Agent.*

The most frequent result of a lack of behavioral alignment comes in the terms and conditions of the listings that the listing agent does secure. I discovered this when I was working with a very successful agent in Dallas, Texas, who had a listing agent. When we were analyzing her inventory of listings, we found that the majority of the listings that had a low probability of selling in the next 30 days had been taken by her listing agent. We calculated that, on average, the listing agent took the listings at 109 percent of value and for a 31 percent shorter term. The lead agent was expending considerable resources to market the properties for a longer time, secure price reductions, and sign extensions to the length of the listing term. When we looked at the client surveys after completed transactions, the client satisfaction level scores for these clients were in the high 60s. The non-listing agent clients had satisfaction ratings exceeding 95 percent on average.

The vexing part was that this was a very experienced listing agent. She knew what she was doing, and she had reasonable sales skills—much better skills than the results indicated. The problem had to be her behavioral style, since the lead agent was a high dominant/high influencer. The listing agent was a high steady with a middle influencer score. The listing agent's behavioral style was worlds apart from that of the lead agent. She couldn't replicate what the lead agent was doing because of her behavioral style. Once we knew the problem, we could create targeted training and standards that improved her performance dramatically. We saw the poor numbers rise over time. They never matched the lead agent's, but they improved.

I then took a look at all my clients who had listing agents and found that the most effective lead agent/listing agent teams were the ones where the lead agent and the listing agent had similar behavioral styles. If you are reading this and want to check your team, we have a free assessment tool on our Web site at www.realestatechampions.com/disc.

Pros and Cons of Having a Listing Agent

By having a listing agent, you can leverage yourself through her. You can increase the number of appointments you have and even schedule simultaneous appointments. You could be off listing the Joneses while your listing agent is working with the Smiths.

This expansion has the effect of increased the number of listings sold, but it will also influence your buyer-controlled sales. Because of the increase in listings, you will increase the number of ad calls and sign calls, which will increase your leads, buyer prospects, buyer clients, and buyer sales. With increased listings sold and buyer sales, you will also increase your past client ranks in a shorter time, which will increase referrals. You will also usually see a decrease in cost per transaction, which will make each transaction more profitable.

You will raise your image and increase your brand recognition in the marketplace. With more listings on the ground, you will become better known as a real estate agent in the marketplace. This will increase the unsolicited call-in appointments that say, "I see your sign everywhere." Your quality of life will be enhanced because you aren't the only plowhorse hooked to the yoke to pull the business. There is some safety in numbers, as long as the other horse is hooked to the yoke with you and isn't shoving you down or pulling the plow crooked.

Your time away from the business will be more relaxing, and the business will operate while you are gone. The period before an agent without a listing assistant goes on vacation is a fire drill at best and total chaos at worst. Inevitably, everyone is going to want to list just before you want to take time off. Whether that's the influence of Murphy's law or just that your focus and intensity rise just before you are heading off on vacation, the days leading up to time off are usually some of the busiest of the year. The lead up to your time off will be more controlled with a listing agent.

The time while you are gone will also be more effective for the business. I always had people who wanted to list their home calling when I was away. My team's first objective was to get them to wait. If that jeopardized our opportunity to list the property, we sent in the team. That was usually a buyer's agent or another agent in my office with whom I would split the listing if it was more than my buyer's agent could handle. If you don't have a listing agent, it's rare that you will list new property while you are away. You might generate buyer sales or listings sold, but you won't take any new listings. The net result is a drop in your listing inventory while you are away enjoying your family time.

If your team has managed to delay a few listing appointments, you will have a work backlog to attend to when you return. You will come back relaxed and recharged, only to jump into the frying pan that has been on the stove heating up while you were gone. You will not be able to make a slow, smooth transition back into the business. You will need to be back on your "A" game the minute you hit the front door of your office. A solid listing agent makes the period of time before, during, and after a vacation much easier for the lead agent. Without a listing agent, you may sometimes feel that the time off wasn't worth the extra effort invested before you went and after your return. That won't happen with a listing agent.

The cons of having a listing agent are as significant as the pros. The most glaring ones will happen to many agents before they even make a dime of profit from a listing agent. This makes the risk of adding a listing agent to your team far greater than that of adding a buyer's agent.

First, you will need to invest significant resources to find high-quality potential candidates. You will have to pan a lot of riverbeds to find a gold nugget. You want the person to have the right attitude already. You can't train someone to have a good attitude. Also, the listing agent's behavioral style must be similar to yours. Again, that's something that training will not solve. Either she has it or she doesn't.

Finding a listing agent by delivering flyers to all real estate offices, sending e-mails through the MLS system or board of Realtors, or doing direct mailings using the board of Realtors' mailing lists takes discipline, practice, money, and time. Even using a strictly word-of-mouth campaign through your company, your broker, your mortgage company, the title company, and even other agents you know or do business with will be an investment of your resources. If you stick with it long enough and consistently enough, you will eventually find the right person. You can't be impatient. You are really looking for a rare individual, not Johnny Anybody. The wrong hire is worse than no hire.

The investment in training is far more significant for a listing agent. The amount of your time and energy that you must invest to make this person a top performer for your team in the listing area will be hours each week. You will need to role-play, coach, book appointments for her and yourself, and go on her appointments with her for a period of time as well as going on yours. She will need a lot of work with you, or she will blow a lot of leads and opportunities that you would have landed before she reaches even the basic competence level.

A nonnegotiable item for me would be a *noncompete contract*. I would never hire anyone for this position without one. The resources you will invest in finding and training a listing agent are enormous. The training, skills, and intellectual property you are giving her as your listing agent are priceless.

Champion Team Rule: *You are not in the business of training and equipping your own competition.*

If you don't use a noncompete agreement, I guarantee that your listing agent will leave you and compete with you in the open market in the future. Many will leave you and not only compete with you in the open market, but also compete with you for your own stable of past clients. This is especially true for the clients that the listing agent did business with directly and has a relationship with.

A drawback to a noncompete agreement is that some high-quality candidates won't sign one. You could lose some good people. My view is that you have now ferreted out the people who would have left and left quickly. The people who object to a noncompete agreement will leave as soon as they feel they have learned enough to make it on their own. Once they reach that point, they hit the road. Many of them already have that figure in their head when talking with you. They think, "I will spend 12 months learning the business from the best, and then I will go out on my own." When they get to the point where they start to have some success, their ego grows, their timeline gets cut in half, and they are gone one morning without any notice.

Another disadvantage is that you will sometimes be saddled with listings that you would have turned down or that have terms and conditions that aren't in your favor. You will be forced to deal with overpriced listings where you have to invest your time to get the price reduced. In the interim, you will have to market these listings knowing that the money you are spending on marketing is being wasted because the listings won't sell at their current price. You will have listings you wish you didn't have in your inventory because of their condition, the motivation level of the seller, the price, the area, or the type of property (e.g., a manufactured home in a trailer park). Your options are either to bite the bullet and hope everything comes out OK or deal with the problem head on with the seller, correcting the issue or referring the listing to someone else. Referring it to someone else runs the risk of alienating both the seller and the listing agent on your team.

All of these situations will affect your bottom line negatively in terms of time invested by you and your staff to deal with the issues, marketing dollars spent on each property, and lower odds of your achieving a sale and earning a commission. The listing agent can have the attitude that she will get any and all listings she can because it's not her resources in the form of marketing dollars, staff time, and your time to fix the problems that are being used. She has all the potential upside of earning a few dollars with none of the downside of increased costs and lower odds to cover out of her own pocket.

Setting the Standards

The most important standards are in two areas: the *activity standards* and the *quality standards*. The activity standards are the listing agent's prospecting, lead follow-up, conversion, and overall sales ratios. You should have set standards for each of these areas to ensure the listing agent's success. You will probably also want to set practice standards, so that she raises their skill level to the highest possible level quickly, while costing you the least in blown opportunities.

X Theory of Success. It always takes us X amount of time to become proficient at anything. That X will be different for each one of us based on our internal, God-given gifts and the previous experiences and skills we have that complement what we are trying to learn.

As an example, it might take some of you reading this book 100 practice sessions to really perfect your listing presentation, so that you can deliver it with power and conviction, handle all of the objections that will naturally come up, and convert the seller to sign the contract the night you are there. I might be less skilled than you and have a tougher time perfecting it. My effort section of the learning curve might be larger and steeper than yours. I may need to practice it 200 times before I get it perfected. The issue isn't that I take twice as long as you to achieve the X level of success; it's that I have an idea of where X is, and I am working toward it regularly.

Y Theory of Choice. I now have a *Y Theory of Choice* decision to make. Since I know I will have to practice my presentation 200 times, I have a choice to make on how long it will take me to get to X. That is the Y Theory of Choice. I can take ten years, five years, two years, one year, or perhaps even just six months. If I practice my listing presentation only when I am live in front of sellers, and if I am in front of sellers three or four times a month, it will probably take me more than five years to get to my 200 times. That, unfortunately, is the mistake that most agents make. They have a poor attitude, and they lack the commitment to speed up the time frame for hitting X. Their Y Theory of Choice is way too long to build a successful career. Your success is determined by crossing the finish line X and using the shortest amount of time Y to get there.

A far better approach, and the one that a Champion Agent would apply, is to use a combination of presentations in front of sellers and a larger number of practice or role-play presentations to speed up the learning curve process to reach the *X Theory of Success*. My personal goal years ago, once I discovered the X and Y Theories, was to do a listing presentation every day. If that presentation was live in front of a seller, wonderful. If it was a role-play presentation, that was fine, too. For a little over six months, I did a listing presentation each day. My role-play partner (my wife, Joan) got very tired of hearing my presentation. In fact, she could probably have done it better than most agents because she had listened to it hundreds of times over a six-month period.

As I got closer and closer to my X, I got much better at my presentation. As I got close to the peak of the learning curve (about four months into my six-month daily routine), a transition happened. The number of practice presentations I did started to diminish, and the number of real presentations in front of motivated sellers increased. By combining the X Theory of Success and the Y Theory of Choice, I increased the speed at which I reached the Champion level of production, and so will you if you apply the same principles to your listing assistant to improve her performance and income.

The quality standard involves the type of terms and conditions the listing agent must have on the listings that she takes. There should be a standard deviation of list price to true value for the homes she lists that she can't go above. She must know what this level is, and it is her job to make sure she doesn't go above it. There will also need to be standards for listing length and market dollars invested, and for whether you do broker open houses or regular open houses. You don't want your listing agent overpromising to the client. You want her to secure listings just as you would.

The market you sell in will determine these standards. In a market where everything is selling, the standards can be a little more flexible. You might allow your listing agent to take a listing at 110 percent of value. When the inventory rises, competition for buyers increases, and the number of sales per month drops, the standard might be pricing at no more than 100 percent of value. You will have to watch the market and track the trends in the marketplace to establish your standards.

The Compensation Plan Is Different from That for a Buyer's Agent

I seem to be one of the few people who believe that the compensation split arrangement with a listing agent must be different from that for a buyer's agent. The truth is, it has to be different because of two clear business differences.

1. The position—with a listing agent, you become involved in the life of the transaction.
2. The cost—with a listing agent, you incur expenses to bring the transaction to close.

On a buyer's transaction, your team incurs its largest cost in closing the transaction. Your team and you really enter the picture only to service the client once there is an accepted agreement between the buyer and the seller.

With a listing, to get to that same point, you have to advertise the property to other agents and consumers, communicate with the seller, and assume some risk that you won't get the property sold and all your time and expenses will be uncompensated. When the buyer's agent brings in a transaction to the team, everyone is usually 30 to 60 days away from a paycheck. With a new listing, the time to everyone's paycheck is further away. In fact, the paycheck from that new listing may never come. If the listing agent didn't acquire the listing from a motivated seller for the right terms and conditions, you might not get paid. Your risk as the lead agent is clearly greater.

In addition to your risk being higher, your costs are higher as well. More staff time will be needed to keep the seller happy at this stage, and as much work will be needed with the seller as with the buyer down the road after an accepted contract is reached; in addition, the cost of marketing, advertising, communication, open houses, Internet listings, virtual tours, pictures, signs, flyers, and home magazine ads all will come out of your part of the commission. You can't apply the standard 50 percent split that many lead agents use to compensate buyer's agents and still be profitable.

For example, if only 50 percent of the listings that your listing agent takes sell, I can guarantee instantly (without looking at your P&L or any of your costs of business) that you are losing money on every listing he takes. I had a client in Florida whom I worked with in calculating her cost per transaction, the time she invested in every transaction, and the number of homes her listing assistant took that failed to sell. We added those costs to the costs of the listings that did sell and factored in the commission split to the buyer's agent. My client was losing $750 for every listing that the listing agent took for the team. She had been convinced that her listing assistant was a big asset to her and her team before we looked at reality. The truth was that the listing agent was a big asset to himself.

You must create a compensation plan using the core numbers of average commission check, cost per transaction, and time invested per transaction to arrive at a split arrangement that enables you to earn a profit. That's certainly easier to do when your average commission check is higher. These calculations will help you arrive at a fair split that works for everyone. The amount will generally fall in the range of 15 to 35 percent of the gross commission earned, depending on your costs and gross revenue.

Another option is to have the listing agent pay a fixed cost per transaction to cover your costs associated with doing a transaction. If the listing agent is willing to share the risk and lower it for you, he should receive a greater reward.

Telemarketer or Prospecting Agent

The telemarketer or prospecting agent's primary job is to use the telephone effectively to set appointments. These appointments are predominantly for listings. Telemarketers will not usually be calling your past clients and people in your sphere of influence unless your database of business is so large that you can't reach all these people regularly by yourself. If that is the case, you should determine the segments of your past clients and sphere members that the telemarketer will be calling. It should be the lowest-value group of past clients and sphere members—the ones that are least likely to send you business based on their past performance, their relationship with you, their influence level in their job and community, their behavioral style, and your feelings about them. Don't give away your best people to someone else. My belief is that a lead agent will never be able to give away all his prospecting responsibilities to others. You will always need to maintain a list of people that you will need to contact and connect with regularly.

Setting the Standards

The standards are pretty simple. There are daily, weekly, and monthly goals for dials, contacts, leads, and appointments. There is a set schedule of time in and time out. You will also want to track telemarketers' numbers in hourly increments. You will find that they are more effective at certain times. You will also see that their ratio of contacts reached to dials will be better at certain times. When they fall below the standards, corrective action and training are necessary. You don't need six months of data to know whether a prospecting agent will make it or not. Giving someone new 90 days to produce is enough time to take out the newness and production fluctuations.

Compensation Basics

You will need to pay the prevailing wage for a telemarketer in your area. In many areas, this is in the $10 to $15 per hour range. Then you will need to devise a compensation plan that rewards some of the steps in the sales process. There should be a bonus for an appointment she dialed. That amount can be nominal, like $50 or $100. The prospecting agent needs to see some monetary reward for getting the appointment. The money is paid only for a qualified appointment.

I have a client who added a prospecting agent to her staff and began booking loads of appointments. When we analyzed the results of those appointments 30 days later, her close ratio was horrid. This happened because the quality of the prospects was substandard. If you are going to pay on an appointment basis, which I recommend that you do, you must qualify the appointment yourself. Your time is too valuable to use it going out on garbage appointments and additionally paying someone money when you do. I guarantee that you will cancel a percentage of the appointments that the telemarketer books for you. Even with a good telemarketer, that percentage could be 15 to 20 percent. You don't want to waste your time and resources.

The largest bonus needs to come after a closing. Again, you want to go back to your average commission check, cost per transaction, time invested per transaction, and net profit per transaction to calculate what you can afford to pay the prospecting agent. It most likely will be in the range of 5 to 15 percent of the gross commission. You might be thinking, "Why pay at that level when a referral fee is 25 percent or even 35 percent in many cases on third-party referrals?" Don't forget that you are giving the prospecting agent a safety net in the form of a base or hourly income. Her risk is less because of that steady paycheck and the appointment bonuses you are paying. Your risk is greater because you are paying that base compensation whether she books one appointment or twenty in a month.

As long as you create a structure using your key numbers, whether it's for a telemarketer, a listing agent, or a buyer's agent, you won't get caught with more production but no profit.

C H A P T E R

Use Assessments to Improve Your Odds

Most large companies use assessments to evaluate the quality of candidates for specific job openings. However, the natural reaction of most small business owners, especially real estate agents, is, "There's no money in my budget for testing or assessing people." I am truly baffled by most agents' attitude regarding assessments. They typically feel that a large company can afford assessments, but they can't. My view is that small companies need to use assessments even more than large companies do. You read that right, but let me explain.

In a large company, the cost of one bad hire (as a percentage of revenue wasted and training dollars spent) is minute. For a small company, the percentage is monumental. Because you are doing the training personally in the early stages of building a team, the strain on your valuable time is significant.

Champion Team Rule: *In a small business, you can't afford to make a hiring mistake.*

The cost of hiring the wrong person, when amortized over your limited available time, your small sales volume, and your small revenue model, is larger than it would be for a large business. Investing a few dollars for every hire to make sure that you have the right person is money well spent. In addition, knowing how to motivate each person you hire behaviorally will enable you to work better and more efficiently with the people you do hire in less time.

Interviewing Is Not Enough

When it comes to interviewing, many people have the skill of knowing what a potential employer wants to hear. After all, they have probably been through the interview process a number of times during their career. Unless you are a professional interviewer, the odds on your selecting the right candidate are between slim and none, and slim just left town.

People put up a false front when they are interviewed, and they are certainly putting their best foot forward. Many interviewees are unwilling or unable to look at themselves objectively. They aren't mature enough to be able to convey the truth about their faults—because everybody's got them. We, as interviewers, can be swayed and often fail to remain objective. We can be swayed by our need to get a person on the team now. We can be swayed by an emotional need or an emotional appeal. We can be swayed by the inter-viewee's financial need for the job. We can be swayed by physical appearance.

Interviews by themselves are not an exact science for employee selection. There are certain people who do not interview well. They would make marvelous employees, but they struggle to convey that during an interview.

The Real Value of Job References

In today's litigious world, employers can't afford to say anything negative about a former employee. The information you will receive from a work reference is usually limited to the hire date, the last work date, and possibly whether the person is eligible to be rehired. That information is of little value to you. You can check the candidate's accuracy and honesty in reporting the key dates. You may be able to find out if there was a problem with his previous employment if his former employer is willing to share his rehire status with you. However, his rehire status will not guarantee that he wasn't fired. It also won't tell you about the qual-ity of his work because you won't know why he is not eligible for rehire. You will have to find that out on your own by asking the applicant at the interview.

Even though, as a prospective employer, I want more information from previous employers, I am unwilling to share more than the basics of name, rank, and serial number with other employers. Sharing my views and opinions or having my office manager do so will only open a Pandora's box of trouble.

Align Job Descriptions with Behavioral Style

What if you could predict, in advance, how a person would react to certain job performance tasks? What would that knowledge be worth to you as a lead agent? What if you could predict how someone will deal with challenges, make connections with others, deal with change, and respond to rules and procedures? What if you could align those key issues that we all face in the business world on a daily basis with the right individual and the right job? You would dramatically influence, in a positive way, someone's job performance and the results he achieves.

When you evaluate the individual jobs of the different members of your team, each position requires different skills, attributes, behaviors, and actions. A transaction coordinator needs to be more focused on rules and regulations. She needs to be able to keep the other agents adhering to the deadlines and timelines of the contract. She has to follow or establish certain systems and procedures and clearly know the consequences of not following them and how that affects the quality of client service, stress load during the transaction, and the smoothness of the transaction.

A listing coordinator needs to have a greater ability to interact well with clients than a transaction coordinator does. He needs to be organized, while at the same time being creative. In order to perform the many tasks in from of him, he needs to be stable, predictable, and steady in his work habits.

When you can observe the desired behaviors, temperaments, and needs of the people holding each of the positions on your team, clearly defining the type of natural thinking, actions, and behavioral tendencies a person would need to have in order to excel in each job, you will be able to attract prospective candidates more effectively by designing ads that people with certain behavioral styles will respond to more frequently. You can then secure applicants more quickly and effectively. In addition, you will have acquired a pool of applicants that is small but of high quality based on the positions you have available.

Match People to Tasks

The best approach to finding the right people for the right job is to analyze each position and the tasks that position requires. As the lead agent, you have to go below the job description level and look at tasks. What are the tasks that need to be completed? What type of person is best suited to perform those tasks? How does an employee's behavioral style align with those tasks?

In Jim Collins's landmark book *Good to Great*, he shared two clear concepts to consider when dealing with team members and teams. The first is, you have to get the right people on the bus. The bus in this analogy is your business. You have to have the right people as team members or employees. Being a great company takes great people. Getting the right people on the bus and the wrong people off the bus is essential to the success of your company.

The right people can transform your business through their skill, passion, and commitment. I have found them almost anywhere. Dan Matejsek, who is one of my senior vice presidents, sat in the same row as Joan and I in church for a few years.

He has transformed our online strategies, tactics, lead generation, and sales to an amazing level. He has created numerous revenue streams that didn't exist before he came to Real Estate Champions. My best advice: When you encounter a person who is a Champion Performer or whom you can mold into one, quickly hire that person. If you don't have a position open, make one and hire that person… now!

The second concept that Collins trumpets is getting people into the right seats on the bus. The truth is, even if you have the right people, if they are in the wrong seats, you will not achieve the explosive growth and other objectives you have for building a team. Having the right people is only half of the equation. You must have them doing the right tasks.

That's why I believe you have to start by determining the tasks that need to be done. Design the positions based on the tasks that need to be done, then determine the behavioral profiles of people who would be most likely to be naturally skilled at doing those individual tasks. Then you can go out into the employment market to select your candidates.

If you are a lead agent who already has team members, your approach to maximize performance and production should be a little different. Again, you should start with a list of tasks that need to be done. Then you should analyze the behavioral styles of your current team members. Finally, match the tasks to your team members' behavioral styles. The time you will need to invest to get this area right is more than most agents actually invest in building their team.

Right people + wrong positions = failure

Right people + right positions = success

Forcing Adaptation Can Kill a Team

The reason people become frustrated with their jobs is the need for adaptation. When people have to change who they are naturally in order to perform certain functions required by their job, they become frustrated with their work. They perform at lower levels. They use up large volumes of energy just coping with their job. This sends them home burned out, frustrated, and ready to kick the dog, the cat, or even the kids when they get home. Just as I shared in *The Champion Real Estate Agent*, the revolutionary discoveries we have developed in building the lead agent's business around his behavioral style have to be taken a step further with your team.

In Chapter 19 of *The Champion Real Estate Agent*, I share how an agent needs to build his ideal business. I look at the challenges you will experience based on your individual behavioral style and the specific solutions that can be applied to help you build your business so that it is aligned with your behavioral style. I would also suggest that you consider investing in our program "Building Your Ideal Business." In this program, you will receive comprehensive training (with marketing and sales strategies included) that will help you construct your business in the areas of sales, prospecting, presentation, lead generation, lead conversion, marketing, and servicing your clients. All of this information is personalized for your behavioral style. You can design a business that fits you perfectly—like a glove. If you want to know more, go to www.realestatechampions.com/buildingyouridealbusiness.

You or your staff members will lose effectiveness and productivity when you are in a constant state of adaptation. If your staff is in a state of adaptation, you will see high staff turnover and low performance, which leads to additional challenges and, in extreme cases, the poisoning of all members of the team. Adaptation can kill a team. Your objective is not perfection, however. In such a multi-task-oriented business as real estate sales, it would be impossible to align staff members with their jobs perfectly, so that they never have to engage in tasks that are outside the realm of their behavioral style. Your objective is to achieve a high level of alignment so that you can minimize the amount of time that you and your staff spend adapting. If you can achieve an 80 percent alignment, you will have produced a high-performance team.

Your First Hire—Find the Ideal Behavioral Style

I will admit that I have some very strong views on who lead agents should hire first. More often than not, the first hire most agents make is way off behaviorally. Their focus is on someone who will interact well with their clients.

> **Champion Team Rule:** *You're not looking for a relationship, you are looking for production.*

Too many of us hire someone because she has strong communication skills. "We have someone who we know will 'love on' our clients," is a phrase I hear often. The truth is that your first hire should be for production. By production, I don't mean sales production, but paperwork production. Agents who achieve success in their career are usually not the most organized people. There are, of course, some exceptions to that rule; you may even be one of them. By and large, however, salespeople are good at connecting with people, not at detailed paperwork. What we really need is someone who excels at paperwork production and can come behind us to clean up our messes. We don't need someone to "love on" our clients and prospects. That's our job. We need someone who can make sure that all the behind-the-scenes work is getting accomplished, so that the service that was promised is delivered.

Your first hire needs to have a combination of the steady and compliant behavioral styles (see the discussion of the DISC profile later in this chapter and in Chapter 5). She needs to have high scores in both of those areas. The higher her scores in these two areas, the better the fit. What you will end up hiring is a dependable team player who is a logical, step-by-step thinker and is service-oriented. This person will have high standards and will want others to follow those standards. She will be a comprehensive problem solver who is very objective in her approach. This person will really be the anchor of the team. She will be the solid foundation on which all other team members (whether service support or sales members) rest.

> **Coach's Tip:** *Your first hire must be behaviorally aligned. I have seen few teams that are highly successful without such a person. I have seen many teams that are successful* because they have such a person.

The Magic of a Coordinator 6, 20, or 21

I can admit I was lucky. I stumbled upon a coordinator 6 early in my career in building a team. I wasn't really looking for her. In fact, I didn't even know what I was looking for. I hadn't done the extensive study and research that I have since. The DISC assessment we use at Real Estate Champions is so exact that we can break down behavioral styles into extremely targeted categories, hence the numbers 6, 20, and 21. When Julie Porfirio joined my real estate sales team, everything changed. She is a coordinator 6, which means that she is someone who has extremely high scores on both the steady and the compliant scales. Julie, in fact, scores 100 percent in both of those areas. She was and still is (some fifteen years later) magical for me and my company, Real Estate Champions.

People like Julie who are high in the steady and compliant categories can transform your business. They are tenacious in getting things done. Their organization level is really unmatched. Their loyalty to you as a leader and to your business vision is exceptional. Their natural behavior is to be tireless in working behind the scenes in system development, implementation, and adherence.

Why Hire These People?

These people won't have to adapt their behavioral style in order to function at a high level in supporting your efforts. They are good listeners, patient, stable, sincere, team players, accurate, analytical, precise, mature, fact finders, and courteous, and they have high standards. Just take a moment to reread this list of the characteristics that these people have naturally.

They are all things that most successful salespeople are not! They create a great overlay because they have all the things that most salespeople struggle with. They complement our strengths and shore up our natural weaknesses. Most salespeople hire someone like themselves when they hire their first assistant. They don't look for someone who is really the opposite of their behaviors and characteristics.

People with the characteristics given earlier will influence other people in your organization through their high standards. They will be role models through their actions, not their words. You won't have the "Do as I say, not as I do" problem that you might have with other types of people. Their dependability and attention to detail will speak volumes to others. Their ability to follow transactions through to completion will allow you to focus on your job of bringing in leads and sales. As a lead agent, you won't wake up in the middle of the night wondering if a certain task has been done. If you have hired a coordinator, you know it was done.

Pros and Cons of Coordinators. With coordinators, as with anyone, there are pros and cons. There is the inevitable yin and yang of human behavior. As with all of us, their greatest strengths can also be their greatest weaknesses. I have developed a chart of the pros and cons of coordinators for you to review (Figure 8.1).

As you can probably see from Figure 8.1, the good far outweighs the bad. The cons can be controlled, and the pros will make your business explode. In the best scenario, as I had with Julie, you can toss a coordinator the keys of the business and go get more sales. You won't have to worry about accomplishing your goals in customer service and serving your clients. It will be done.

Pros	Cons
Ability to set and accomplish high standards of work and conduct	Can become offensive or stubborn
Sensitive to problems, rules, errors, and procedures	Difficulty in establishing priorities because, to them, everything is a priority
Can make tough decisions without letting emotions interfere	Can focus too much on details
Ability to understand and preserve the need for quality systems	Can yield to avoid controversy
The skill to begin a project and take it to completion	Changing quickly is a challenge
Works for a leader and a cause	Too focused on standard operating procedures
Leadership through consideration to all others on the team	May become introverted and bunkered when overwhelmed

Figure 8.1 Pros and cons of coordinators.

Blink and You Can Miss Them

I almost blinked with Julie. What a disaster that would have been. After years of hiring for myself and helping many of my clients evaluate their team members and new hires, I have found that it's easy to pass over a coordinator. Unfortunately, they are easy to miss.

They aren't the best interviewers. They are not programmed to promote themselves. They don't want the limelight, so they won't toot their own horn. They are courteous and professional at the interview and with others, but you won't walk away saying, "Wow, I've got to hire this person." They will blend in more than they will stand out. If you are looking for someone who will grab you at the interview and say, "Give me the job," they won't do it. They have a quiet intensity that really can't be measured. It has to be seen in action to be appreciated. The only way to measure it is through a DISC assessment.

These people also don't communicate the way most salespeople do. They are slower and more thoughtful in their speech. They are more cautious in their approach and their emotions. The modulation in their tone is nonexistent. Some are even on the edge of being monotone. They do not communicate the way you and I do.

When I first interviewed Julie, I really wasn't sure about her. I wasn't sure if she was strong enough to handle me or the growth that was coming. I wasn't sure if she could keep after someone when she needed to get things done. I questioned whether she could get the other agents to do what we needed in terms of the paperwork in a timely fashion. When I hired her, I told her that she was going to have to eat a bucket of nails every day, so that she would be tough enough. The truth is, she had that toughness in her the whole time. She just didn't show it at the interview. She showed her toughness through courtesy, consistency, attention to detail, and tenacity. If I had blinked, I would have missed her.

You Need Only One

You don't need a whole team of people who fit this behavioral profile. My view is that you have to have one. You don't have to have more than one, but you do have to have at least one. The size of your team will dictate the number of coordinators you need. For most teams, one will be enough. Realize that what you are looking for behaviorally will not be easy to find. You will have to interview and assess a number of people before you find a coordinator. They are not as easy to find as apples off the tree.

You will also want some team members who will interact with your prospects and clients in a long-lost-friend sort of way. The coordinator will be professional and courteous, but she will be more focused on completing the list of tasks she has to do today than on shooting the breeze with you or your clients. Coordinators are task-oriented, not people-oriented. They will focus on getting things done before they focus on the people. Once you have a coordinator, you may want someone who will focus on the people.

Your Second Hire—Your Choice

You could hire another coordinator as your second hire in administration. The two of them would work well together because they would both think and act similarly. However, you might want to select someone who would offset both your weaknesses and those of your coordinator assistant.

Task-Oriented or People-Oriented—Your Choice

We can break up the DISC behavioral styles into two groups. First, there are the people who are task-oriented, who want to get things done and achieve results. These people have high scores in the D and C areas. Then there are those who are people-oriented, who think of relationships first and how everything affects those relationships. They have high scores in the S and I categories.

If you have a coordinator, you already have someone who is predominantly task-oriented. If you have strong scores in the dominant (D) category (as I do), that means that you are task-oriented as well. To improve your customer relationships and customer service, your second hire should be someone who falls into one of the people-oriented quadrants. Someone who is in the relater area who has a combination of I and S behavioral styles or someone who scores in the supporter area would be ideally suited to help the team. What you want to do is build a team that runs the full gamut of being able to service clients, while achieving a high level of results.

Now… What Position?

If you have hired a relater or a supporter, you can place this person in a position where interaction with clients is high. Giving this person the listing coordinator position and giving the coordinator 6, 20, or 21 the transaction coordinator position is advisable.

A relater or supporter can communicate regularly and consistently with current clients and prospects. A coordinator can make sure that the rules for closing the transaction are being followed by making sure that the lender, other agent, attorney, title and escrow company, buyer and seller, repairpeople, inspectors, and appraisers are all doing their jobs in a timely manner.

Evaluate Buyer's Agents Behaviorally

Using behavioral assessments to help screen and select buyer's agents can dramatically save on training and replacement costs. It's really easy to get excited about a buyer's agent at the interview stage, only to find out later that he is unable to sell, convert leads, create leads, or close for the contract. Or you might find that he is successful in a short period of time, but then leaves your team to go out on his own. You have then invested in him, but once you are in a position to recapture all of the time and money that you invested, he leaves without so much as a thank you.

When you are evaluating the behavioral style of the buyer's agents, you want to evaluate them on the following styles:

D: Dominance
I: Influencing
S: Steady
C: Compliance

These four behavioral styles and the way they are blended will determine how your buyer's agent will react in certain situations. I believe that there are one very good combination of behavioral styles, some good ones, and some disasters waiting to happen in terms of sales, service, and longevity of being on the team. Let's look at each of these possibilities.

Any time you have a potential buyer's agent who has a high compliant score, you will need to be cautious about hiring her. In many studies that have been conducted worldwide, less than 10 percent of top-producing salespeople have the compliant score as one of their top two scores in a DISC assessment. My view is that your chances of getting solid sales performance out of someone in this category are limited.

You may be an exception to this rule. In that case, my message to you is, Congratulations! You must be exceptional because you have beaten the odds. Why try to roll the dice again with someone you're hiring? Also, the time you will invest to bring a person in this category to a level of competency probably won't be worth it.

Another challenging situation is someone with a high dominant score. This person will sell and sell in high volume. The problem with her will not be sales and sales production; the problem will be her ego. People with this characteristic are team players as long as the team is theirs. Their success will be quick and significant. The problem is that you will probably be training your own competition.

The reason I know this is that I am one of these people. I was an assistant to an agent for three months earlier in my career. I brought in a lot of listings and sales in those three months. It was easy for me to calculate "how much money I was making him." That was my attitude, which is the attitude of a dominant. I felt that I was being taken advantage of because of the split arrangement with my lead agent, so I left him and his company and went out on my own. He and I didn't have a formal agreement on how long I would work for him. We had no noncompete contract, so he had spent three months training his own competition. Similarly, you could be hiring someone who will become your competition if you hire someone who has a high dominant score.

Best Behavioral Style for Buyer's Agents

I have studied performance in sales, longevity of service, lead conversion ratios, and referrals generated for hundreds of teams. It's my professional view that people who have a behavioral style with high scores in both steady and influencing make the best buyer's agents. Because of these two behavioral styles, you have someone who is optimistic and enthusiastic about his job and about real estate. People with this combination are people-oriented and service-oriented. They are naturally skilled in verbal persuasion. They are sociable, convincing, trust building, friendly, good listeners, sincere, and steady.

If you hire someone with this behavioral style, you will have someone whom prospects will like and trust right away. You will have someone who is organized and dependable as a service provider. He will tirelessly follow up on the leads that are given to him. He will not produce as many leads as a person with a higher dominant score, but he will follow up with them better. While someone with a high dominant score will get bored or frustrated with a lead that doesn't buy quickly, the steady in this buyer's agent will be like a bulldog with a bone. He will chew on it until he gets it done.

You need to be using a behavioral analysis or assessment to increase the odds that you have hired well. Given your desire to expand your business through people, you must not waste your resources of time, energy, training, and money on the wrong candidates for employment. When you use an assessment, you will spend a few dollars on the front end to save a lot on the back end.

It's like the popular commercials in the 1970s by the Fram oil filter company. The greasy mechanic would always say, "You can pay me now, or you can pay me later." He was saying the same thing I am. You can invest in assessing the people you hire to ensure your success now, or you can invest more money later in turnover, lost performance, blown sales, and hiring and training new people to replace your poor hires.

C H A P T E R

9

Hiring Buyer's Agents

The hiring of buyer's agents has perplexed lead agents for years. I will admit that much of the advice you will receive as you read this chapter comes from my mistakes in personally hiring and firing buyer's agents. Some of the principles, skills, techniques, and evaluations discussed here have resulted from the frustrations produced by the trial-and-error method that my clients initially implemented, which led me to create a more effective process for hiring buyer's agents.

Few agents have any rules or processes to aid them in deciding which buyer's agents are suited to join their team. My goal in this chapter is to give you some solid guidelines and coaching on the crucial evaluations you must make as a business owner if you are to select the right buyer's agent the first time. The cost of hiring the wrong one, taking into account training time, low conversion rate of leads, personal frustration, blown transactions, and going through these steps again with another buyer's agent, is significant.

New Versus Experienced Agents

The first question you must ask yourself is what level of proficiency you want your new buyer's agent to possess. There are valid reasons for hiring only experienced buyer's agents. You can also make just as compelling a case for hiring only new agents. The question is which arena you want to work in. You must create a long-term standard or profile of what a good buyer's agent prospect for your team looks like.

I coach Champion Lead Agents with large practices who will argue this issue of new versus experienced indefinitely. One

> **Coaching Tip:** *If you are a person who really wants control and wants things done your way, you will be better off hiring a new agent instead of an experienced buyer's agent. New agents are easier to control, coach, and monitor.*

Champion Lead Agent swears off new agents, and the other swears by them. I believe you can build a successful practice with either new or experienced buyer's agents. The real question is: which type do you want to work with?

Advantages and Disadvantages of New Agents

When you hire new agents, there is probably a greater element of risk. They don't have a track record in real estate sales. They may have a track record of success in other types of sales that will help, but to suggest that all sales jobs are comparable to an agent's job is a stretch. You will be training a new agent through every step of the real estate process, from securing the lead from an ad call, sign call, or open house to buyer interview presentations, showing property, promoting urgency to buy, and writing and negotiating contracts. Your training program will need to be from soup to nuts. Even with an effective training program, there is a risk that your expenditure of time on training won't produce enough fruit in terms of sales. Figure 9.1 is a short list of the advantages and disadvantages of hiring a new agent.

Brand new, wet-behind-the-ears agents can have a lot of success in the business quickly. The real factor that drives their success is their attitude and desire. If they want to be successful badly enough and are willing to put in the effort to accomplish it, a new agent can achieve more than 30 units in her first year.

Because the learning curve for a new agent in terms of skill development is steep, new agents must be willing to rely on their number of contacts and method of contact to earn their success. They must be willing to make more contacts (i.e., make more calls, reach more people, return calls more promptly) than a more experienced agent might have to. They will need to do more personal prospecting and select a method that gets them face to face or phone to phone more frequently than other agents. Because the quality of their message is

NEW AGENTS

Advantages	Disadvantages
Attitude	Doesn't know how to write contract
Energy	Inexperience
Not beat down	Too trusting of potential prospects
Excited about the opportunity	Lack of market knowledge
No bad habits	Poor sales skills
No back talk	Lower lead conversion
Trust you – why not	No past client/sphere database
	Greater investment of your time
	No marketplace knowledge

Figure 9.1 New agents.

initially going to be substandard, their conversion ratios and the quality of their prospects will be inferior. They will not win by waiting around for better prospects. They will just have to "make do" in the short run until their skill improves.

New agents must be willing to exert the effort to practice and perfect their sales skills. They must role-play daily with someone. They must role-play weekly with you on their ad calls, sign calls, open house scripts, lead follow-up, presentations, showing property, and converting clients to contracts.

Advantages and Disadvantages of Hiring Experienced Agents

Most Champion Lead Agents would rather hire an experienced agent than someone who is new. While I tend to agree with this thinking in general, there are diamonds in the rough that you will lose if you have a blanket philosophy of not hiring new agents.

The basic assumption that most lead agents make is that an experienced agent is much closer to having his act together as a real estate agent. In many cases, this is true; in many others, however, this assumption is disastrous. To assume that an experienced agent who wants to join your team as a buyer's agent is always currently a successful agent is dangerous. If the agent were currently at a high level of success, he would not be talking with you about a position. Most buyer's agents working for Champion Teams would not be as effective on their own. They joined the team for a number of reasons, but the most common one is a lack of leads. They don't have a system that creates enough good-quality leads with enough consistency to sustain their business as sole agents. If they did, they wouldn't be working with you. Don't ever lose sight of that fact. There is a deficiency in an experienced agent's ability that you will need to work to fix.

If an agent's number of leads is low, then you can be assured that he won't have exemplary lead follow-up and appointment booking skills. He hasn't had enough opportunity to do these things. Also, while he has been waiting for the opportunity to work with a live buyer prospect, he probably hasn't been practicing his sales skills. Getting an experienced agent to adhere to your standards of practice, role playing, scripting, and delivery can be challenging. Thus, there are advantages and disadvantages of hiring experienced agents (Figure 9.2).

EXPERIENCED AGENTS

Advantages	Disadvantages
Basic real estate knowledge	Re-training, breaking bad habits
Marketplace knowledge	Independent minded
Experience in sales functions, showing property, ad calls, open houses, etc.	Potential lack of work ethic

Figure 9.2 Experienced agents.

There will be times when experienced agents will revert to their old habits because they are comfortable with those habits. The old habits brought them to your team; you have to let them know that staying with the old habits will get them fired from your team.

Proof Is in the Pudding

Many lead agents are too trusting when it comes to hiring experienced agents as buyer's agents. They frequently take too much at face value, rather than checking. When interviewing a potential buyer's agent with experience, ask her about her previous production. You want to know the number of units sold and sales volume in the last few years. You also must know the sources of her business. Were all the sales handed to her by her lead agent or her broker, or did she create them herself? Was she effective in converting ad calls, sign calls, and open houses to sales? Were there sales that came from Internet leads? How did she do with those leads? Getting the units sold by sources will provide you with the facts about this agent's skills today.

You may be able to go to the MLS to see the agent's production in the last 12 months. Some companies and lead agents, however, want all the production under their name exclusively, so don't eliminate someone with a lack of listings out of hand. Require the potential agent to provide a transaction record from her broker. You might even want the broker to certify the results. There are a number of organizations that need a certified transaction record from the broker when applying for membership or receiving awards.

If potential agents are unable to furnish any type of transaction record, ask them for a 1099. There are many of you who are thinking, "I couldn't do that." Why not? These people are asking you for a highly valuable and prized position with your team. They are trying to negotiate the best commission split possible for themselves. They are trying to convince you that they are players in the game of real estate sales. They are saying, "I will bring income to you and the team that you don't currently have now." They should be willing to prove that they earned what they say they earned, that they are worth what they claim to be worth, and that there isn't any puffing of numbers to make themselves look better in order to negotiate a better deal or secure the position you have offered.

> **Champion Team Rule:** *There won't be a miraculous improvement in an experienced agent's sales performance in the first 30 days just because the agent has joined your team.*

In the short run, an experienced agent's sales performance will be about what it has been. You must see what the agent has actually done in the past because that's what you should expect from him in the next 90 days. There may be a few exceptions to this rule, but they are infrequent. Tell your applicants that the proof is in the pudding.

Lastly, ask them for their conversion rates. Typically, what are the ratios from an ad call, a sign call, or an open house? How often do they get the client to come to the office for a buyer interview? When they have that interview, how often are they able to secure an exclusive right to represent agreement? Most of the experienced agents you will be considering will not be able to answer any of these questions. This gives you an opening to let them know that you track everything, and that you will expect them to embrace your system of tracking activities and results if they want to be on your team. You also want to make it clear that, because of the tracking, you will be able to help them be far better buyer's agents and make more money. All of these statements are true. Also, because of the tracking, they will have no place to hide. Their effort and results will be out in the open. Both you and they will know, without a shadow of a doubt, how they are really doing. They won't be able to hide or cover their tracks if they are off on their activities and production.

$1/2$ Theory—*Cut Everything They Say in Half*

If you are considering an experienced buyer's agent who cannot or will not provide a reasonable level of proof of her previous production, you will need to apply the $1/2$ Theory. The $1/2$ Theory states that no matter what the agent tells you she did in production, cut the number in half. I am not saying that all buyer's agents use fuzzy numbers. I am saying that if you cut a potential agent's production numbers in half, you won't get burned. She will probably have done at least that much.

If the person is worth hiring based on half of her undocumented numbers, you probably have someone who is really worth having on your team. Act quickly to sign her up; just don't make the mistake of taking everything she says at face value.

Attitude Is Everything

When faced with the decision on new or experienced, I often coach clients to evaluate the attitude and character of each individual. Does he have a pleasing, positive attitude? Does he have the work ethic that is necessary to succeed? Is he willing to receive your coaching and counsel? Does he the ability to hold himself accountable to a set standard? Is he willing to work inside your team?

These are all areas that a Champion Lead Agent must evaluate to increase the chances of success with just-hired buyer's agents. You must make these evaluations whether the buyer's agents you are considering are new or experienced. There will be some rocky roads ahead even if you hire someone with tremendous attitude and character. All your staff members can have attitude problems periodically. This is especially true for the sales staff. Their friends, spouses, family, prospects, the marketplace, and other staff members will be influencing them on a regular basis.

═══════════════════════

I had a wonderful buyer's agent who initially had a tremendous attitude, but over time her attitude deteriorated to the point where I was forced to terminate her. I later found out that a friend of hers had been influencing her, telling her that I was taking advantage of her and that she could be out on her own making more money. When she went out on her own, she failed miserably in short order. We ran into each other about a year later. She was almost out of the business and was desperate. She admitted to me that her friend had influenced her badly and told me that she was no longer in contact with that friend. She asked me boldly for the opportunity to come back and be on the team. After a few more discussions and prayerful eval-uation, I offered her an opportunity. She came back and did a marvelous job because her attitude and resentment were gone. She really was grate-ful for the second chance. I was grateful to have another talented individ-ual on the team.

═══════════════════════

A change in attitude is the most challenging type of change for a human being to make. Because attitude is fundamentally a decision that you make each day, the timeline for atti-tude changes is exceptionally short. The philosophy you must apply for all staff members, especially buyer's agents, is if you can't change people, you must change people. I want you to really ponder that concept. If you can't change the attitude, activities, skills, or phi-losophy of your buyer's agents, and if a behavioral change doesn't change what they do, then your only choice is to replace them.

A team leader can't teach attitude. When you are dealing with adults, there are a num-ber of areas that the lead agent is not entirely in control of. The attitude of your staff is one of those areas. You can influence, help, or coach them to establish a better attitude, but the tipping point is located in the six inches between their ears. Attitude is like honesty; there aren't gradient levels. Either you are honest or you are not. You can't be kind of honest. It's like being kind of pregnant.

In evaluating a potential new team member, attitude must play a major role in your decision. Most buyer's agents are hired for the skills they have exhibited, their track record of success, and the potential you believe they have in the future. Most people aren't fired for lack of skills. They are fired because of their attitude. Replay in your brain all of the people you have ever worked with who have been fired or whom you yourself have fired. The vast majority of them will have been fired because of attitude problems.

A word of caution: the right attitude doesn't guarantee a successful result for buyer's agents. You will still experience problems with their sales skills. They will still do stupid things that you will shake your head at, as all human beings do. (All human beings includes you and me, too.) They will make contract-writing mistakes, customer service mistakes, and lead management and conversion mistakes. There will be an endless list of issues.

If they have the right attitude, at least they will receive constructive criticism of their performance correctly. Positive change has an opportunity to take root. The right **Coach's Tip:** *The right attitude gives you a chance of success. The wrong attitude gives you no chance.* person will want the feedback and will want to make the changes necessary to produce at a higher level.

Three Key Evaluation Points

Champion Lead Agents have a limited number of hours in which to evaluate buyer's agent candidates. You must develop an effective, simple system to separate the wheat from the chaff in candidates. Bringing them in for a few days trial, as you would do with an administrative assistant, is much more complex and difficult. You can see how an administrative assistant will perform in short order. It will take you several weeks to see results from a buyer's agent.

My belief is that buyer's agents must engage in prospecting and lead follow-up consistently. The profit for the team comes from the segments of business that the buyer's agents create while working with your inventory of homes. It comes from the ad calls, sign calls, open houses, and call capture return calls. It also comes from their prospecting for referrals from their sphere, their current clients, and their past clients. Any buyer's agent can convert leads that are handed to her on a silver platter by the lead agent. The real question that must be answered is what she will do in these other areas.

One of the critical considerations before hiring any buyer's agent is how much she will prospect. Numerous studies have shown that there is a direct link between prospecting and sales. The most reliable determining factor for sales performance is consistency of prospecting and lead follow-up activities. If you accidentally hire buyer's agents who won't engage in regular prospecting and lead follow-up over the phone, or if you have such buyer's agents on your team now, their sales performance will be (I didn't say *might be*; I said *will be*) in the bottom quarter of buyer's agents—guaranteed.

Let me share with you the three questions that I ask myself before I hire any salesperson.

1. How much will he sell?
2. How soon will he do it?
3. At what cost to me and the company will he do it?

How Much Will He Sell?

We need to be able to determine, in advance, what a buyer's agent's sales volume is likely to be before we hire him. How many units will this person probably sell each month? What's the likelihood that he will be able to increase those sales by at least 20 percent year after year? What price point is he most likely to gravitate to because of his current comfort level? What's the gross commission income that he will probably bring into the company? What will the company's profit on that gross commission income be?

How Soon Will He Do It?

Every salesperson requires a period of time to become acclimated to your team, systems, strategies, marketplace, inventory, sales process, and leads before he can become a revenue-producing member of the team. How quickly will this person make sales? Will he make sales in the next 30 days? Is it more likely that it will take longer than that? Are you turning over any hot, high-quality new leads to him? If you are, your expectation for a sale should be high.

I see team leaders waiting patiently for 60, 90, or even 120 days for the first sale to happen. I don't mean closing, I mean sale under contract. Even a brand new agent should make a sale in the first 45 days—maximum. If you think it will take a buyer's agent that you are considering hiring a lot longer that that, you'd better think again before you hire that person. The risk you will be taking to bring someone in is much greater the longer you think the timeline will be before that person regularly contributes sales to the team.

At What Cost to Me and the Company Will He Do It?

This last question is probably the most subjective of the evaluations. It involves determining the actual cost to you and your company of hiring the new team member. How much time do you feel you personally will need to invest in training, coaching, and monitoring him? What is your hourly value per hour? Multiply those two numbers together. How much administrative time will need to be invested to teach the new agent the systems he must follow? How much time will you need to track, analyze, and evaluate his numbers and sales ratios? How much frustration will you feel when he doesn't "get it" as quickly as you would like, and when he blows leads and good opportunities? How much will that affect you and what you need to do? How much will it affect you when this person gives your clients poor customer service, with the result that your clients aren't happy with you or your team? I guarantee that this will happen to you at some point in time.

> **Coaching Tip:** *Some people will cost you too much in personal production. Understanding the limits of that cost will save you and your company time and money.*

Looking at the cost honestly isn't pretty, but for you as a business owner, it's necessary. My best advice is to double whatever you come up with. Double the amount of time you expect to invest personally in training a new agent. Double the amount of leads you feel the agent will need and ultimately blow to make a few sales. Double the amount of energy, emotion, and frustration you are expecting to expend.

Being able to look ahead of time at the true figures for how much, how soon, and at what cost will save you mounds of headaches in the future. Knowing the potential agent's level of prospecting and lead follow-up in advance will dramatically swing the odds in your favor. There is a secret, little-known assessment instrument that you can use before you hire someone for your team that can help you greatly reduce your chances of making the costly mistake of hiring someone who can't or won't do the necessary prospecting and lead follow-up.

SPQ* Gold®

I discovered this assessment a few years ago, and it has transformed my sales team. It has made hiring salespeople a more exact science than ever before. I have made fewer poor hires and have been able to determine the probability of success with much greater accuracy than before.

The assessment we have been using with great success is the SPQ* Gold®. It measures 12 different categories of call reluctance. It benchmarks a salesperson's probability of success in using the telephone to create and convert prospects. It will let the employer know whether the salesperson has a mild or terminal case of call reluctance. It's another advanced tool in determining the right person to hire, so that you avoid the rehiring and retraining process that is so expensive for small businesses.

I could devote a couple of chapters to fully explaining the proven, tested, and perfected results from the SPQ* Gold®, but I don't have room to do so. Go to our Web site at www.realestatechampions.com/SPQGold to learn more about how this assessment instrument can help you and your team achieve more sales.

The Nonnegotiable Noncompete Agreement

You can't afford to hire any buyer's agent who won't sign some type of noncompete contract. Your intellectual property, team systems, past clients, lead-generation strategies and systems, sales techniques, scripts and dialogues, and other such information are too valuable to expose them to someone who could be your competition in the future. Your investment of time in coaching and training a new agent to a higher level of competency, only to have her leave inside of as little as a year, creates a net loss for you. I can't say this strongly enough, often enough, or passionately enough.

Don't hire any staff member without having her sign a noncompete contract!!!

10

Training the Buyer's Agent

In a large real estate team, the buyer's agents outnumber the other members of the team. They also can account for up to 75 percent of the team's production. Because buyer's agents are really one of the key elements of a real estate team, the training program that you establish for them is one of the most crucial pieces of your success puzzle.

Most lead agents have a training program that amounts to little more than, "Here is your desk; here is your phone; go get 'em." The other option that is often used is to send new agents to a multiday training program that is workshop-based. This is a better option than the first one, but it falls far short of the constant, ongoing training and coaching that really must take place to produce a successful buyer's agent.

If you turn over your leads and lead-generation systems to a buyer's agent who is poorly prepared, you won't achieve many more sales than you already have now. To expect a new buyer's agent (or even someone who you feel is experienced) to take over your leads and lead-generation systems and convert those leads successfully is delusional. (When I use the term *lead-generation systems*, I am referring to anything that creates leads for you, like ad calls, sign calls, Internet inquiries, call capture systems, and open houses. It includes any strategy you are currently using to make the phone ring or to get people to contact you or come to you.)

Don't Waste Your Leads

Until I discovered the secret solution to this problem, I watched hundreds of agents experience a temporary production drop each time they added a buyer's agent. The most dangerous drop in production came when they added the first buyer's agent. You can't afford to waste leads and opportunities, but when you hand over ad calls, sign calls, and other lead-generating sources to someone without proper training, that is exactly what you are doing. There is a significant cost to each lead that is created. What does each lead you create cost you in dollars or in time?

If you were to evaluate the cost of leads, you would need to add up all the expenses you incur to make the phone ring—all the marketing that you do in newspapers, Internet direct mail, and home magazines, and any advertising, whether it's institutional, brand building, or specific property advertisements, in any medium you select. Take that gross amount for your marketing expenses and divide it by the number of leads you produced. You will now have what it costs you to produce an individual lead. As you know, the ratio of leads to closings is not one-to-one. You need to have a number of leads in order to generate an appointment to make a presentation.

Let me show you how important this is to your business.

We calculated one of my clients' cost per lead to be $111. We determined that number by adding up the costs of her Web site, ads, flyers, direct mail, image advertising (billboard), and home magazine ads and dividing the total by the number of inbound calls that were created by these efforts. We then calculated her conversion ratio of leads to appointments, appointments to buyer representation contracts, and buyer representation contracts to closings. It took four leads to get an appointment and two appointments to get a buyer representation contract. Her ratio of buyer representation contracts to closings was almost one-to-one. Her overall average for her personal production was eight leads to one closing. (That is a respectable number or conversion rate for inbound sources to closings.)

However, the cost per lead of $111 times the 8 leads she needed to achieve a closing meant that she was actually spending about $888 per transaction. Her average commission check was $7,800, before she paid her broker split, transaction costs, and time invested per transaction. That meant that her revenue after lead costs was only $6,922. (We calculated the other numbers, and she was still fine; she had a little over $1,500 in net profit per transaction after all the other expenses were factored in.)

The problem arose when we looked at her buyer's agents' effectiveness. When we calculated their conversion rates, they needed almost twice as *many leads as she did to create a transaction. They had a fifteen-to-one overall ratio, so she was investing 15 leads at $111 per lead, for a total of $1,655 per transaction. Then, after subtracting the lead cost from her gross average commission check of $7,800, she had only $6,145 to split between herself, the buyer's agents, and the broker. The broker split was 20 percent, so he received $1,560. That left $4,585 in net dollars to pay the buyer's agent from. She was on a 50/50 split with her buyer's agents, so they received $3,900 (50 percent of the $7,800 commission check). Now she was left with only $685 before being compensated for her time, her assistants, the operating costs of the business, and other such expenses.* She was losing money on every transaction her buyer's agents did. *The difference between her sales skills and lead conversion skills and the lower skills of her buyer's agents created a situation in which where she couldn't make money.*

Train in the Order of Importance and Value

Most agents make a significant mistake when they try to train a buyer's agent. This mistake is not training the buyer's agent in the order of importance and value. They usually train their buyer's agents in the order of the flow of the business. They train them to do lead follow-up, qualify leads, categorize leads, set the buyer interview appointment, conduct a professional buyer interview, close for an exclusive right to represent contract, show property, write a purchase agreement, negotiate a transaction, service to close, and after-sale servicing, in that order. This is the exact opposite of the order in which training should be done. (This is the secret I talked about earlier.)

Champion Team Rule: *Train buyer's agents from the back of the transaction to the front.*

There are two reasons why you should train agents from the back of the transaction to the front. The first reason is that the time investment is greater at the rear of a transaction. Buyer's agents are there to leverage your time. You want to get rid of the largest investment of time first. The bulk of an agent's time is invested in researching property to show; showing property; writing and negotiating a contract; dealing with inspections, appraisals, repairs, and walk-throughs; and attending closings (if you do that). When you look at the difference in the amount of time invested by an agent, the back half of the work done for a buyer client takes at least four or five times as long as the front half of the job.

A buyer's agent could spend a couple of hours in research; 10 to 15 hours in showing property; a couple of hours in writing and negotiating the contract; a couple of hours in dealing with inspection, appraisal, and repair; and another hour at least in walk-throughs and attending the closing. In total, the buyer's agent could easily invest 17 hours to complete the back half of the transaction. Using the buyer's agent to remove this lower-importance, more time-consuming work right away will allow you to keep control of the more important front half of the business, which requires a smaller time investment. You are delegating the lowest-value activities to the lowest-paid competent person.

When you have a new buyer's agent, you should work to relinquish control of these back-end areas right away. Retain control of lead follow-up, qualifying leads, categorizing the leads, booking buyer interview appointments, and conducting buyer interviews. The mistake that most agents make is either to turn over the whole process, including lead follow-up and lead conversion, to their new buyer's agents or to turn it over from the front to the back. That approach is wrong on two counts. The first is that the buyer's agent won't be nearly as effective as you are at converting a lead to a face-to-face buyer consultation. If she were as effective as you, it is questionable whether she would be working with you.

A Champion Agent will have a conversion rate of about 25 percent on buyer leads, but a typical nonperforming or low-performing buyer's agent will convert fewer than 5 percent. If you generate 20 buyer leads a month, that's the difference between five buyer interviews that you book and one that your buyer's agent will book. It's the difference between at least three transactions a month for $15,000 gross commission income and half a transaction a month for $2,500 in commission.

The time you will invest in following up on 20 leads, determining their motivation, booking an appointment with 5 of them, and conducting 5 buyer interviews is less than your buyer's agent will invest to get to one interview. You will convert more leads, invest less of your time, raise the conversion ratio of leads, and sign more exclusive right to represent contracts. What you are keeping control of, in the short run, is the highly skilled sales functions of the initial contact, lead follow-up, booking the appointment, and conducting the appointment to secure the relationship.

Once you have a client on an exclusive right to represent contract, if his motivation is at a very high level, selling him a home is easy. The hard part is really over. The risk of not earning a paycheck is also reduced once a client signs an exclusive right to represent contract. Why waste the leads and opportunities when all you need to invest is a couple of hours a week? Is it worth a few hours a week to increase your income from 50 percent of $1,500 to 50 percent of $15,000?

How you go about training your buyer's agent has a definite impact on your cash flow. If you are turning leads over to your buyer's agents to blow, this has a detrimental effect on your cash flow. As your buyer's agents become more proficient, you can train them in the sales functions and start to turn over these functions, which include all activities up through the buyer interview. To start training them, have them watch you conduct a dozen or perhaps two dozen buyer interviews in person. Then, book the appointments from the leads and have them conduct a couple of dozen interviews with you there critiquing their performance.

Once your buyer's agents have mastered the buyer interview, you can book them appointments and not have to be there. Then you should work to train them in the lead follow-up procedure and techniques. Once they have that down pat, let them do all the lead follow-up after the initial call from you. Then start training them on how to make the initial call to the prospect and book an appointment on the first call. Keep training, testing, and tracking them and monitoring their performance at each stage until they are able to handle the initial contact with the prospect and convert him as well as you do. You can't turn over good leads and good opportunities right away to people who will blow them. Your buyer's agents also will progress faster if they are actually able to conduct business and work with high-quality buyers. If the whole process is turned over to them at once, if they can't convert leads and make appointments, they won't be showing property and making sales. Turning over the back end first also helps you build your value to them, so that they are not as likely to exit and go off on their own.

The Buyer's Agent Is Not Involved in the Closing Transaction

The key in training the buyer's agent in this area is how his role changes to a behind-the-scenes support role. You, as the team leader, want your buyer's agents to step away from the transaction for two reasons. The first is that you want them to invest their energy in securing another purchase contract. One of the benefits few lead agents sell to buyer's agent candidates is that they will be able to do more transactions. They don't need direct involvement in closing the transaction. They can use that time to create more transactions.

The buyer's agent is a much more highly paid person than the members of the administrative staff. The buyer's agent has a more direct opportunity to create new sales and new revenue for the company. The goal is for the buyer's agent to turn over the file to the administrative staff and go create another file.

Far too often, the buyer's agent continues to be involved with the transaction and the client in more than a behind-the-scenes support role. He stays intimately involved at a level that causes problems for the team. His role should really be to check in with the client every week or two to see how she is doing at getting ready for the move. He should also ask for referrals of additional people that he could serve. He needs to check to see that everything is OK and to make sure that the closing coordinator is doing her job well. If he receives a negative response, he should convey these concerns to the closing coordinator, so that she can solve the problem. If the closing coordinator needs help, then she can bring the buyer's agent back in to assist her.

The second reason you want the buyer's agent to step away is the need to transfer the client's loyalty from the buyer's agent to the team. You don't want to have a fight for this client's loyalty on your hands in the future. By having the buyer's agent move to a support role, you will be more effective in showing the benefits of the team.

I would also advise that you, the team leader, make a few personal calls to the client to check up and see how she is doing and how your staff is handling her needs. The calls serve as a demonstration that you personally care about her as a client, and that you care about the quality of the service she is receiving from your team. It also opens the door for a referral discussion with her.

Dealing with Inspections and Appraisals

The buyer's agent should be the person representing the client and the team at inspections. The buyer's agent should be writing the repair and contingency removal addendums as well. If the standard practice in your area is for an attorney to perform that function, then the buyer's agent should coordinate with the attorney. The closing coordinator is responsible for reminding the client and the buyer's agent of any deadlines.

Requiring the appraisers to gain access themselves is the most time-efficient result for the buyer's agent and the team. Arrange for the seller to meet the appraisers, pick up a key for access at your office, or have the listing agent meet them. There are numerous options that are better than having a buyer's agent invest an hour of his time to meet an appraiser.

Building Urgency in the Buyer

A skilled buyer's agent should already have handled the misconception many buyers have that if they look long enough, they will find the perfect home. If they still believe that old wives' tale at this stage, the buyer's agent is in trouble. The best advice I can give for creating urgency is to use anything you can. Whatever is at your disposal, use it: the impending interest rate increase, the scarcity of inventory, the quality of the deal, the ideal time frame for the client, and the market trends in the last month that indicate a need to act. You must be able to teach the buyer's agent how to build urgency in the buyer.

The definition of a great salesperson is someone who has the ability to convince a client to do something that is beneficial to the client *or* to get the client to do it faster. You are there to persuade the client that acting now on this home is really beneficial to her. (If it is not beneficial to your client, you shouldn't force her into a purchase… ever!)

You Snooze, You Lose

In trying to create urgency at this stage, you will need to deal with the buyer's feeling that she can wait. We have all seen situations where a buyer lost the home she really wanted because she didn't take competitive action now.

We must teach buyers that the speed with which they make decisions matters. The best-priced, best-quality, competitively priced properties won't wait for a buyer to act. A good listing can't be kept secret from the other agents in the marketplace who are trying to make a sale. People will find out about it and sell it. When the marketplace has limited inventory, it is easy to build urgency.

A Champion Salesperson can also build urgency to take action in a more neutral marketplace, where not all of the listings sell or sell quickly. He has the mindset and the skill to be able to build urgency in a prospect anyway. A Champion builds urgency through the value of the property, the length of time and the amount of hard work expended to even find the property, the inventory levels, and how closely the property aligns with the buyer's needs, wants, and desires. All of these lead to the client's taking competitive action sooner. We don't know exactly when the property will sell. Educating the purchaser on the need to take action now on a good or even great property enables strong revenue growth. The best properties sell fast.

The Rules of Selling Real Estate.

1. *Good properties sell fast; great properties sell overnight.* Most buyers need to move more quickly and take more decisive, competitive action. In any marketplace, the best-priced inventory will be gone in a matter of days or a few weeks. The challenge is that, even at three weeks, we don't know when the home will sell. When your buyer finds something through you that you know will be sold quickly, don't forget to drive the point home—this home won't last.

2. *If you wait, you may lose it. If you sleep on it, you may not sleep in it.* A buyer needs to know that with the best properties, even overnight consideration is a significant risk. You need to ask the buyer, "How will you feel if you lose it?" and "What's your disappointment value?" The disappointment value is what it is worth to the buyer to not be disappointed in the morning when she finds out it's gone. What's it worth to avoid that feeling?

When you do convince the buyer that she must take action and do it now, you also must be able to convince her that she must be competitive in taking that action. Taking action by writing an offer that is not competitive or not within a reasonable distance of fair market value most likely will produce a negative result that she won't want.

Consumers have been taught by someone like their parents or their Uncle Ned to never offer full price, that you are a fool if you offer full price. While negotiating has a place in real estate sales, if the property is a good value, why risk losing it to save a few thousand dollars? At times, depending on the inventory in and the frenzy of the marketplace, the client may even have to offer more than full price to secure the property. When you counsel the client, you have to be able to convey the true cost of the difference between her projected low offer and the full-price offer.

Too many buyers see the lower offer as a huge savings to them, rather than what it is. For a well-priced home in a competitive marketplace of good homes, the buyer may save at best between 2 and 3 percent of the sales price of the home. That 2 to 3 percent is really just additional money that the buyer ends up borrowing. For example, if the buyer managed to save 3 percent on a $200,000 home, that would amount to $6,000. The real cost of borrowing that amount at a reasonable interest rate would be $35 a month, or $1.13 per day. That is probably the best that a buyer can do when she is competing for a high-demand home in a good marketplace.

When you factor in the tax savings and inflation of the dollar, the effective cost drops well below a dollar a day. What home that a client really loves isn't worth a dollar a day more to be sure of ending up with it?

> *Is it worth the risk?*
>
> *or*
>
> *Are you willing to lose the right home over $1.13 a day?*
>
> *or*
>
> *My experience with _____ number of clients is that they don't miss the money, but they do miss the home if they don't end up buying it.*

If you allow your clients to engage in this type of thinking, then you may be faced with the problem of the house they didn't get. Once they have a house that they liked one and have fallen short on it, they will compare every other home they look at with that one. It will be like fighting in the jungles of Vietnam where you can't see the enemy clearly. All you hear are the bullets whizzing by, and all you smell is the napalm.

Many buyers also believe the myth that they can always start low and come up later. This is the cousin of "never offer full price." You will often hear them together. The view is that sellers always make a counteroffer. They want to sell their home, so they will engage in a dialogue with us on paper back and forth.

I remember early in my career working with a sales manager from a car dealership in southern California who had moved to Portland. He wanted to make low offers and negotiate everything. After a few rounds, when he saw that he was not going to get anywhere on the price, he started in on the furniture and personal property. Fortunately, I was smart enough to put the two parties in separate conference rooms in the same office. Also fortunately, I was working with a good listing agent. We must have created almost 10 counteroffers in an hour of back-and-forth negotiating. It was early in my career, and I hadn't prepared my buyer for how the seller would react to his haggling the way car salespeople do. The seller was getting insulted and upset. This was especially true when he bottom-lined the price, and my buyer started in on his possessions. As I said, it was my first year in the business. I didn't have the control of the client that I would today.

Sellers Can Be Emotional about Their Homes

Sellers can easily be insulted by a low offer and become defensive and illogical. They often will counter with a higher price than they really want just because of the initial offer. You must ensure that the buyer understands the seller's options when he receives a low offer.

1. *Become insulted and fail to respond.* I would frequently counsel my sellers to reject significantly low offers outright because of the limited probability of finding a middle ground or meeting of the minds. Also, because both the seller and I knew that this was the best value in the marketplace for that type of home, we knew that someone would purchase the property for the asking price or close to it. Waiting might cause the seller less stress and less hassle. When we selected the rejection response rather than countering, it was sometimes because of the skill of the other agent. Did that agent have the skill to go back to the buyer and make the case for the value of the home? Some sellers will reject, rather than respond to a low offer.

2. *Get defensive or hostile.* The seller could defend his position or value in hostile terms. If you manage to secure the agreement of all parties at this stage, you still have

the home inspection, appraisal, and turnover of possessions to work through. It sets the stage for a more combative transaction.

3. *Be more difficult to negotiate with because of the initial offer.* The battle lines can be drawn when the buyer makes a low offer. The seller can dig himself a foxhole about price, repairs, and possessions and may not be willing to come out to find a middle ground that is a win for everyone.

4. *Not care if he sells it to the buyer at all.* This situation is again caused by a low offer. I can be influenced by the listing agent's ego or the seller's ego. The buyer loses all opportunity to acquire the home at any price.

The way to combat the misconceptions about low offers is to explain what can happen to the seller. Take the time to educate the buyer to understand the risk that she is taking when she pushes the seller into any of the four categories previously discussed.

Then, lead in with the key questions to ask a buyer when she is considering a low offer.

Question 1: What will it take to be the seller's best buyer?

Sellers want the best buyer for their home in terms of sales price or net proceeds. They also want a buyer who requires little hassle, extra work, and emotions for them. With some sellers, being able to identify with the buyer has value to them. While most sellers want the most they can get from the sale of their home, there is a large group that would rather identify with the buyer. This can be especially true for people who have lived in the same home for a long time and raised their family there.

Question 2: What will it take to avoid offending the seller?

If you offend the seller with an initial offer, you have a long uphill battle ahead. The probability of your getting paid for your effort now and the probability of the buyer's purchasing the home she wants is contained in this question. You must be aware of the possibility of offending the seller and try to avoid it if at all possible.

Keys to Showing Property Well

The next step in training your buyer's agents is to teach them to show property. Few agents have ever been trained to show property well. One of the keys to showing property comes from the buyer consultation. By gaining enough knowledge about the buyer in advance, you can select properties that are better suited to her specific wants and needs. Being able to ask questions as you show the property to gauge the buyer's interest in and excitement about this property compared to the mental picture of the home she desires is critical. You need to be able to guide the buyer through exploring her options and deciding if this is her new home. You must ask questions like:

1. How do you feel this room would fit your furniture?
2. Is this the type of kitchen nook you were hoping for in your new home?
3. Bob, this garage seems the right size, doesn't it?
4. Which area of the backyard would you put the children's play area in?
5. We talked about how _____ was important to you. Does this _____ meet your needs?
6. If you had to make a decision today between _____ and _____, which would you choose?

Use the One-Up Technique for Success

It's imperative that you teach all your buyer's agents the one-up technique. The one-up technique can help dramatically decrease the sales time and the number of homes shown. It can significantly decrease the buyer's and the agent's confusion as well. The one-up technique allows clients to focus on only one home at a time as the home they may be purchasing. They aren't allowed to consider a dozen, four, or even three homes at once. As a home is being shown, it is being compared to the "up" home. The question is, which of the two homes meets the clients' needs better? If they had to purchase one of the two, which would they purchase?

If the one-up technique isn't used, the client will usually begin to mix up the rooms, features, landscaping, and finish work of the homes she has seen. She will create this combination of the perfect home she is looking for. Once she has created this perfect home from the jumbled-up parts of all the homes she has seen, it's increasingly difficult to bring her back to reality. The number of homes needed to be shown increases, the time to writing an offer increases, and the quality of the initial offer usually decreases because the client feels that she has settled for less. As a result, she makes a low offer.

Reduce the Number of Homes Shown

The truth about real estate agents is that our commission income is fundamentally fixed. When we decide to work with a particular client, we know what we will earn more than 95 percent of the time. Sometimes, a client will go up in price point to acquire what he really wants, but that isn't a regular occurrence. The vast majority of buyers purchase at very close to the maximum they can afford. Even when we do an outstanding job or our client manages to secure a discount because of our hard work, our negotiating skills, the seller's motivation, or the fact that he is buying a distressed property, our commission income will not change significantly.

The real variable, once the exclusive client relationship has been established, is the time you invest to earn the commission. It's the span of time you invest in terms of days, weeks, or even months before you receive your commission. It's also the volume of time invested. The more properties you show and research for your client, the more time you will invest. By reducing the number of homes that need to be shown, your buyer's agents will increase opportunities to earn more income for themselves and the team. Try to increase productivity through better time management tactics and better sales skills.

It is important to set a clear standard with the client. Establish the standard that you are investing more time up front to be able to service him more effectively; by knowing his wants and desires, you can select more suitable properties that are more targeted to those wants and needs. These properties will also be the best for the client in terms of condition, price, features, amenities, and value. The buyer's agent will prescreen these properties, so that the client will see only the best in the marketplace.

Finally, and most importantly, when you are trying to focus the client and reduce the number of showings to increase service quality and the team's net profit, you need to inform and educate the client that if the right home isn't found in the initial group of homes shown, the ones you show him in the future (other than brand-new listed properties) will only be of lower quality and value than the ones the buyer's agent is currently showing him. If this situation occurs, you must inform the client that when a brand-new listing comes on the market, he will need to act swiftly and competitively. There won't be a lot of negotiating room if the property is priced at close to fair market value. Is the client all right with the truth of the marketplace?

You might also consider training the buyer's agent to establish a standard number of homes that she will show before your clients select and purchase the right home for their family. This technique gives the buyer's agent a further guide to follow. It also opens up the dialogue of, "Where are we at? Am I missing something? Do we need to raise our price or lower our expectations because we have seen more than the _____ that it usually takes for my clients to find the right home for them?"

Move the Prospect to Client Status

A buyer's agent needs to know that she should work only with clients. She also needs to know exactly what a client looks like and what services all your buyer's agents provide to your clients. A client is someone who has made a commitment of exclusivity to you in return for a predetermined set of services and benefits. A complete, mutually beneficial exchange of commitments has been agreed upon by both parties. That, in essence, is what a client is. The vast majority of real estate agents who work with buyers fall far short of this reasonable definition of a client. The only way to achieve a true client relationship with a buyer is to conduct a buyer interview or buyer consultation.

Buyer Counseling Interview

For most agents, the buyer interview, buyer consultation, or buyer counseling session (whichever term you want to use to describe your meeting with a buyer face to face in your office to secure an "exclusive right to represent" contract before you show property) is less structured and planned than a listing presentation. Most agents completely "wing" this critical meeting that will set the tone for the working relationship with the buyer (if they conduct it at all).

If you have a simple agenda for the meeting that you hand to the buyer prior to beginning your discussion, this will enable you to conduct the meeting and convert and commit the buyer to your service more quickly.

Sample Agenda

1. My role in helping my client
2. My specific services and benefits
3. Current and emerging market conditions
4. Your financing options
    a. The value of preapproval
    b. Earnest money deposit
    c. Life of a loan
5. Discussion of your wants and needs in your next home
    a. Preferred style
    b. Preferred features
    c. Preferred location
    d. Price and payment penalties
6. Selection assistance services
7. Representing you to the seller
8. Professional negotiation as your agent
9. Communication and closing coordination
10. Servicing you after the sale for life
11. Exchange of commitments

After establishing your role with the prospect, then move into a segment of the discussion of your services. (This assumes that you have already asked the prospect sufficient questions to qualify her desire, needs, ability, and authority to proceed with a purchase.) An option before you define your services and benefits is to take a refresher trip down the qualifying trail to confirm your understanding of the prospect's expectations.

Three Core Messages

There are three core messages that need to be conveyed in the My Services section; they need to be the first things discussed with a buyer. Most agents never discuss these concepts. These three messages are directly linked to building the value of your services and obtaining exclusivity of your services in return. They are:

1. All real estate agents are not the same.
2. It really matters who represents your interests.
3. My market knowledge is superior to other agents'.

Agents Are Not All the Same

One of the primary messages used by inferior agents and discounting agents is that agents are all the same; there is essentially no difference between Champion Agents or Champion Teams and other agents. You need to convey that each agent operates an independent business and applies different techniques to arrive at the purchase of a home. One may employ a Kia-level strategy regarding service, amenities, and experience, while another uses a Mercedes-level strategy. You want to create a clear distinction between what you do and what other agents do. An analogy outside of real estate that illustrates service and quality differentials is highly effective. I have found that car comparisons are easy to use because car companies have spent billions of dollars over the years branding their products and establishing the fact that cars and car dealerships are not all the same. Your job, at this stage, is to show and demonstrate the differences between you and other agents and to counteract the prospect's preconceived feelings and beliefs that all agents the same.

You could even use the meeting you are conducting as a demonstration that you are different. Your desire to create a delighted client is so great that you conduct these meetings to ensure a successful outcome for the client. Most agents just want to stick the client in a car and sell her a home as quickly as possible. Your philosophy differs from that of those other agents. You hold yourself to a higher service standard than that.

> *"There are tremendous differences among the agents you can work with. Each agent operates independently and approaches his business in a different way. There are differences in knowledge, skills, strategy, attitude, experience, communication, negotiating style, and, ultimately, results. I spend time with you up front to clearly understand your objectives and needs to ensure a successful relationship. Does that make sense?"*

It Really Does Matter Whom You Select to Represent You

In this section, you are building the value of your service and moving it away from that of the guy who looks up properties to show and opens doors. A Champion Buyer's Agent knows that those are the least valuable parts of his service. Any agent can plunk a few keys on the keyboard of a computer and possess an MLS key.

There is a story about a senior executive who was having problems with his computer. The company called in a technology expert to fix his problem. The technology expert looked at the computer diagnostically for a few minutes. He then reached into his briefcase for a small hammer; he tapped on the computer three times, and it was fixed. He then handed the senior executive a bill for $500. The executive said, "I won't pay this; you were only here five minutes. That's outrageous! I want you to itemize this bill." The technology expert then itemized the bill. It read: "$2 for tapping on the computer and $498 for knowing where to tap!" What you are trying to tell the buyer is that it's easy to get a hammer and start hitting the computer. God knows there have been many times when I have taken more than a small hammer to my computer! The buyer needs to know that you are one of the few agents in the marketplace who knows where to tap.

The agent a buyer uses to represent her interests in securing a house can affect:

- The home you select
- The long-term appreciation you generate through your home
- Your financial position years down the road
- Your ability to avoid legal pitfalls
- How your offer is presented
- The financing you receive
- The stress you experience during the transaction
- The timeliness of the closing
- The communication during and after the transaction
- The price you pay for a home

Given all these factors that an agent influences, it's easy to demonstrate how important the decision about who will represent her interests in her purchase will be for the client and her family. There are also factors that affect the client financially and emotionally. There are security issues as well. These factors can have negative consequences that can extend well into the next decade. Selecting the wrong agent now won't just affect her purchase of this house but can affect her purchase of her next few houses, as well as long-term financial security for her and her family.

You could ask the client which of these issues or factors concerns her the most. What is important is getting the client to understand, at this juncture, that selecting the wrong agent can cause two, three, five, or even more of these areas to be heavily negative for her. At this stage, you must let the client know that you understand how important your job really is to your clients. Therefore, you have developed a process to ensure that all their buying factors are in your favor.

> *Do you see an agent's influence and the effect on your home purchase if the agent isn't the right one? Doesn't it make sense when I say that it fundamentally matters whom you select to represent your interests?*

My Market Knowledge and Service Are Superior to Other Agents'

Many of the factors listed previously are intertwined with market knowledge. The home the client selects, it's appreciation, the client's long-term financial position, how the offer is presented, stress, and the price the client pays are all connected to market knowledge. You have to prove that your market knowledge is topnotch. When looking at market knowledge, there are two core areas.

1. *The study and evaluation of the supply and demand aspects of the marketplace.* A Champion Buyer's Agent views the market in terms of how the law of supply and demand connects with the marketplace—right now. Educating yourself and then your clients on this demonstrates value. It also enables you to have a solid discussion with your clients about how the market can change quickly. If a lot of houses sell quickly in the next 30 days with a limited amount of new inventory coming on the market, the selection will be smaller, and the client's bargaining power will also be reduced. There are few agents who really understand the effects of the law of supply and demand on the marketplace.

   A Champion Agent tracks active inventory at predetermined price points. He tracks the number of homes sold monthly at those price points as well. Additionally, he monitors the list price to sales price ratios and days on the market numbers. Finally, if he is a true Champion, he will calculate the absorption rate or available months' worth of inventory remaining. This figure can be easily calculated by dividing monthly sales into the current inventory numbers. This will give you a clear, quantifiable measure of the competitiveness of the marketplace that the buyer will encounter. It will also convey the breadth of selection the buyer can expect to encounter in the marketplace. If your marketplace has six months' worth of inventory, the buyer can expect a good selection of homes to choose from. If it only has one month's, the volume of homes to select from is diminished. One market is like a Wal-Mart Super Center; the other market is a corner 7-11 convenience store in terms of inventory and selection.

Completing this type of analysis quarterly or monthly gives you a tremendous snapshot of how competitive the marketplace is currently and how competitive the client will need to be. The reason I used the word *snapshot* is because the analysis is for one moment in time. You have to make that clear to a client. Too often, people feel that our analysis, whether it is for a buyer or a seller's competitive market assessment, should be good forever. It's just a snapshot of now.

> *Do you see why my clients can make better decisions? Is it clear how this creates an advantage for my exclusive clients? Is this the type of service you are looking for?*

2. *Transaction process knowledge.*   This is the other subsection of market knowledge. There are few agents who have actually created a step-by-step process that they follow in serving the client, a checklist that moves the client along the path to home ownership. What steps do you take before securing a property for your client? What steps do you take once you have secured the property to ensure a timely, low-stress closing?

There is a process for a transaction that allows the buyers to experience less stress and anxiety. Most purchasers experience, at best, what I describe as controlled chaos. The transaction and the clients are being thrust into emergency deadlines because the lender, the attorney, the other agent, or even the buyer or seller didn't perform in a timely manner, and the agent found this out a little later than he should have. A smooth transaction is certainly one of the benefits that clients will receive from working with a team. You, as the lead agent, have established a service model system that yields delighted clients. You have staffed that model with highly trained professionals to provide more service to your clients. There will be greater consistency of service; more frequent communication; better protection of clients through the buying process; and low risk of exposure to poor contract writing, losing a home they really desire, and overall dissatisfaction. Clients receive all of these extra benefits and services at no additional cost. In fact, the seller pays all of these costs.

> *Our clients experience a well-timed and structured process that leads to our end objective of a smooth closing. Having helped _____ people in my career and over _____ in the last year, you can rest easy that, with each step of the process, we will complete it timely and with excellence and will communicate the activities all throughout the transaction.*

Close for Exclusive Commitment

Being able to secure a full exchange of mutual commitments from the prospect to work exclusively with you really separates the top buyer's agents from the marginal ones. The ability to convey the benefits and value of working with your team and having the confidence and conviction to ask for the order really set the stage for a tremendous relationship now and also in the future. It enables buyers to clearly see the differences and value of your team and will cause them to want to send their friends, family, and associates to you and your team.

The biggest area of gaining an exclusive commitment that buyer's agents need training in is getting the elephant in the room on the table. The elephant is the commission your team will be paid for services rendered.

For there to be an effective relationship between the buyer's agent and the buyer client, the two parties must exchange a mutual commitment of loyalty. Buyer's agents are committing to a high service standard. The only way a prospect can receive that high service standard is to work with you on an exclusive basis, forgoing all other previous, potential, and possible relationships with other agents. A buyer's agent will need to explain the scope of that commitment-based relationship.

After this discussion with the prospect, he either becomes a client or is deemed non-qualified. It could be that the prospect qualifies in every way in terms of motivation and financial capacity. However, even though he has the proper desire, need, ability, and authority, he lacks the will to exchange commitments with you.

Fair Exchange

It's paramount that a buyer's agent have the strong personal beliefs and sales skills to be able to persuade the client of the fundamental fairness of his committing to an exclusive agreement; that the client will receive better service and a higher level of service and benefits through exclusivity; that it won't be fair, based on your compensation plan, for her not to be the buyer's exclusive agent; and that only the best agents work exclusively, and any agent who doesn't expect it is a poor agent. At the core, an agent won't work diligently at her job if there is a question of whether her paycheck will be good in two weeks.

The buyer needs to understand that your team operates an exclusive practice. Your buyer's agents don't work with anyone and everyone who walks in the door, calls on the phone, or hits your Internet site. Your team is highly selective about the clients that you represent in the marketplace. The benefit of exclusivity is that your team can provide a higher level of service and counsel to your clients. The only way your team can follow through on all the services and commitments the buyer's agent talked with the clients about earlier is to work with a small group of clients rather than a large group of people.

> *Bob and Susan, I want you to know that I don't work with everyone who calls or even with everyone I meet with. To be able to provide the services I provide, and that you indicated you want, I have to choose my clients. The big benefit for my clients is this approach allows me a greater amount of time to invest in my client's total satisfaction. My clients end up securing the best homes in the marketplace at the best values in the marketplace. In the end, by working this way, the clients save time, frustration, even money and especially stress because I am able to give them the attention they deserve. Based on our discussion this far, do you see the benefit in that?*

You need to fundamentally educate your clients on how real estate compensation really works. There are still many people who think we get paid in some other way, rather than through the transaction. They don't realize that we are like a personal injury attorney who gets paid only when the case is won—when the transaction closes and funds are collected.

> *Bob and Susan, I want you to understand that I work on a contingency fee basis. That means that this meeting and all the services I will provide to you will be in the hope and expectation that I will be paid at closing in the future. It's a risk as an agent I am willing to take with the right clients. I have had situations where I did a tremendous amount of work, and the transaction didn't close. So, all that work, time, effort, energy, counsel, and advice went out the window as unpaid. Just like you, I have a mortgage payment and other bills. I owe it to my family and 2 children to ensure I work in a manner that serves my clients well in addition to ensuring my compensation. The benefit is I want to do an outstanding job for you, so I do receive payment at the conclusion of your home purchase.*

One of the best techniques to teach your buyer's agents is what I call the "I am like you" technique. In the "I am like you" technique, the buyer's agent wants to show the prospect the many similarities between him and the prospects. The only difference really is his job and how his compensation structure works. Most prospects are not in sales. Even if they are in sales, few of them are in 100 percent commission sales where there is no base salary, no company car, no health insurance or retirement account, and no safety net of any kind. Those are the differences. The similarities are numerous and should be verbally listed for the prospect.

Your buyer's agent, just like the prospect, has goals and dreams in life. He has a mortgage, car payments, credit card bills, and other financial obligations. He may be married and may have a spouse or significant other to support (or at least a family budget to contribute to). He might have children to provide for, as well as dreams for their future in the form of college savings or help in the future when they want to buy their first home. Your buyer's agent owes it to himself, his family, and his future to work in a manner that serves his clients well while also ensuring his compensation. The only way a buyer's agent can ensure his compensation is to ask for it. A very effective way to ask is through the "I am like you" technique.

Explaining *Agency* to the Client

When you execute a great presentation, it should be benefits-based. It should clearly answer the question, what's in it for them. It should have trial closes throughout the presentation to build momentum to the close. It should be delivered with enthusiasm, conviction, confidence, and assertiveness.

This part of the presentation should be the assertive part. Most buyer's agents approach this crossroads and wimp out. If your buyer's agents have followed the Champion process I have laid out for them thus far, they have earned the right to secure an exclusive right to represent contract.

> *Bob and Susan, I will commit to providing you with every single service we talked about that you agreed you wanted. All I ask and require is that you commit to working exclusively with me. Can you do that?*

The key, once you have asked the question, is to be quiet, to not utter a single word. Let tension build if you must, but don't say anything. I think one of the biggest mistakes that ordinary, or even good, salespeople make is right here. A Champion Buyer's Agent asks a great closing question and waits for the response.

One of the key differentiators between good and great in the presentation is the silence after a direct question. Too many salespeople fear dead space in a conversation and think that they have to fill it up. That need to fill the void will keep your buyer's agents from greatness in sales. The void of silence causes our client or prospect to think. At this moment, the sale is made.

Coach's Tip: The difference between great and good is very little. It's the last inch or two that separates great from good. It could be the smallest detail that gets overlooked by most people, but that the person who wants to achieve greatness never overlooks.

Arthur Rubenstein, the world-famous pianist, was once asked, "How do you handle the notes on the page as well as you do?" He responded, "I handle the notes no better than many others, but the pauses… ah! That is where the art resides." Your sales process needs to be like a great piece of music. It causes a reaction and an emotion on the part of your client or prospect. The real artistry is in the pauses. It's in the void of quiet after the question. Don't run through the pauses with another question or statement. Let the power of the pause take over. Rubenstein would let a note resonate throughout the hall. Let your question resonate in the conference room, the living room—wherever you are making your presentation.

If you step into the pause, you invalidate, or soften, the last question. You are at the moment of truth. You will find out valuable information about your client or prospect at that moment. The power of silence is deafening. Make sure to use it to your advantage. Becoming a Champion Buyer's Agent requires watching the little things.

If, after pausing, waiting, waiting, and then waiting again, you still can't get a commitment, you have to move in another direction. I am a firm believer in getting a buyer client to sign an exclusive right to represent agreement without conditions. If you can't get the agreement without conditions, put the condition in the contract for them.

The main argument people use for not signing an exclusive right to represent agreement is that they don't want to be tied up. They play the "what if" game in their head. What if the agent doesn't perform? What if I decide not to buy now? What if a friend calls me about her house? What if I find a FSBO? They come up with all kinds of examples. The probability of any of them happening is about zilch, But they want to still hang on to that low chance, just in case. Then you put in the condition on their ability to cancel the agreement.

I will commit to you the service we have talked about if you commit to buy exclusively through me. You can cancel our agreement at any time if you tell me first, if you call me personally or meet me personally. Does that meet your approval?

I want you to pause and think. When you found out that someone you had spent a lot of time with had bought from another agent, when did you find out and from whom? Usually, we find out just before or after the deal closes. We also find out from another party: our lender, their lender, or another agent. We rarely find out from the buyer. The buyer usually doesn't have the guts to call us and say, "I found a FSBO, found another house, bought it through the listing agent, or you were doing a poor job." She just goes away and hides, hoping that you never find out.

You have two options once you reach this point and once you have a commitment: you can move forward to discuss exclusive agency, and you can get the buyer to sign an exclusive agency agreement with that condition in there.

The natural tendency for most buyer's agents is not to execute a buyer agency contract. They don't want to force people or "sell them." Your company policy must be that buyer agency contracts are always used. I have had clients at Real Estate Champions who got so frustrated with their buyer's agents' failure to get the contract signed that they actually created a different compensation level for cases where their buyer's agents failed to get a buyer agency contract signed. The buyer's agent received 10 percent less in commission.

Coach's Tip: According to NAR, in 2004, over 64 percent of transactions involved an exclusive buyer's agency relationship with the buyer. If you are thinking this can't be done in my area, 64 percent is a significant number of people who accept and operate via exclusive right to represent agreements.

You might think this is harsh, but those clients didn't have the problem ever again. When it affects their pocketbook, it's amazing how fast something buyer's agents had said couldn't be done happens.

Your other option is to look the client straight in the eye and say, "Let's shake on our agreement." A handshake commitment is better than nothing, but it falls far short of a written document of exclusive agency.

Reaffirm the Relationship

At its core, the exclusive relationship is centered on three fundamental statements:

- You will use me if I find you what you want, right?
- You will use me if you find what you want, correct?
- You will use me if another agent finds you what you want, right?

Without an affirmative response to those three fundamental questions, you will want to put Roy Rogers on the CD player and sing "Happy Trails" to them. If you get a pause, stall, or balk, you can go back and explain the value page again, reemphasizing the value you bring to the transaction—demonstrating each service and why it's worth it.

In the end, your final argument could be, why not? Why not use someone else's time, experience, knowledge, expertise, and gas to find the right home? It costs the prospect nothing; the seller pays for it.

If you can't get someone to commit exclusively, which would be rare if you follow this process, I would deem that person unqualified and move on to the next prospect.

Press Hard—There Are Three Copies

In training buyer's agents to really master the buyer counseling interview, they will need to see you conduct it probably at least 20 times. They will need to see it live numerous times to understand the agenda and the flow of the presentation. They will also need to be present because you will want to make the hand-off of the relationship to them during the presentation. It's easier when they are present. After they have seen you conduct the interview numerous times, you will then need to sit quietly, take notes, and observe their initial 15 to 20 interviews. You are there to critique their presentation, not to step in to save the presentation and secure the prospect. Your buyer's agents will probably learn more from the ones they lose than from the many that they secure. You must be willing to let them skin their knees on these. It will cost you a few bucks in the short run, but it will make you lots in the long run.

Lead-Generation Systems

At this point, you have kept the most important job that takes the smallest amount of time. You have already transferred all of the more service-oriented, time-consuming jobs to the buyer's agent. Now she is ready to learn how to fully deal with ad calls, sign calls, Internet leads, call capture leads, and the host of other sources of leads. The first step is determining the order in which you intend to train your buyer's agents on each source of lead generation. Which ones do you want to transfer to them first? There are two ways to evaluate which to transfer to them:

1. The ones that infringe the most on your personal energy, family, and quality of life
2. The ones that have a lower conversion ratio

A word of caution: don't transfer too much too soon. You will see a drop in conversion because you are more skilled than they currently are. You could see a drop in revenue if you make the transfer too quickly. My advice would be to transfer the Internet leads first. Internet leads have the lowest conversion ratio in the real estate industry. The volume of leads is large and is growing with each passing day. The quality has remained the same or degraded over time.

You might also train your buyer's agents to handle the call capture calls on nights and weekends next. You might consider keeping these calls for yourself during normal business hours when you are able to take them. This would allow your buyer's agents to cover when you don't want to handle these calls, but you aren't going to give up too much, so the risk of production drops is lower and controlled. The last lead-generation system I would relinquish would be ad calls and sign calls. These calls are the highest quality with the highest conversion ratios of all sources. When you are ready to begin training your buyer's agents on these calls, you might consider transferring responsibility to them only on nights and weekends and keeping them during the normal business hours that you work to keep leads and conversion up.

The training you give your buyer's agents must be focused on taking the prospect on a sales call and driving her to a face-to-face presentation. Teach them to bring up the value of the service you offer right there on the initial call, so that the prospect has the desire to meet with you. Buyer's agents need to learn to convince the prospect on that initial call that an appointment with you raises the probability that the prospect will understand the marketplace better, receive a higher level of service for no additional cost, secure an advantage when negotiating, acquire a better lender for a smoother transaction, secure money in the short or long run, and, ultimately, receive the representation that he deserves and should expect.

All of these are valid benefits of booking an appointment for a face-to-face buyer consultation. The truth is, consumers perceive a true professional as someone that they meet with by appointment only. They willingly set appointments with their doctors, dentists, attorneys, and accountants. Being able to convey that the value of your team is equal to that of these other professionals in their lives is paramount.

The typical agent is trying to secure a phone number and an e-mail address so that he can send the prospect stuff. The stuff is usually marketing pieces, personal brochures, and properties via e-mail. There is a laundry list of garbage that we send to prospects and they throw away without ever looking at. The truth is, this trend is more prevalent in real estate teams than anywhere else. That's because most teams have more marketing stuff to send.

Unless you can prove and clearly show that your marketing materials, philosophy, sales strategies, and track record are superior, you will rarely convert a buyer by e-mailing properties to her based on a profile.

If you secured the prospect through an ad call, sign call, open house, or the Internet, you must assume that other agents have all the information you do. If you manage to convince the prospect to share her e-mail address, you must assume that five other agents have it as well. Whoever meets the prospect face to face wins.

When I say appointment, I am not talking about an appointment to show property. I am talking about an appointment to conduct a buyer interview; to determine the prospect's desire, need, ability, and authority; to assess the odds of your servicing this client and earning a commission. Pretend for a moment that you are a personal injury attorney. As a personal injury attorney, you offer a free consultation. The reason you want the consultation is to determine the probability or odds of winning the case. A Champion Buyer's Agent's focus is the same. We are evaluating the prospect based on the odds of achieving the client's goals and serving him well. We also are evaluating how much we will earn; how soon we will earn it; and what it will cost us in time, effort, energy, emotion, and dollars invested.

A Champion Agent knows that the primary objective of a sales call, either inbound or outbound, is an appointment. The truth is that Champion Agents have more appointments than other agents. They make more money because they have more appointments. Lower-performing agents look at the Champion Agents in awe. They think there must be something magical about the way they operate. The truth is that their philosophy, skills, and focus are more fundamentally sound. They know clearly that the objective is a greater number of appointments.

Lower-performing agents are too much in need of "the deal." They often show need, even desperation to secure a new client.

Champion Team Rule: *When you need it more than the prospect does, you lose control.*

If the buyer's agent needs the deal more than the client needs your team, that agent has lost. It's hard for buyer's agents to take the risk, create a little tension, and close assertively if they need the deal to cover their mortgage or other bills. To be effective and successful in sales, they have to be willing to risk losing the prospect or client. This willingness is shown first by asking people for an appointment to meet. It is followed by the conviction with which the buyer's agent asks the prospect to work with your team using the service system that he has laid out for the prospect. Your team and the buyer's agent are the experts, so why not use your system for service? It's hard to guarantee successful results if you use someone else's system or approach to home purchasing, especially the buyer's.

A Champion Lead Agent is an agent who is in command. She is in command of her business, the prospect, the client, the service she provides, and how she provides it. She is also in command of her time and her knowledge. Most other agents are on demand. They are at the beck and call of the prospect, the client, another agent, or other people in the transaction like the lender, inspector, and appraiser. The need for the deal can cause an agent to lose all control. Being willing and able to walk away from a prospect if he doesn't follow your procedures in doing business increases the odds that you will earn your value. As an agent trying to reach the Champion Lead Agent level, you need to act as if you are a Champion now—already.

Teaching a buyer's agent to use strong dialogue to convert the prospect to a face-to-face appointment is clearly the objective. It's about being able to deliver scripts with excellence that will explain to prospects the benefits of meeting with you or your buyer's agent. The prospects clearly know that there are benefits of meeting with your team. However, getting them to come to your office for a buyer consultation requires delivering the benefits that *they want.*

> *In order for me to provide you with the highest level of service and representation, we simply need to meet. Would _____ or _____ be better for you?*
>
> *or*
>
> *I have helped _____ number of families in my career and over _____ just in the last year, and my clients have found that by meeting with me, they have a better knowledge of the current marketplace and greater opportunity to live in the right property for them and their family.*
>
> *or*
>
> *In order for you to maximize your initial equity position and minimize your up-front investment in a new property, we need to meet. Would _____ or _____ be better for you?*
>
> *or*
>
> *I have been able to acquire properties for my clients at _____ of the asking price when the market average is _____. This saves my clients, like yourself, thousands of dollars. You end up buying a home for less money with less money out of your pocket. For me to be able to save you thousands like my other clients, we need to spend a few moments together. Would _____ or _____ be better for you?*

Once your buyer's agent has demonstrated that she has the skill to convert the leads to face-to-face appointments, you can turn over the whole lead follow-up and all lead-generation systems to her to handle. When you add additional buyer's agents, you need to repeat the steps and strategies that I have outlined and given you in this chapter. Once you have taken one buyer's agent through these steps, you have the option of having that buyer's agent train the future ones. Be careful; you want to make sure that the buyer's agent who does the training isn't cutting corners.

If you currently have a team of buyer's agents, you will need to determine which stages of the sales process they have achieved mastery in. My suggestion is that they are less skillful than you think. You will probably want to start them from the beginning and move them quickly through the training, up to the buyer interview stage. It is unlikely (in my experience) that they are beyond the buyer counseling interview training stage.

11

Setting Performance Standards

One important key to building a team of Champion Performers is establishing and maintaining performance standards. The only way to measure performance is with objectivity. The only way to achieve objectivity is through predetermined standards and measurements. Champions and people who desire to be Champions don't mind performance standards. In fact, they prefer having them because they want to see how they are doing relative to their goals and the production of others. Most Champions are competitive with themselves and others.

═══════════

When I played racquetball as a child learning the game and as a young adult at the professional level, I didn't merely want to win. I wanted to destroy, demolish, and crush the competition. My goal was to create the largest margin of victory possible. I was singularly focused on winning the tournament. That was the performance standard. The standard in my head was: there is first place, and there is losing.

I was cleaning out my garage recently, and I found a few boxes of trophies, plaques, and awards from my racquetball career. As I was taking a trip down memory lane, reliving the years of struggle to become a Champion in racquetball, I realized that all of the awards I had saved were first place. I remembered that early on I had started the habit of not taking home any award that was less than first. I left the second- and third-place awards behind because they weren't up to my performance standard.

═══════════

The world of real estate sales is very similar to my world of athletics. There isn't ever a second place. Either you secure the seller or the buyer and lead him to a contract or you don't. When you and your team finish second, you have no income. Because you are the Champion Lead Agent, you must set the minimum performance standards for the team. All

Coaching Tip: *You will first see results based on what you* **inspect; results based on what you** *expect* **will come second.**

of your team members must know what they are expected to contribute to the team. Additionally, if you sit down with each individual to determine her personal performance standards, in most cases you will find them to be higher than you expected.

The first step is having strong expectations or standards, but the real power comes from the inspection process. The acts of reporting, evaluating, comparing, and monitoring are really the power source for increased performance in human beings. This is especially true for salespeople. Salespeople are so optimistic that they are able to put on their rose-colored glasses and never take them off, even in the face of looming disaster.

Two Rules for Increasing Performance

To raise our own performance and that of others on our team, we must establish some type of activity management system. A system that monitors and reports each staff member's activities based on her position or responsibility is best. For salespeople, the activity management system must count and report contacts, leads, and appointments and the corresponding conversion ratios for these activities against the results of units sold and revenue generated. This type of reporting and monitoring is rarely done by even very good teams in the real estate field. There are many reasons why; lack of knowledge, difficulty of system setup, and lack of time are frequently cited. One of the most obvious reasons is that when the agent initially entered real estate, his broker never required it, so he was not taught the importance of measuring activities from the early stages of his career.

When you are dealing with your support staff, you again need to be able to establish objective standards for them and to monitor, report, and evaluate their performance. Are your support people establishing the right priorities for the day or week? Are they completing the things with the highest priorities before the close of business for the day? Are they getting enough done in terms of quality, priority, and volume to advance your business? Are they helping you achieve your objectives and priorities for your day by protecting you from distractions and interruptions?

> **Champion Team Rule:** *When performance is measured, performance improves.*

You must be willing to devise measuring systems for your own performance and that of your staff. This is especially true of your sales-focused staff, i.e., buyer's agents, listing agents, and telemarketers. Performance rarely improves without measurement to identify the where, how, and why of the needed improvements. Improvements won't be sustainable unless people know the specific how of the improvement. Knowing how the improvement it will be accomplished is essential for replication. Without measurement, the how is merely a guess!

> **Champion Team Rule:** *When performance is measured and reported, performance improves faster.*

When you require not only the measuring but also the reporting of performance, you will see performance improvement speed up. Issues that you thought would take six months to correct fully may take only three months. You may save yourself three months of lost revenue, lower sales, and the time and dollars for increased training, and have more satisfied employees at the same time.

Establish Measurable Benchmarks

It is essential that you create meaningful targets or benchmarks for each staff member that are tangible and traceable. These benchmarks are quite different for the sales-oriented team members like buyer's agents and listing agents. The benchmarks for these production-oriented staff members need to be aligned with the standard an agent should aspire to.

Buyer's Agent Targets. For a buyer's agent, there should be a set standard or benchmark for the number of units sold. The minimum standard should not be below two transactions a month or 24 units in a year. If a buyer's agent can't do two deals a month, he shouldn't be on your team. With the leads that a Champion Lead Agent creates (the ad calls, sign calls, open house opportunities, and Internet leads), 24 units a year should be easy to obtain if the buyer's agent has determination, desire, and a little discipline.

The 24-transaction minimum benchmark can easily be achieved through 48 buyer consultations or buyer interviews. Buyer consultations or buyer interviews need to be conducted in your office. The buyer's agent needs to be adept at explaining his role, his services, and the benefits of doing business with you and your team. He needs to be able to convey the truth about the conditions and opportunities in the marketplace. The buyer's agent must be able to explore the client's wants, needs, desires, and expectations for her next home and for the agent she is selecting to represent her interests. He must then be able to ask for an exchange of a commitment of loyalty on the buyer's part for his service guarantee.

There are two main reasons for poor buyer consultations or buyer interviews. The first is that most buyer's agents never get a prospect to such a meeting. They run around, show property, and attempt to build rapport with the prospect using the same tired process that most other agents are attempting to use. They don't push the prospect enough or show the prospect that an appointment for a consultation with them carries significant value to the buyer. They don't communicate the value of the appointment to a high enough degree to gain the prospect's desire to meet with them. In essence, those interviews they do achieve won't be very effective because they don't conduct them frequently enough to achieve a reasonable level of competency. No one is naturally outstanding at anything without a reasonable level of practice, time, repetition, and discipline. People can be naturally gifted at something. They can have previous experience that is transferable, but they don't become Champions or world-class through osmosis.

The second reason the buyer consultation yields less than desirable results is that the presentation isn't planned. For most buyer's agents, even when they manage to get a face-to-face meeting with a prospect for a buyer interview, the structure of that interview (agenda, scripts, dialogues, trial closes, value-building segments, questioning, and qualifying) is so undefined and unorganized in its delivery that the odds of their success in securing an exclusive right to represent contract are diminished.

Having a set agenda for your meeting with a prospect and knowing what to say and how to anticipate each agenda item will enable you to stay on track; this provides a better, more complete articulation of services, benefits, and values that the prospect will understand more easily. Knowing what to say and the order in which to say it will raise the conversion ratios of prospects to committed clients. At the low end, a buyer's agent with a reasonable understanding of the structure and delivery of a Champion Buyer Interview will close more than 50 percent of the prospects he meets with face to face to an exclusive right to represent contract. I have seen highly skilled buyer's agents who have practiced, rehearsed, role-played, and debriefed their presentations regularly close in excess of 80 percent of the buyer consultations they book.

Administrative Staff Targets.   It is more challenging to establish benchmarks for administrative staff. Areas that need benchmarks for them will be communication with your clients and prospects (quantifiable by survey scores), productivity, and reduction in your involvement in production-supporting activities. The most valuable benchmark relates to productivity and getting priorities accomplished. Are these important administrative people establishing the correct priorities based on your view and your business? Do they understand what your priorities for the business are, and are they working accordingly? Do they know what your priorities for the day are, and do they always complete them before going home? *Always* is a very limiting and exclusive word to define this. Always will give you a clear picture because you are comparing their performance against 100 percent adherence.

You might want to establish a benchmark for frequency of communication with a client. The assistant should be handling a large majority of the communication with clients. He should be sending out written reports and advertisements, showing feedback, and making weekly or biweekly courtesy calls to clients. I would suggest that you, as the Champion Lead Agent, make a call to your clients a minimum of once a month; however, twice would be even better. Is there enough communication between your team and the client who is listed, pending, or searching for her new home?

Another benchmark could be survey scores. Use a survey to determine how you are viewed by the clients whose transactions you just completed. Your administrative team is one of the greatest influences on customer satisfaction and referrals of anyone involved in the transaction—other than you. Using a scoring benchmark in these customer service areas will help you improve service and drive up referrals (Figures 11.1 and 11.2).

Develop Simple, Accountability Systems

Measuring, reporting, and accountability are connected with a chain the size of that used for a ship's anchor. It's forged with links of iron that are unbreakable. Having a measuring and reporting system that buyer's agents must use daily creates the accountability that is needed. As a Champion Lead Agent, you must use this tool with frequency and consistency to change the natural behaviors of your buyer's agents and listing agents. You must measure the benchmark or goal against the results achieved each day.

Create a daily, weekly, and monthly tracking sheet that mirrors Figure 11.3. This will enable your agents to create the connection between their activities and results. Start making every member of your sales team accountable daily. All team members must hand in this report to you at the close of each day. They must also compile the daily numbers to create a weekly and monthly report as well.

You could have your administrative staff do the number crunching, although I don't recommend that at first. The members of your sales team need to be hit graphically with why they are where they are in their business. By calculating their own numbers, they will begin to see the link between their activities and the results they achieve. Having to count and compile their own numbers speeds up the learning process.

Date

Dear Clients,

Congratulations on the sale of your home! We are always striving to improve our customer service. Please take a moment to complete this evaluation. Your response will help us improve the overall quality of service to you and other clients in future real estate transactions.

Please circle the number that is most descriptive of the service you received from me and my team.

	Unsatisfactory			Satisfactory	
1. How well did we do at staying in touch with you throughout the entire process?	1	2	3	4	5
2. Personal Attention: Did you feel important?	1	2	3	4	5
3. Escrow Coordinator: Were they helpful and professional, and did they keep you informed?	1	2	3	4	5

1. Did you feel we adequately explained the listing process and what you could expect during the listing period? Why?
2. Did you feel we understood you and your real estate needs? Why?
3. Would you feel comfortable recommending our services to your friends, associates, and family? Why?
4. Would you use us again? Why?
5. Were the people we referred to you helpful, professional, and available to answer all your questions?

Lender: Yes   No   N/A
Inspector: Yes   No   N/A
Escrow: Yes   No   N/A

6. When you think about this real estate experience, what stands out most in your mind?

_____

7. What could we do to improve our service and provide an excellent real estate experience?

_____

8. Any suggestions for improvement or comments are appreciated. _____

_____

9. Is there anyone you know of who is interested in buying or selling a home in the future?
   Their Name?_____ Phone Number?_____
10. May we use you as a reference: Yes No

Comments:

_____

We've enclosed a self addressed, stamped envelope for your convenience.

Thank you,

Your Name and Team
Company
encl.

©2007 Real Estate Champions, Inc.

Figure 11.1 Client survey—sale of client's home.

Date

Dear Client,

Congratulations on the closing of your new home! We are always striving to improve our customer service. Please take a moment and complete this evaluation. Your response will help us improve the overall quality of service to you and other clients in future real estate transactions. Please circle the number that is most descriptive of the service you received from Dirk and his team.

	Unsatisfactory			Satisfactory	
1. (Buyer's Agent name)'s overall knowledge of real estate:	1	2	3	4	5
2. How well did we stay in touch with you throughout the process?	1	2	3	4	5
3. Personal Attention: Did you feel important?	1	2	3	4	5
4. Escrow Coordinator: Were they helpful and Professional, and did they keep you informed?	1	2	3	4	5

5. Did you feel that (Buyer's Agent name) understood your real estate needs? Why?

6. Would you feel comfortable recommending our services to your friends, associates, and family? Why?

7. Would you use us again? Why?

8. Were the people we referred to you helpful, professional and available to answer all your questions?

Escrow   Yes   No   N/A
Lender: Yes   No   N/A
Inspector: Yes   No   N/A

9. When you think about this real estate experience, what stands out most in your mind?

_____

_____

10. What could we do to improve our service and provide an excellent real estate experience?

_____

_____

11. Any suggestions for improvement or comments appreciated.

_____

_____

12. Is there anyone you want to refer to us who is interested in buying or selling realestate?
Their Name?_____ Phone Number?_____

13. May we use you as a reference?   Yes   No
Comments:

_____

_____

We've enclosed a self addressed stamped envelope for your convenience.

Thank You,

Your Name and Team

Company

encl.

Figure 11.2 Client survey—closing on client's home.

Activity Tracking Sheet

Activity	Goal	Results
Contacts Made		
Leads Obtained		
Listing Appoinments Scheduled		
Qualified Listing Presentations Completed		
Buyers Interview Appoinments Scheduled		
Buyers Interview Appoinments Completed		
Qualified Offers Written		
"Real Working Hours" Invested		
Prospecting Hours		
Listing Hours		
Showing Hours		
Offers Hours		
Rate the success of Year Day (1-10 scale)		
Comments:		

©2006 Real Estate Champions, Inc.

Figure 11.3 Activity tracking sheet.

When you know their numbers, you will be able to do a much more effective job of coaching and training them. You will know exactly where their skill deficiencies are located, so you can address them. If your agents are getting enough leads but no appointments, you know that their phone skills in creating a compelling reason for the prospect to meet with them face to face are not at the level they need to be. If they are securing buyer consultations but have limited exclusive right to represent contracts, the problem involves either qualifying the prospect or their buyer presentation. Remember that the presentation also encompasses objection handling and closing skills.

List the Top Ten Prospects and Their Contract Time Frames. Another simple accountability system is to get your agents to list their top 10 prospects and time frames to contract each week. You want these weekly reports and check them against the previous week. Make sure to have the agents identify the people who are going to buy or list with them this week. If Bob Jones appears three weeks in a row as someone who will buy this week, there is certainly a problem. If the buyer's agents or listing agents have a steady diet of new leads and lead opportunities, it's really easy for them to lose track of prospects.

The administration and support area of your business also needs some simple accountability systems. These are focused on a task list or prioritization system. Being able to hold your support staff accountable for completing the most important activities in the production-supporting area of your business is paramount for a Champion Team.

Establishing your daily priorities will help you make each day a "10." I am giving you a tool that I created a few years ago that really enables you to get maximum value from your time. Figure 11.4 is our Real Estate Champions Daily Priorities Tool.

Real Estate Champions
Daily Priorities Tool

Priorities	Category	Activities
A-1		1.
A-2		2.
A-3		3.
A-4		4.
A-5		5.
		6.
B-1		7.
B-2		8.
B-3		9.
B-4		10.
B-5		11.
		12.
C-1		13.
C-2		14.
C-3		15.
C-4		16.
C-5		17.
		18.
D-1		19.
D-2		20.
D-3		21.
D-4		22.
D-5		23.
		24.
E-1		25.
E-2		
E-3		
E-4		
E-5		

©2006 Real Estate Champions, Inc.

Figure 11.4 Real estate champions daily priorities tool.

Step 1: List the activities that need to be done for the day.

When you are listing activities on the right-hand side of boxes, you are brainstorming to get your thoughts down on paper. Just focus on what needs to be done—all of it. Do not let your mind think about importance or order of completion. If you do, that will stop the brainstorming process.

Step 2: Categorize the activities that need to be done.

Most people, once they create a list of activities, number them or put them in order. The Champion categorizes them to determine their level of importance. Assign each activity to category A, B, C, D, or E.

> **A**—Something that has serious consequences if you don't complete it today.
> **B**—Something that has mild consequences if you don't complete it today.
> **C**—Something that has essentially no consequences if it is not completed today.
> **D**—Something that can be delegated to another person on your team or an affiliate.
> **E**—Something that should be eliminated because it is unnecessary.

Once you have categorized all the activities using this system, you are ready for the final step.

Step 3: Prioritize the activities in each category.

Select the A category activities and determine which activity is the most important, the second most important, and so on. Number them and write them in the squares on the left-hand side.

Establish the habit of using this tool yourself and having your staff members use it. You want your staff members to give you their prioritization tools before they leave for the day, so that you can inspect the progress of their performance and task completion each day. Having them also give you tomorrow's prioritization tool at the same time allows you to review their decisions concerning the priorities they set in advance. This technique allows you to hold them accountable for selecting the highest-priority activities first. They will learn more effectively from you what the real priorities are for the day and your business.

Ownership Is Important in Team Building

Ownership is the real buzzword in team building. If an individual has ownership of his production numbers, a project, or a solution to a problem, he will work to create a more successful outcome for the team. If he feels personally vested in the results, customer satisfaction, and financial performance, the net results for the team will always be better.

There is a balance between ownership and entitlement. Entitlement can develop when one member of the team acquires too much personal pride and takes the position that she is irreplaceable, that the team could not function without her contribution. Team members with an entitlement mentality are a danger to themselves and to the success of the team. It's truly like a highly contagious disease that can be caught easily by anyone who is exposed to it.

Ownership is empowerment of the team member. You are giving him his own area and results to control. A buyer's agent could own the results of a subdivision you are representing or the results of an open house. He could own the interactive voice response system for lead generation. In this case, he would need to respond promptly when calls come in and track the results in terms of contacts, leads, appointments, and revenue that he achieves from the IVR system. Breaking the responsibility up into specific areas or divisions of your business creates an ownership mentality.

I have a number of Champion Lead Agents who have teams that have a division head for each area of their sales operation. These agents are running large teams, and the division heads in the sales area report to them and are responsible for sales, appointments, leads, conversion ratios, and contacts in each area. I have some clients who have such divisions as inew construction and development; expired listings; FSBOs; buyer seminars; farming; professional relationships like those with divorce attorneys, probate attorneys, and financial planers; and foreclosure properties. These division leaders have an ownership mentality and are building revenue by creating divisions for the team using the name recognition and power of the team.

Key Numbers for Your Team's Success

One of the most challenging aspects of having a team is achieving the right balance between sales, revenue, and expenses to provide a reasonable net profit. The vast majority of teams' profit and loss balance sheets are far from being balanced. The problem for most lead agents is lack of financial control and failure to know the key numbers that must be monitored to ensure your control and net profit.

You must realize and accept that sales is a margins game. The margin is between the investment of resources, time, and capital and the expected return in money and satisfaction. You need to have a vehicle you can use to test the margins easily and effectively. I developed the seven key numbers because so many agents struggle to control their business, control their time, and control their money while still achieving a controlled quality of life.

Hourly Rate.   This is the amount of money you generate every hour that you invest in your real estate sales business. Multiply the number of hours you work in a day by the number of days you work in a week by the number of weeks you work in a year. You will arrive at a total number of hours worked that is between 1,500 and 4,000 hours (4,000 hours is a bad number, but I have seen it). Divide the *gross commission income* you earn by the total number of hours worked. This would be your hourly rate or hourly value. Use the gross because you bring that level of income into your company.

Your buyer's agents and listing agents must understand their hourly rate as well. They need to make wise decisions concerning their time in order to increase their income. Knowing their hourly rate will help them say no to low-level prospects.

Average Commission Check.   You need to know your average commission check or average earnings per sale. If you want to test your sales margins or revenue versus expenses on a per-transaction basis, you need to understand your average commission check. Take the gross commission income again and divide it by the number of units you close. If you represent both the buyer and the seller in a transaction, be sure to count them as two trans-actions. Your assistants must know their numbers as well. Often, their averages will be less than your personal average. This is usually the result of a lower average sales price.

Average Sales Price.   The average sales price will tell you in which one or two segments of the marketplace you generate the most business. As an example, if your average com-mission is low, you work most often in the entry-level or lower middle of the price point. This number will demonstrate where you are currently more effectively investing the bulk of your time or where you are investing the most marketing dollars. Once you determine the number by taking your gross sales volume (again counting sales volume twice if you represent both the buyer and the seller) and dividing that by the number of transactions you do, you will have your average sales price.

When you know your average sales price, you can consciously move it higher or lower depending on the market conditions and the return on investment you desire. There could be a difference in average sales price between you and your buyer's agents or listing agents. I highly advise you to track and know this number. This number also will illustrate how effect-ive you are in proving your value to a client. When you divide your average sale price by your average commission check, you will know what you charge on average for your services. You must repeat this process for your buyer's agents and listing agents as well. You really want to check the listing agents carefully. You might find they are far below you in terms of securing listings with full commission when they start. You might also find that if they do the negotiat-ing, the fee adjustment comes at the negotiating stage. Most lead agents don't know that. It's a fast and easy way to know how well you and your team are defending your fee structure.

Cost per Transaction.   The average cost per transaction will tell you how successful you are as a business owner and how much net profit you should expect. To calculate it, take the total costs of your business (i.e., the cost of your cell phone, marketing, advertising, signs, gas, car, insurance for your car and business and even health insurance—it's a deductible expense—your assistant's compensation, anything that is a legitimate business expense) and add them up. Then divide the total expenses by the number of units you do. That will create a cost per transaction. (Your cost per transaction will go down as your units increase.) This is certainly one of the values of having a team.

Marketing Cost per Transaction.   What you spend on marketing and advertising divided by the number of units you close is your marketing cost per transaction number. (A listing agent will have a larger number here than an agent who works predominantly with buyers.)

Time Invested per Transaction.   How much time, on average, do you invest in every transaction? I believe a real estate agent wears two hats in his business. One hat is "lead salesperson"; that is the hourly rate you should be paid. It's what you are worth per hour. You are also the CEO or the owner of the company. As such, you deserve a profit for your work. The profit is what is left over after everything is paid for, including your hourly rate. You will live on and spend your hourly rate. The creation of wealth and financial independence comes from the profit you generate. When you have a team, you will invest some amount of time in each transaction. You will be investing some amount of time in overall training as well. These need to be factored into the costs of executing your business.

Net Profit Goal per Transaction.   I believe you must have a goal for what you will net on average for every transaction you enter into. You can't afford to leave this net profit to chance. My goal was $1,500. (It would be higher today because of the increase in the average sales price.) If I couldn't net $1,500 from a transaction, I referred the opportunity to another agent. Maybe the client wanted to overprice her home, which would increase my marketing cost per transaction, days on the market, and the investment of my time in talking with them week after week about lowering their price.

The client might be a high-maintenance type of client. These clients want overkill on reporting, calls, and customer service. Their expectations are outlandish. This again would increase my time invested per transaction, reducing my net profit. I am only going to make about $1,500 net dollars in profit. By referring the prospect, I know that I can generate a 25 percent referral fee of $975 for investing about 10 to 20 minutes of my time with limited other expenses.

Coach's Tip: *If you have a client who is overly demanding, challenging, and even problematic, you are better off referring rather than representing.*

Develop Commission Plans Based on Your Key Numbers

The secret to developing an effective commission plan for buyer's agents is your ability to use your seven key numbers to calculate the split arrangement. You must determine what amount of the net profit you are willing to share after all costs are paid for. You must also include in your costs the value of the time you have invested in managing, coaching, and training your staff members to improve their performance. The costs also must reflect the amount of time you will personally have to invest in each transaction to guarantee its closing for the team and your buyer's agent.

Champion Calculation

Let's say your average commission check through a buyer's agent is $6,000 gross, and you are on an 80/20 split with your broker; the revenue you receive would be $4,800. Then your average cost per transaction is $1,500 to cover your car, cell phone, administrative assistants, advertising, marketing, and other expenses. You are now down to $3,300 before you factor you time in as a cost. You make $250 an hour, and you factor in three hours of training, education, and coaching for each transaction your buyer's agent does. You now have a final net profit of only $2,550 left to split with the buyer's agent. How do you split that up? If the split is too low, you won't be able to attract skillful buyer's agents to work for you. If you aren't going to make something, why bother?

Gross commission	$6,000
Broker split	$1,200
	$4,800
Cost per transaction	$1,500
	$3,300
Champion Lead Agent's Time	
Invested per Transaction	$ 750
Net Profit	$2,550

The truth is, unless your average commission check exceeds $10,000, generating more than a small, short-term net profit is challenging. You will usually be in the range of $500 to $1,500 per transaction after the associated costs of your time and the cost per transaction are covered.

Your ability, as a Champion Lead Agent, to set complete and compelling performance standards will create the opportunity for your team to reach the Champion Team level. Without these concrete performance standards, your team will always fall short of the mark for Champion Team status.

PART III

TEAM LEAD GENERATION

12

Tried-and-True Lead Generation Techniques

Champion Lead Agents require their team members to focus on activities that produce specific results through specific avenues of lead generation. With the advent of new forms of lead generation, the tendency is to neglect the old standards. Most entrepreneurs are attracted to the new, cutting-edge, technology-based forms of lead generation. Since we are entrepreneurs at our core, we fall into that category. I would caution you against that narrow view.

A Champion Team Leader will require his buyer's agents and listing agents to devote a portion of their time to the tried-and-true lead-generation techniques. He will demand that they practice and perfect their skills in the open house, ad call, and sign call arenas. Some of the best-quality leads still come from these sources. You might not create as high a volume of leads as you can from your Web site, but the quality and convertibility of the leads will be significantly higher. In the terms I used earlier, the number of contacts may not be as large, but the method of contact is better because you are either face to face (as in an open house) or phone to phone (with an ad call or sign call). The quality of the prospect is also better, on average, because a prospect reaching you by e-mail can remain anonymous. With a phone call, however, you are more likely to be able to secure an appointment to make a presentation or to collect the prospect's contact information for follow-up. You may receive an ad call from someone who has been receiving e-mail property matches from other agents for six months but has no loyalty to any agent. If you are skilled, you can get the appointment and secure the client.

Lastly, the quality of the message, in all likelihood, is much better with an open house, ad call, or sign call than with the magical Internet lead. It's challenging to write compelling enough copy to cause someone to act. It's much easier and more efficient to build your value and build urgency through your words, tonality, and body language.

Generate Leads through Open Houses

Think of the open house as the Realtor's equivalent of the retailer's "loss leader." It attracts people into your business. In the same way that a store manager offers milk at a discounted price in order to draw shoppers into the store, a real estate agent invests time and money in an open house in order to build traffic, attract prospects, and cultivate sales of other products.

When I was selling real estate, I wasn't a big fan of open houses. I wanted to keep my Fridays, Saturdays, and Sundays free so that I could spend those days at my vacation home. Obviously, I couldn't have it both ways, and so I opted out of open houses. However, a lot has happened since then to change the way Realtors work. The impact of the Internet, the time-draining effects of dual-income families, and an overall greater difficulty of identifying high-quality prospects combine to put an new emphasis on the importance of open houses, as the following sections explain.

Online Real Estate Marketing

The explosion of online real estate marketing and shopping activity has led to a dramatic drop in the number of phone-to-phone and face-to-face meetings between real estate agents and their prospects. The open house provides a proven way to gain clear and easy real-time access to prospects who are ready to buy or sell homes.

In today's wired world, real estate consumers no longer need to reveal their identities in order to acquire information about available properties. They can cruise and click through hundreds of sites, requesting additional information from scores of agents via e-mail without ever making a personal contact.

As an agent, when you receive an online inquiry, your only options are either to hit "reply" and send back an e-mail of your own or to put them onto an autoresponder series to communicate with them impersonally over a longer period of time. In doing so, though, you face the unavoidable barriers that are part of cyber-communication:

- It's hard to distinguish yourself via online correspondence. Your e-mail note will look very similar to the notes the consumer will be receiving from dozens (or more!) of other agents and teams.
- If the consumer forgets that she requested information from you, your reply may be perceived as a spam mailing. (A Penn Institute survey found that 22 percent of

people have reduced their use of e-mail and 53 percent are less trusting of e-mail because of concerns about spam.)

- E-mail provides a quick, convenient, cost-efficient way to answer a prospect's inquiry. But when it comes to determining the buyer prospect's desire, need, ability, and authority to buy, or to determining the prospect's motivation and time frame, or to distinguishing yourself from the countless other agents in the Realtor community, an open house exchange provides a far more effective route.

Motivated Buyers Frequent Open Houses

The ever-growing number of dual-income families has put leisure time at an absolute premium. Motivated buyers frequently attend open houses—on their own, as couples, or as families. When they do, you have the advantage of watching them react to a home. You can learn a lot by observing them in the house, noting the features that interest them, overhearing their concerns, and visually tracking their reactions. You also have the chance to visit with them, which is the beginning of turning a casual open house visit into a lasting business relationship.

Do-It-Yourself Home Shoppers

With the growth of the Internet as a tool for home buyers and the increase in the number of discount or fee-for-service models, there are some changes that we must embrace. The result of these changes is that more and more prospects are taking parts of their home searches into their own hands:

> **Coach's Tip:** *When do-it-yourself home shoppers drop into your open house, you're safe betting on two things: they're serious about finding a home for sale, and they aren't represented by an agent. In other words, …they're great buyer prospects!*

- They actively search out listings online.
- They aggressively shop the swelled ranks of FSBOs.
- They spend their weekends doing home-shopping "leg work."
- They attend open houses in droves.

Plan Your Open House

I find that many Champion Lead Agents don't have a system for open houses. When they start expanding their team, they have been shooting from the hip for so long that they don't establish a process, system, or strategy for open houses. Most hold them because the sellers want them, rather than analyzing which would be the most effective houses to hold open. What price range is most active? What price range do they want buyers in? What do they want to earn in commission? You can't hold a $200,000 home open and expect to secure $400,000 buyers.

We all know that actually selling the home your buyer's agents are holding open is rare. The NAR has kept statistics on open house sales for years, and the numbers always come out between 3 and 5 percent. Selling the home you hold open is a long shot. Since the odds against you and your team are so great, why select the home you hold open based on which seller makes the most noise? You need to select which homes to hold open based on the quality of the homes, the quantity of leads you generate, the geographic area, and the price range of the buyers.

If you have a strong presence in a certain geographic area, you certainly want your team members to hold open houses when you have listings in those areas. If you have a $150,000 listing and you don't want your buyer's agents to be working with $150,000 buyers because the gross commission of $4,500 is too low for you and them to net a reasonable return, you can't let them hold a $150,000 home open. Selecting the right home through your analysis of the marketplace and your business is essential.

No one comes to an open house to meet the agent. Therefore, as you prepare for an open house, think of the home you're featuring as the show. Choose a home with star power by using these techniques:

- *Select a home in a high-demand, low-inventory area.* Scarcity is a well-proven marketing strategy. People line up to get into crowded restaurants. They respond enthusiastically when told they are limited to "one per customer." And they will show up at your open house in greater numbers if the home you're showing is one of only a few for sale in a well-regarded neighborhood.

- *Do your homework before selecting the home to feature in your open house.* Study the inventory levels in the neighborhood you're considering for your open house. Obtain the prices of recent sales to be sure that your home is within the acceptable range. Research the number of days that recent sales and current listings have been on the market. Then compare your findings with research on nearby neighborhoods to be sure that the home you're considering competes well.

  Every marketplace can be broken down into the following real estate price categories: lower-end, lower-middle, middle, upper-middle, and upper-end. Build your real estate practice around the upper-middle price point position to allow yourself the greatest sales flexibility and business success.

- *Look at the risk-reward balance.* All prospects require similar amounts of time and energy, yet those that result in the sale or purchase of an upper-middle or upper-end property deliver far more commission revenue.

- *Maintain your positioning flexibility.* If you position yourself to serve the upper-middle price range, you won't get pigeonholed. You won't get painted as that snobby Realtor who sells only the upper end, and you won't get tagged as the agent who works only the low end. You can easily move among all five price segments, migrating to wherever the market is most robust at the moment.
- *Focus on a quality clientele.* By specializing in upper-middle properties, you'll attract high-quality middle-range prospects who aspire to own more exclusive properties even if they can't quite afford them. In addition, you also attract buyers with the financial ability to migrate to the upper end.
- *Focus on quality lead generation.* By working the upper-middle price bracket and holding open houses that serve the upper-middle price category, you set yourself up to collect buyer and seller leads and grow your business within that lucrative price range.

Four Rules of Open Houses

Many lead agents don't remember doing open houses either because it was so long ago that they did them, or because they never did them or never did them well. They have never established a set of rules for making an open house as successful as possible. You must have a system, checklists, and forms that can be used to improve the results of the open houses that your team conducts. As the lead agent, you need to select the houses that your team members are to hold open. You must make sure that your team members do the work before the open house to increase its success and their conversion rates. (They can't just show up on Sunday with signs in hand.)

Invite the Neighbors to Increase Activity. Many agents achieve greater open house results from neighborhood marketing efforts than from general public exposure. As you plan your open house announcement strategy, pay special attention to your nearest prospects by marketing to those who live right around the house you're showing. Follow these steps:

- *Consider a neighborhood "sneak preview."* Invite neighbors into the house during the hour before the home opens to the general public.
- *Send at least 25 invitations* in order to generate an adequate neighborhood response. Better yet, hand-deliver the invitations. Before you allow yourself and your buyer's agents to assume that door-to-door delivery is too time-consuming, remember that this simple touch will increase the invitation response rate dramatically.
- *Use neighborhood events to gain access to prospects in restricted-access neighborhoods.* Restricted-access neighborhoods include gated communities or condo complexes that require the public—including real estate agents—to gain permission

before entering. This barrier makes prospecting in these areas difficult at best. There-fore, whenever you achieve a listing in a restricted-access neighborhood, leverage the opportunity by staging an open house neighborhood preview that allows your team to meet and establish relationships with surrounding homeowners.

Do Your Homework Before You Open the Door.   Require your buyer's agents to do their homework. Have them select about half a dozen available homes that are similar to the open house in price, amenities, neighborhood, and geography. They need to spend some time studying the properties to ensure that they understand the differences among them. The best approach is for them to take the time to preview each one of these homes personally. It should take only about five minutes per house. This will prepare them to shift the discussion with a prospect to another home. If a prospect suggests that the home they are holding open won't work because the backyard is too small, they will be able to describe this other house that they previewed and the large yard it possesses.

Because only 1 out of 20 homes for which you hold open houses actually sell through the open house, your buyer's agents must have other properties that they know well for prospects to consider. Create flyers or feature sheets for these properties. You need to have something that prospects can take with them. The purpose is to remind them of your team and the home that they looked at. You want to remind them of your team most, since they probably will not buy the home. Keep the feature sheets simple, with a picture of the home and the information about bedrooms, bathrooms, square footage, and amenities. Place your picture and your contact information on the feature sheet.

Don't forget to have a guest book or sign-in sheet where you can record your prospects' contact information. Make sure it has a place for name, address, and phone num-bers (work, home, and cell). Also, be sure to collect prospects' e-mail address. Getting complete contact information leads to higher conversion ratios. Also, be sure the guest book or sign-in sheet has the approved "no call" language, so that when they sign in, they are allowing you to call them back unfettered (Figure 12.1).

Collect Complete Contact Information.   Your primary objective during the open house is to meet guests and sell them on meeting with you. Your measurement of success is how many appointments you book for after-the-open-house buyer interviews, which are meet-ings during which you determine the prospect's motivation, time frame, wants, and needs and the prospect learns how you work and what services you provide.

Successful buyer interviews conclude with a prospect commitment, which takes the form of a signed buyer—agency agreement. The single best way to obtain a buyer inter-view is to convince the prospect when you are face-to-face at the open house that you are the best available real estate resource based upon

OPEN HOUSE PLANNING WORKSHEET	
Planning Step	Notes

ADVANCE PLANNING
Select the right property/Factors to consider
  High-demand area
  Attractiveness of home
  Curb appeal
  Proximity to major street
Set open house objectives
  Number of visitors
  Number of leads
  Number of buyer interviews
Set the open house hours
Plan neighborhood events, including:
  Sneak peak event
    Establish date/time
    Determine number of invitations
    Decide whether to mail or hand deliver
  Other neighborhood events
Plan directional sign strategy; choose sign locations
Plan advertising and write ads
Assess curb appeal; advise seller re: suggested improvements	

DAYS BEFORE THE OPEN HOUSE Place open house ads Prepare and produce flyers or home feature sheets Research up to six similar properties to share with prospects Advise seller of hour to depart prior to open house	
OPEN HOUSE DAY Prepare house by opening blinds, turning on lights, and arranging music, candles, etc. Place guest book or sign-in sheet and pen in entry area Put out flyers or home feature sheets Put out and carry a supply of business cards	
FOLLOWING THE OPEN HOUSE Send hand-written note to each attendee Send requested or promised material to prospects Make phone calls to set appointments	

Figure 12.1 Open house planning worksheet.

1. Your superb knowledge of the marketplace
2. Your high level of professional service
3. Your ability to deliver a buyer advantage in the marketplace
4. Your ability to facilitate the best lender arrangements and the smoothest closing transaction
5. Your experience in saving buyers' money in the short run through lower sales prices or initial down payments, or in the long run through reduced payments
6. Your commitment to delivering the quality representation that the prospect truly deserves

The big difference between highly successful and marginally successful agents can be measured by the number of appointments they schedule and conduct daily, weekly, monthly, and annually. When you host an open house, keep your eye on the prize, which is the chance to sit down after the event in a one-to-one appointment with the most valuable asset your business can acquire: a high-quality prospect.

As you work to develop prospects, consider these tips:

1. *Invite attendees to sign the open house guest book or sign-in sheet.* Many guests may be reluctant at first to provide you with the information that you want and need—their names, addresses, e-mail addresses, and work, home, and cell phone numbers (see Figure 12.2). (You'll find, though, that the longer you talk with visitors, and the more they see that you can provide them with valuable information, the more willing they will be to provide the information that allows you to follow up.)
2. *Present your business card to introduce yourself and create a professional impression.* Use the simple act of offering your card to open a dialogue with the prospect. Then once you get a conversation going, begin to acquire information that you can use as you convert the guest to a buyer or seller prospect. Use the following techniques:

   - Ask the prospect a time-frame question: How long has she been looking? Has she seen anything she liked? How soon is she hoping to be into a new home? *(The answers will tell you not only about the prospect's time frame, but also about her motivation.)*

     > **Coach's Tip:** *If someone says that he has been looking for six months, you know that either he is not highly motivated or he is slow to make a decision. Either one is not a good answer.*

   - Ask the prospect a dream question: What are you looking for in your new home that is missing in your present home? What features do you want in your new home? Describe your perfect new home for me. *(By getting prospects to share what they want, you open up the dialogue. You also show you care and are here to help.)*

Welcome to Our Open House!

Please let us know who we have had the opportunity to serve today by signing in.

Sales Associate: _____
Date: _____
Address: _____

Name (Please Print)	Address	City	State	Zip	Phone (Home, Office or Mobile)	E-mail Address	How did you hear about this Open House? (Slings, Internet, newspaper, etc. Which site/newspaper?)	Do You own a home? Yes/No

By providing us with your name and telphone number, you grant us permission to contact you via the telephone.

Thank You!

©2006 Real Estate Champions, Inc.

Figure 12.2 Open house sign-in sheet.

- Wander the house and stay close to the prospects without hovering over them. You have a secondary responsibility to protect the home and the seller's property. If the open house guests are in the master bedroom and you are in the kitchen, they could be in the jewelry box and you wouldn't even know it. *(Make sure that you are in the general area of your guests at all times. If the bedrooms are at one end, meander down the hallway and ask a question, simultaneously checking on the whereabouts and interests of your guests.)*

- Ask them to buy. Before open house guests leave, ask them to buy the home. If you have not secured their information yet, you have nothing to lose. If they are not interested, ask them what it is about the home that causes them to feel it's not right for them. *(Doing so opens up the opportunity for you to share information on other listings.)*

Set Appointments with Open House Attendees.   There's no single magic figure, but my recommendation is that you aim to achieve interviews with at least 25 percent of the guests who provide you with follow-up contact information. To achieve interviews, consider these steps:

- Ask for the opportunity to meet.

> *Bob and Mary, in order for you to maximize your initial equity position and minimize your up-front costs in securing a new home for your family, we simply need to meet. Would _____ or_____ be better for you this week?*

- Most people at open houses also are sellers. They need to sell their current homes in order to make the purchase of a new home possible. Ask to come by and take a look at their home.

> *Bob and Mary, would you be offended if I came by to take a look at your home? Would _____ or _____be better for you this week?*

- If you cannot secure a face-to-face appointment, aim to at least set a specific time that you can contact attendees by phone. Then you can work to at least acquire an over-the-phone appointment for a specific day and specific time to speak next.

Send Handwritten Thank-You Notes

The first step after an open house is to send handwritten thank-you notes. Send a hand-written note to anyone who attended that you collected contact information from.

If the prospect requested additional information, or if you offered to send him something, send it separately from the handwritten note. Send the additional information after you mail the handwritten note. Don't assume that your home was the only open house the prospect attended. I guarantee that he has attended other agents' open houses. I know it's a competition between you and the other agents for who is most skilled at lead follow-up.

Contact the Prospect

Call the prospect in the afternoon or evening of the day your handwritten note arrives. That should be the second day after the open house, usually on Tuesday. The objective of the call is to book a buyer presentation appointment in your office.

Call the prospect again later in the week, say Thursday or Friday. Tell him that you have found a property that is similar to what he is looking for in a home. Tell him that you would like to meet with him to evaluate its suitability. This meeting needs to take place in your office. Remember, you are in competition with other agents. Whoever gets the prospect into her office first dramatically improves her odds of acquiring a commission check.

You want to repeat this process for a few weeks. If you have not been able to get the prospect into your office within a few weeks, the quality of this prospect is probably lower than you should be working with. It's time to cut him lose and move on to more motivated buyers.

When you prospect open houses, some of the leads you will acquire will be people who are hoping to move, but never will. You are not looking for "hope-to" prospects. You are looking for "have-to" prospects.

ABCs of Ad Calls and Sign Calls

To be successful as a team leader, you must be sure that the members of your team are ready for any and all opportunities that come their way. They must be trained to seize those opportunities and convert them to results. Even with the advent of numerous new lead-generation strategies to attract new buyers and sellers, ad calls and sign calls are really still among the best sources for generating new business!

I have found that the vast majority of real estate agents have never really been trained to engage with the ad call or sign call effectively. We often acquire the skill to convert ad calls or sign calls over time through operating our real estate practice. The problem with using that approach for yourself or your staff is that it takes too long! You will also blow countless opportunities to increase your income by converting these calls to quality prospects and then to clients.

I embrace the philosophy that the prospect must have a reasonable level of motivation to make an inbound phone call. In fact, the motivation of these leads is markedly higher than that of an Internet lead or even a call capture lead, on average. You should expect to receive a much higher conversion ratio on leads from ad calls or sign calls than on many other varieties of leads.

The Truth about Conversion

The average conversion rate on sign calls and ad calls is pathetic. The key reasons for the low conversion numbers are these:

1. Lack of recognition of the importance of these calls
2. Inadequate training of sales staff
3. Absence of the appointment mindset
4. Lack of perseverance through the "no"

Lack of Recognition of the Importance of these Calls. As the Champion Lead Agent, you must get the members of your staff to understand that ad calls and sign calls are the highest-value leads. One could argue that referral leads are higher, but referral leads are generally more variable in their motivation level and time frame than ad calls or sign calls. Referral leads might be less competitive in securing an exclusive relationship, but the time frame to purchase or sell will be longer, on average, than that of an ad call or sign call.

Coach's Tip: *A significant portion of your buyer's agents' production in the 1/3 category that they must produce should come from ad calls and sign calls. If your buyer's agents are lacking in production, you can be assured that much of their lack of success is caused by limitations in their skill at converting ad calls and sign calls.*

Inadequate Training of Sales Staff. Buyer's agents must be able to quickly ask for a face-to-face consultation and be able to continue a meaningful dialogue with the prospect without giving away too much information about the home that led the prospect to call. They must recognize that once the prospect acquires enough information, the next sounds the buyer's agent will hear will be a click followed by a dial tone because the prospect hung up.

Some of you reading this may object to the possible cat-and-mouse game you might need to play with the prospect. You must recognize that just blindly giving callers all the information they desire over the phone will not produce any leads at all! There must be a disciplined, organized strategy to secure the prospect's contact information. Without it, you don't have a lead. To assume that a prospect will call you back because you were nice and didn't put any undue pressure on her to reveal herself is tantamount to a belief that the world is flat.

One of the biggest mental mistakes real estate agents make, in general, is not embracing a salesperson's mentality. In order to be able to serve and sell and earn an income, you must know whom you are selling to—in short, who the prospect on the other end of the line is. Your buyer's agents must understand that their primary job is securing face-to-face appointments. Their secondary job is securing phone appointments. Their tertiary job is at least collecting full contact information for lead follow-up.

Absence of the Appointment Mindset.   You must train your buyer's agents that every prospect or lead must be compelled to meet with them. They must eventually (and the sooner the better) gain a face-to-face audience with the prospect.

Lack of Perseverance through the "No".   The average prospect says no to a salesperson far more often than the salesperson asks for the order. All the studies in sales indicate that the average consumer conveys a no to a salesperson at least four times before a yes is granted and a sale is made. How many times do you or your sales staff ask after the first, initial no? Since we know that we should expect at least four nos from a prospect before we receive a yes, why not move through the nos on the initial call? Why should you make three, four, or even five lead follow-up calls before booking the appointment with the prospect? The truth is, nos are nos, whether they all happen in one call or over the course of ten calls. You just need to get beyond the nos quickly.

Sixty percent of all sales are made after the prospect has said no four times. This is true even when the salesperson is merely trying to sell the prospect on the value of just meeting with him. Salespeople quit long before the consumer is ready to buy what they are offering.

44%   Quit the first time the prospect says no
22%   Quit the second time the prospect says no
14%   Quit the third time the prospect says no
12%   Quit the fourth time the prospect says no
92%   Quit asking the prospect to commit or act before the majority of sales are made

The reality is that only 8 percent of salespeople ask enough times to easily sell a majority of products and services.

Champion Team Rule: *A mere 8 percent of salespeople control 60 percent of the business—just by asking more often!*

Coach's Tip: *My best advice is that you role-play with your buyer's agents. Expect and inspect their willingness to go beyond the initial discomfort of being rejected by a prospect. For their income and yours, you must move them beyond the fear of the second, third, or even fourth no on an ad call or sign call. You might even consider having them tape some of their ad calls and sign calls.*

Scripts That Raise Conversion

My belief is that most buyers in today's world have been exposed to enough sales-people. They have been exposed to enough real estate agents as well, so they are often more prepared for the interaction than the agent is. Their real desire is to get off the phone with the information they want in hand as quickly as possible without revealing too much about themselves.

The problem with this approach is that, in the end, people using it receive lower-quality service. They just don't know it. They also approach the ad call or sign call with more apprehension than they did in the past. That's the result of our desire, as real estate salespeople, to ask them this laundry list of questions to "qualify them." I don't believe that over the phone in the first minute is the time to "qualify" the prospect.

A better approach is to work to secure an appointment with a prospect first. When you do this, you have been granted permission to ask that prospect questions. You are now an insider, rather than an outsider. Use your questions to keep the dialogue flowing. Use bridging words that help build relationships like: *I understand, that's interesting, tell me more, I need your advice, wouldn't that be exciting,* or *I'm on your side.* These are all feed-back response words that will turn whatever you ask the prospect and his response into something that feels to him like a real exchange.

In order to increase your conversion rate, you must have a flowing dialogue with the prospect. You also must ask for an appointment to have a buyer consultation interview. You need to offer them enough value to lead them to want to meet with you, then ask for the appointment directly. Here are a couple of scripts that work well.

> *Bob, I am currently helping my clients acquire property at _____% of the asking price when the market average list price to sales price is _____%. The value in this for you would be a savings of $_____ in your pocket by working with me over any other agent you might select. Would _____ or _____ be better to meet, so I can demonstrate how you can save this money?*

> *Bob, I have helped _____ families in my sales career and more than _____ just in the last year. Most of these people had dreams, expectations, and desires just like you and your family. What my clients found was that by our simply getting together briefly, they had more knowledge, information, and power, and they acquired the right property at a lower price with better terms and conditions. Would _____ or _____ be a better time for you and me to meet?*

Use Other Properties to Increase Sales

Countless times, I have encountered salespeople who were not prepared when dealing with ad calls or sign calls. This lack of preparation goes beyond the lack of sales skills that I explained in previous sections of this chapter. It extends to inventory knowledge as well. In short, most agents' only hope is for the property the prospect called in about to be exactly what she wants. The truth is, the odds that the prospect will buy the home she called about are limited. According to the NAR, the sales that come from ad calls or sign calls on a specific home are less than 10 percent. If you aren't prepared to entice a prospect to look at another property, your sales from ad calls and sign calls will be low.

When you take an ad call or a sign call, you must know intimately at least three other properties that are similar to the home the prospect called you about. My definition of intimately would be that you have previewed the properties and neighborhoods, and you have the MLS printout of these other properties with you at all times, so that you can talk with the prospect at an expert level; in other words, you, at a minimum, have a working knowledge of these properties. Your sales tactic with the prospect is that you know about some properties that she is probably not currently aware of, that your market knowledge and understanding of the pulse of the marketplace in properties like the one she called about are exemplary. You are trying to give the prospect the impression that you offer exclusive benefits that she can't get anywhere else. I guarantee you that, by having the knowledge of other similar properties, you are offering the prospect something that other agents are not.

Go for the No

There are only three potential responses you can get from a prospect; you can't get a fourth. The three are yes, no, and maybe. So, which of the three is the worst? I ask that question frequently, and the response I get from most average agents is that it is no. In fact, the worst response is actually maybe. Maybe requires additional investment of resources. (For most teams and agents, the average conversion rate of a maybe is a pretty low number.)

My best coaching advice is to go for the no. Press for the no from the prospect. When a prospect understands that it's OK for her to say no to you, she will be more willing to be open and honest with you. The reason that we as real estate agents don't go for the no is that we need the deal. We need to convert this lead, and we become wimps and accept a wimpy lead because we are too attached to getting the deal. We also don't want the prospect to consider us too pushy. We want to give her the freedom and comfort to take her time in making a decision. However, we must recognize when we are wasting our time, emotion, and energy on a nonsale. Are we watering a dead plant and hoping that it is alive? Suppose you are on the phone with a prospect that you know is a good possibility. You have created some value and connection with the prospect. It's time to go for the no! Your buyer's agents will go for the no with probably half the intensity and focus that you do. They must see how committed you are in going for the no. You need to drill them on this practice through role playing regularly.

> *Mr. Jones, it has been a pleasure talking with you for _____ minutes. I have invested this time with you because I know that I can really help your family. I would like the opportunity to serve you, but I am sensing some hesitation on your part. Do you mind my asking you what that is?*

> *Mr. Jones, I need your help. I have enjoyed our conversation of the last _____ minutes. It's clear to me that I have some market information, exclusive properties, and market knowledge that would be invaluable to you in securing your ideal home. I would like to know if there is an opportunity for me to serve you, or is the timing not quite right at this point?*

These scripts do a masterful job of going for the no professionally. By using them, you can ferret out the concerns, objections, and conditions that are holding the prospect back from meeting with you. This will enable you to turn the maybes into decisions for or against.

Close for the Appointment

When you have conveyed the value of your team's service or the perception of exclusivity sufficiently, the close must be connected with it. The telephone is really a salesperson's primary appointment-setting tool. Before your buyer's agents hang up the phone, they have to ask or close for the appointment.

If they have made a reasonable presentation of your team's value on the ad call or sign call, the close should be a natural ending to that. Having a handful of closing scripts that are approved by you for your buyer's agents is essential. You don't want your team members winging the close. They must use approved scripts. Following are some of my personal, highly effective ones.

> *Our team has helped more than _____ families since its inception, and more than _____ families last year acquired their ideal home. We have found that, by meeting with us, our clients find they have a higher knowledge of the current and emerging market conditions and a higher probability of securing the right home for them and their family. Would _____ or _____ be better for you to meet?*

> *Our team has been able to secure properties for our clients at _____% of the asking price, on average, when the overall market average is _____%. This saves our clients, like you, thousands of dollars. <State name of client,> for a home in the price range you called on, we would save you an additional $_____ over the other potential agents you could work with. For me to be able to help you save that $_____, like our other clients, we need to spend a few moments together. Would _____ or _____ be better for you?"*

Control the Call

The only successful technique for controlling the call is through questions. In any sales situation, the person who controls the asking of questions controls the sales situation. You must have a set process for your buyer's agents to follow in their questioning. Again, not having approved questions that each of your buyer's agents uses every time he encounters an ad call or sign call will be disastrous for conversion rates. You must control the call through questions.

According to a study, 80 percent of all salespeople do not prepare a list of carefully produced questions in advance of the sales call. In order to be able to advance your team, you must construct an approved scripts and dialogues book for your business. You must focus on having 100 percent adherence to those scripts and dialogues. The members of your sales staff must be required to carry their scripts and dialogues book with them everywhere. There needs to be a zero-tolerance policy for people who "wing it."

This study also stated that 90 percent of all questions asked by salespeople during the average sales call are closed-ended questions. You won't achieve team success in sales if your sales staff aligns with this statistic. To be successful in sales, you must ask open-ended questions. To keep the dialogue going with a prospect, open-ended questions are imperative. Without them, you won't be able to talk with a prospect long enough to build enough value to get a personal meeting. A salesperson won't learn the necessary openings or problems that need solving and can be solved by your team's presentation without asking high-quality, open-ended questions. Real estate salespeople who want to achieve the highest results must master the process of asking open-ended questions.

High-Quality, Open-Ended Questions.   These questions are specifically designed to help your buyer's agents engage the prospect, so that they raise the odds of their booking a face-to-face appointment with more prospects.

- Tell me about your perfect time frame.
- Tell me about your ideal home.
- Could you tell me one of the three top features you want in your next home?
- What amenities have you put on your wish list?
- You certainly know better than I do the requirements you have for your next home. Would you share them with me?
- Obviously, price range, payment amount, and amenities are critical issues for any home buyer. Besides these, what else is important to you?
- I'd like to get your opinion on something. What are the most important amenities you are looking for in your next home?
- Can you do me a favor? What caught your eye in the ad you read?
- Can you do me a favor? What caused you to call after seeing our sign?
- Can you help me out for a moment? I try to gauge the results of my advertising, so what prompted you to call on this ad over the hundreds of others in the paper?
- Can you assist me for a moment? As a business owner, I work to understand what causes prospects to call. Can you tell me what it was in the Internet listing for this home that caused you to call on it rather than the thousands of others on the Web?

All of these questions work to keep the dialogue flowing with a prospect. They can buy you and your buyer's agents additional time to convert the prospect. They should be used in addition to the typical buyer qualification questions that focus on time frame, motivation, financial capacity, type of property wanted, and location of the home.

13

Using Technology to Generate Leads

The use of technology in real estate agents' practices worldwide has advanced at an alarming rate over the last 10 to 15 years. When I started in real estate in 1990, most agents were still working off the printed MLS book that we received every two weeks. We were required to keep that big book of listings in our possession and never give it a buyer. Stamped on the front of the book in big, bold letters was, "Don't give out, or you will be fined $500!" Most agents gave that book to every buyer they worked with for their review. We have come a long way, baby!

The more things have changed in those last 18 years, however, the more they have stayed the same. Even with the advent of massive advances in technology, our business is still tied to the sales skills and sales strategies of individual salespeople and teams. Technology will never replace the personal service, personal interaction, and market expertise that we deliver to our clients and prospects. It has changed (or advanced) the delivery vehicles that we might select to deliver our value, but not our value itself.

There are some technologies that we need to embrace and others that have limited value for our business. My objective in this chapter is to shine the light of truth on a number of opportunities that are well suited for a Champion Real Estate Team.

Interactive Voice Technology

With the explosion of technology in the last 15 years, we have seen many new lead-generation systems come and go. Interactive voice response (IVR) systems have stood the test of time in the last 10 years. They have become an important source of leads for Champion Teams. This type of system, when employed correctly, can quickly become one of the strongest sources of new leads.

I was one of the first agents in my marketplace to embrace an IVR system. I recognized that a buyer would call a recorded message more frequently than a real estate office, so my lead volume would increase. I also felt it would be a service to the seller that offered me a strategic advantage over my competition on the listing presentation.

My volume of leads increased over 205% on a monthly basis. Over a period of 12 months, I did an additional 20 transactions that I could source back to the IVR system. It allowed me to expanc my buyer's agent team because the lead volume had increased so substantially. All those results stemmed from a $1,000 investment.

IVR technology is a must for people who want to build or advance their team. It gives you the necessary tools to enable you to increase your lead volume to a level that can feed a few buyer's agents with regularity, as long as you have an effective marketing strategy that will expose prospects to your listing inventory.

You will experience favorable results if you have a reasonable level of listings to market. You certainly won't generate a large number of calls if you have only a few listings. For most agents, call volume really begins to climb when they have more than 10 listings in active inventory. If you don't have 10 active listings, borrow some from someone to market. You don't sell a prospect the home he called on anyway. Who cares if it's someone else's inventory you are using to build your team production? The clear objective is to make the phone ring.

IVR is a system that captures the phone number of an inbound caller when he calls a predetermined phone number. This phone number is usually a toll-free number, and because you are paying for the call, you have a right to the caller's phone number.

Within the toll-free number are extensions that lead to voice mailboxes where you can record messages that callers can access. The voice mailboxes (or extensions) can be used for marketing individual properties, explaining your services to buyers or sellers, or targeting specific prospect groups such as expired listings, FSBOs, or nonowner-occupied properties. You can link an IVR system with any marketing strategy you are currently using to generate leads, and it will create more leads for your team. Advertise your toll-free number everywhere you would normally advertise and market, including your mail-outs, Web site, classified ads, FSBO campaigns, or expired listing campaigns. The goal is to create lead traffic to your system, so that you can capture phone numbers that you can call back.

The volume of leads you generate from an ad in the newspaper or home magazine will usually increase fivefold when you use IVR technology. All your ads need to be written in a manner that will direct people to call your 800 number and enter a code. (More people will call the recorded message because they think they won't have to talk with an agent.) Using home magazines with call capture technology is even more effective. The home magazine, which has a one-month shelf life, will often lead to a greater increase than the fivefold increase we see with classified ads. It is not uncommon for an agent who has a high-single-digit inventory of homes to get a couple of hundred calls a month to her IVR system with the right marketing approach.

The system will also generate leads and opportunities while you sleep. It's like having a 24-hour marketing department that churns out leads for you to follow up on. More leads and 24-hour service sounds too good to be true. Of course, there are obstacles, as well; it's not all rosy, but the benefits are significant. It takes time to record messages and create marketing strategies. It takes effort to compile the numbers to determine your sales ratios and return on investment. It takes commitment to call all of the people who call you. Sometimes you will need to make multiple calls before you reach someone.

Dealing with the *Do-Not-Call Registry*

A call capture or IVR system is also valuable because it allows us to create leverage by accessing people who are on the federal do-not-call registry. When these "do-not-call" prospects call our system about a home, our free reports, podcasts, or general real estate information, we secure their number with our system. We then fall under the 90-day inquiry period provision of the law. This inquiry period allows us to contact them for up to 90 days after their first call to us, even if they are on the do-not-call list.

Using an IVR system to specifically target people on the do-not-call registry is an effective prospecting strategy because you know that these people have had limited personal contact with real estate agents, since most agents will not dare call them back. When you use this technique in connection with a high-probability source of business like expired listings, you have a wonderful combination to generate listings with. You are combining a limited-access strategy with a high-probability prospect. You won't have much competition for the business, and you will be working with a prospect who has a demonstrated need.

By using the IVR technology, you also alleviate one hassle of the do-not-call registry: the fact that the law requires you to document that the person called you first. Your IVR system takes care of noting when the first call was made. A word of caution when working with people on the registry: the 90-day inquiry period will be cut short if they tell you not to call again. If they do that, by law, you can't call them again unless they engage you again through your IVR system.

Deal with the Increase in Contacts

I think the biggest mistake we agents make when utilizing IVR technology is neglecting to contact all the people who call in. We get busy and fail to schedule the time to return prospects' calls. Certainly, a Champion Agent wouldn't do that, but every day, countless agents fail to make follow-up calls to their IVR leads. This is especially deadly when we put sign riders with our call capture number on our property signs.

I believe sign calls provide the highest-quality inbound "do it now" leads. If you fail to call back all of the people who inquired, then you will be missing some of your highest-quality sign calls because they will be mixed with the others. If you are struggling to return the calls, dump the use of the sign riders on your properties, so that you can separate the sign calls from the other calls.

One of the challenges with using IVR technology as a marketing strategy is dealing with the increase in the volume of leads whose quality you are not able to assess effectively. If you ran a standard marketing page in a home magazine directing people to call you for more information, the number of calls would be less than you would get with an IVR, but the quality would be higher. When people call a real estate agent's office, they are expecting to talk with a sales agent. The likelihood that they are not being represented by an agent when they call in is higher. The conversion ratio on that type of lead should be very high as well. Ad calls and sign calls generate a higher probability (there I go again using that word *probability*) of making the sale.

If you are driving every response to your ads and signs to your IVR number, you are mixing most of the people who would have picked up the phone and called you directly into a large pool of warm and cold leads. The only way to find those golden, high-probability leads is to call everyone who uses your IVR system. I required my buyer's agents to call them all, no matter what. I watched and monitored each buyer's agent's progress in this area. I didn't want to lose the easy leads that had gotten mixed in with the more challenging ones.

You must be careful not to focus solely on buyers who call in and forget that some of them are also going to have to sell. I have seen agents who secured the relationship to buy for a prospect, but lost the listing because they forgot to ask for it. Some of the people calling will want to sell as well, especially if you integrate your direct mail to sellers with a call to action to listen to your free market update report, your strategy for achieving top market value for their home, or the 10 mistakes most sellers make when selling their home. All of these are drawing cards for sellers to call your IVR system. These are especially helpful when you will be marketing in a targeted area like nonowner-occupied properties, first-time home buyers through rental lists, or some similar market segment. It's equally effect-ive for expired listings by people who are on the do-not-call registry. You can lead them to make an inquiry that lets you call them back. With this technique, you will probably be the only agent who can follow up with these people by phone.

Another mistake agents make is leaving long, rambling messages about their proper-ties. With most IVR systems, you are charged by the minute. The longer your message, the more money you will spend to create the lead. The caller's number is captured in the first few seconds. A several-minute message only runs up your monthly service bill.

Drive Prospects to Reveal Themselves

Your primary focus in integrating IVR needs to be on creating a lead that you are able to process through a fundamental sales channel. Prospects today reveal very little information about themselves. This reduces the odds of conversion for you, increases your costs, and provides prospects with a lower-quality service experience than they expect. The vast majority of agents (and teams) are investing too much time, energy, dollars, and overall resources in developing low-level service systems to move leads through the sales process. They do this primarily through property-matching e-mail marketing or other forms of e-mail marketing. The results of this huge expenditure of resources have been, at best, mixed. I am sure I am going to get a nastygram from someone saying that I am wrong. Please save your time and your stamp unless you have concrete proof in the form of numbers and sales ratios. The return on investment through this process, once you count all the expenses, is usually low. We need to move away from thinking, "I get a few deals from this."

Let me remind you that the real goal with any technology-generated lead is just the same as that with a standard lead: to establish a fundamental sales channel process to be followed so that you can secure full contact information, thereby enabling you to implement a solid lead follow-up strategy. That strategy encompasses phones, direct mail, e-mail, potential faxes, and face-to-face follow-up.

The value of an IVR system is that it requires all prospects to reveal them-selves. If all your calls were coming directly to your buyer's agents through ad calls or sign calls, what percentage of the time would you expect your agents to acquire the prospect's phone number? I don't know your standard or what your

Coach's Tip: *I really believe that IVR, done right, is the single most powerful tool a team can put in place to drive a large volume of leads to the buyer's agents. You might want to check out the Web site www.callcapturesuccess.com for more information and a special offer for Champion Teams.*

team is actually doing in this area, but my guarantee to you has two parts. First, over 90 percent of you reading this right now don't know the percentage of phone numbers your buyer's agents get from prospects compared to the number of calls that come in. Second, even if you are one of the less than 10 percent who do know, it's a whole lot less than the 100 percent of the ad calls and sign calls that it would be if you used an IVR system.

Hidden Benefits of IVR Usage

For the Champion Lead Agent, the biggest hidden benefit of using IVR is the ability to track results and performance improvement. These benefits alone create significant value for you from incorporating IVR technology into your strategy.

You will clearly know the effectiveness of the ads you are running. You can directly link inbound calls with dollars spent. You will then be able to monitor conversion ratios of calls to leads, leads to appointments, and appointments to exclusive representation contracts and eventually to closed units, commission dollars, and closed volume. Having the power to track the results of your marketing efforts easily and effectively has tremendous value.

The other hidden benefit is performance improvement for your sales team. The fundamental truth about salespeople is that you must know the sales ratios of performance in contacts to leads, leads to appointments, appointments to represent contracts, represent contracts to purchase agreements written, purchase agreements written to purchase agreements accepted, and purchase agreements accepted to closed transactions in units, commission earned, and sales volume. Without this comprehensive approach to performance numbers, your education, training, and coaching won't produce the fruit you desire.

Coach's Tip: *As the Champion Lead Agent, you need to know all of these numbers and ratios for your team members. This information can help you pinpoint where your education, training, and coaching need to be focused.*

For example, if your sales agent is calling back almost all of the IVR calls, and you are getting a reasonable volume of those calls from your marketing, but the number of calls converted to face-to-face buyer consultations is low, the field of choices is limited to basically two:

1. *The quality of the leads is poor.* The poor quality of the leads could be related to either lack of motivation or an unacceptable timeline. The leads could be longer-term leads, which are more challenging to bring in for a face-to-face meeting. You might need to reevaluate your marketing strategy by changing your ad copy and the vehicles you are advertising in.
2. *The quality of the agent's sales skills is lower.* The other possibility involves the delivery of the return call and the lead follow-up. It focuses squarely on the agent's sales skills in the areas of quality opening statements, raising value to compel the

prospect to meet with you, closing for the appointment, asking for the appointment multiple times on the same call, dealing with any objections to booking a buyer consultation interview, and reclosing and continuing the appointment.

Quick Callbacks Improve Your Odds of Success

Calling all the inquiries improves your odds. Calling them back close to the time they called you will improve your results as well. Using a fax printout of yesterday's or this week's captured numbers dramatically diminishes the return. Make sure you subscribe to a system that has an instant notification system. That way, when a phone number has been captured, the phone number and the property the person called about (indicated by the specific voice mailbox number) are sent to you instantly via your pager or your cell phone. E-mail notification is better than no notification, but it falls far short of cell phone or pager notification. What if you are not at a computer to be able to retrieve the e-mail message? (If you use a BlackBerry or Treo, e-mail notification might work for you, since you carry that access with you.)

The best rule to follow in responsiveness is to call people back in less than 15 minutes. That speed of response increases the chances that they are still at the phone number they called from. Anything you can do to raise your reach percentage, you should do. Act quickly!

You might startle a portion of the people with your quick response. In most cases, they are not expecting you to call. There are a number of techniques that are effective in getting prospects to open up. Once you call them back, my favorite is what I call the customer service call. You approach them softly with, "This is a customer service call to the person who recently called our real estate information line. Were you the person who called? How did you like the service? Did you get all of the information you needed?"

Once you get through those early questions, just move into a standard buyer script to convert the lead and book a face-to-face appointment. I really like the customer service call approach. It is softer, and you will get less negative pushback. You will get fewer responses of, "How the heck did you get my number?"

Creating leads through IVR is an excellent way to increase your number of leads generated, as well as lead sources. It's also an effective strategy to help your buyer's agents increase their business. You can produce more leads, so they can increase their income and skill.

Use Voice Broadcast for Efficiency

Another new technology that most call capture or IVR systems also provide is voice broadcast. This system is highly efficient at leveraging your efforts to a targeted group of prospects. The key is that you must have permission to contact them. These people can't be on the do-not-call list.

If you are a lead agent who has a large sphere and past client group, recording a message and broadcasting it to your group can save you a significant amount of time. You are letting technology do the dialing, listening to the phone ring, waiting, listening to the message, and delivering your message to the contact's voice mail or answering machine. If the person you are calling actually answers, the service hangs up and doesn't deliver the message, so the person doesn't know who called.

Some of my clients are using this technology to increase their dial-to-contact ratio. They are reducing the amount of time they spend prospecting because they are spending more time actually talking with prospects. If they want to make 10 contacts a day, they load 30 people a day into a voice broadcast. The voice broadcast goes out right before their prospecting time block. They are then able to quickly receive a report on messages delivered and messages not delivered.

There will usually be between 9 and 12 people (out of the original 30) who didn't get the message. The overwhelming reason why a message wasn't delivered is that someone was home. The agents now call the 9 to 12 people who were home to transfer personal value and ask for referrals. This system is a tremendous time saver for Champion Lead Agents with too much to do and too little time.

The Internet Lead Bonanza

The Internet is one of the forces that is changing the real estate industry rapidly. There has been a massive shift in the marketing of properties away from print advertising and to the Internet. We have seen a tidal wave of new businesses (good and bad) that have entered the real estate arena to "help" agents with the Internet.

The Internet is a great tool, but that is all it is—a tool. For some agents, it is an essential tool for their business success. For others, it is a very minor piece of the puzzle. The Internet is really a lead-generation vehicle. It's like direct mail, classified ads, or any other indirect income-producing activities (IIPA) that we could use. Creating and implementing Internet marketing strategy is clearly IIPA.

The first connection is the *number of contacts* you generate. The Internet can increase your exposure to people. These aren't contacts by my definition, but many agents would view an Internet visitor as a contact. The *method of contact* is of low quality, however. The copy on your Web site has to compel someone to do something. The results of direct mail and Internet traffic are somewhat parallel; they are not very compelling in terms of getting someone to act, book an appointment, or even reveal some information like a personal phone number. Fortunately, the number of contacts can be large enough for some agents to make up for the lower quality of the Internet, as opposed to the phone. You can drive a lot more visitors to your Web site than you can make phone calls. The quality of the people and the conversion rate on the Internet will always be lower, however.

The *quality of the prospect* is the next area of connection. You must sift through the prospects to determine who's a looker and who's a buyer. Again, this is very hard to do because many of the people are stealth and want to remain that way. That means that their motivation, on average, is very low.

The *quality of the message* is last. It's hard to have a compelling message explaining what makes you different, why someone should hire you, and what benefits the prospect will receive from you using only text and a few previews. You certainly do not have the ability to really determine prospects' desire, need, ability, authority, and service expectations, so that you can modify your presentation to the highest level.

Quality and Quantity Issues

The two main types of issues we face with the Internet are quality and quantity issues. We want to drive visitors to our site, so that we increase the odds of generating leads from it. We want to increase the quality of the prospects, so that we can separate the really good buyers and sellers from all the rest. We want to achieve a reasonable conversion rate, which is much higher than the 1/2 to 1 percent we are now seeing from the Web.

There is a delicate balancing act between quality and quantity. The two must be addressed in the proper order. If you had to choose one, which would you choose to emphasize first—quality or quantity? Before you select, let me tell you the truth about the Internet: the volume of traffic is important. At the end of the day, he who has the most visitors usually wins. We build these beautiful Web sites, but no one sees them. We have to drive traffic to make money with the Internet.

Once we have traffic, we have to get people to stay and leave a trail. We need them to at least leave a trail of bread crumbs, such as their first name and e-mail address. You could attract a couple of thousand people to your site each month but end up with only two or three prospects. I am not talking about clients; I am only talking about prospects. You now have to do the work of moving these people up the loyalty ladder to become clients by first converting them from visitors to buyers. There are lots of nameless people surfing the Web. We don't know anything about them; we don't even know they are there until we get a Webtrends report. All we know is that they are willing to invest their time to come and visit our site.

We begin moving them up the loyalty ladder by offering them a free report, newsletter, or something else that a buyer or seller would deem valuable enough to warrant leaving us at least his first name and e-mail address. We need to walk them up each step of the conversion track. With each level or step they take, the probability of our earning a commission check grows. The object is to move them from visitors to prospects, prospects to clients, and clients to referral sources.

The more complete the contact information we get people to leave, the higher the probability that we can move them up to the client stage. More information increases the opportunity of moving them to a fundamental sales channel of send, call, and see. I would rather have the name and phone number of a single prospect than 100 names and e-mail addresses. I will make more money with a name and phone number.

Two Schools of Thought

There are probably a number of people who have the view that *any* lead is better than *no* lead. I don't happen to subscribe to that viewpoint. Leads must be looked at in the context of quality and quantity. I will take 10 leads with phone numbers over 100 Internet leads where I only have an e-mail address to communicate through. How about you?

Leads (even the Internet variety that you might put on some type of autoresponder system) still take work. They also require a basic investment of either your time or that of someone on your team. They can also cause complacency. The creation of large volumes of low-quality, low-convertibility leads creates a level of comfort in even the most disciplined salespeople. This level of comfort and satisfaction is a dangerous thing for a salesperson who generates all her income directly from sales transactions to have. I guarantee you that personal prospecting by you and your team will drop when you have an overabundance of low-quality leads. The Internet lead is the epitome of these leads.

Some of you might be saying, "I get lots of business from the Internet." It's true; there are many agents who do very well from their Internet strategies. The question is, what's the cost of acquiring these leads on a per-lead basis? What is the conversion rate on these leads and the cost to provide your service to the client? What's left when all is said and done? Is this the best model you can invest your time, effort, energy, emotion, and dollars into in your given business and market?

Either you embrace the percolator view, where you are there to generate the majority of your Internet sales through dripping on the prospect electronically, or your objective is to take the stealth prospects and aggressively work to get them to reveal themselves fully. Fully revealing themselves, in my definition, would be for them to give you their phone numbers (work, home, and even cell) and the address of their current residence (or business or both). This gives you the opportunity to control the results of your efforts and increase the delivery of your message and conversion of the prospect.

The Wait and See Prospect

This is the prospect who gives you only an e-mail address to correspond through. There are a number of obvious problems with the communication method being words only. In communication, only 7 percent of the meaning is conveyed by the words. This method forces us to be 93 percent ineffective! Our message can easily be misconstrued because of the prospect's mood when she reads it. Differences in language use and even education can create a problem in communication. If your overall education is higher than the prospect's, she may feel that you are talking down to her. Explaining advanced concepts through the written word alone proves more problematic. You are also unable to deflect questions that you don't want to answer at present because you haven't built enough value for your services.

Because tonality contributes 38 percent of the total communication between two people, you are clearly losing that advantage of oral communication. You also lose the ability to clarify a point in real time or ask questions to elicit more information now. You are forced into a long timeline with less emotional engagement of the prospect. Your body language provides 55 percent of communication. This is a complete nonfactor if you are plunking at the keyboard to type a response to the prospect.

The most deadly element that most real estate salespeople don't even know about is delivery issues. Delivery issues with e-mail are becoming more significant with each passing day because of the overabundance of spam in all of our inboxes. The open rate for an e-mail that is sent to a double opt-in list is currently less than 38 percent. Yes, you read that right—38 percent. A double opt-in list is defined as anyone who asks for something from you via e-mail; you reply and ask if the person is that he wants this; he replies by clicking the link and confirming his yes. You know that this person really wants your information, expertise, guidance, counsel, and help. Only 38 percent of all the people who go to this effort actually open your e-mail.

The Stealth Prospect Revealed

The most effective strategy is to work to get the stealth prospects to reveal themselves. I would encourage you to work with these prospects with greater urgency than you do with the wait and see prospects. Once you get the stealth prospect to turn off the cloaking device, you can take dead aim at serving him.

One thing I have to touch on lightly is that there also must be an element of persuasion. Having high-value content for a targeted audience isn't enough by itself. You must, through persuasive sales copy and Web conversion elements, persuade the folks who visit your Web site to become prospects. For this, I recommend that you contract with a good copywriter—preferably one who has Web site design experience. You can find such a person online at www.elance.com or any other contract labor source. The key is to find one who is good at persuasive copywriting and design for the Internet; those are the prerequisites for hiring. Check out people's past projects to see if they fit your style, and maybe even contact their references. A great copywriter could make you hundreds or thousands of dollars for every dollar you spend. I know; I have one of the best on my staff.

Again, get visitors to take information that is valuable by offering free reports. Give them access to information like "The 10 Mistakes Sellers Make When Selling a Home." This is a report that lists these mistakes and gives ways of avoiding them. Someone who pulls that type of report is at least considering a sale. Another example of a report could be

"How to Guarantee You Get Your Home Sold and for the Highest Price Possible!" A report like this would lead visitors through the steps to ensure both the sale and a top dollar sales price. This type of provocative title piques interest and leads people who are considering a change in their housing to take action. There are similar reports for the buyer's side as well.

We are trying to get people to raise their hand, even if they are unsure and are just starting the process. We are trying to generate a volume of leads at this point. Free reports are a good first point of contact. There are thousands of them that have already been produced, so don't sit down to write them. They are easy to get through most direct-marketing companies.

Newsletters are also a very effective means of communication. There is immense power in an e-mail list of people who read your material regularly. Your job is to provide them with value in that newsletter. I would encourage you to do a newsletter monthly. Start with a generic or template version. One of the reasons that agents don't produce newsletters is that their ego leads them to want to write the material personally. They want it to be unique and original. I understand that. I write all the material in my "Coach's Corner" newsletter. It's no more effort today to send it to 800,000 subscribers than it was when we had 5,000 subscribers. It's the same amount of work to write, edit, and do the layout as before. The resulting sales and exposure, however, are much better now. It's part of my job to create intellectual property; you don't need to.

The ability to communicate with an audience consistently is extremely valuable. Some of my marketing results come from the consistency of the message delivery, as well as from the message that is delivered. It's easier for an agent to be consistent if she starts with a template newsletter. Test it out; evaluate how much or how little work it is, and see if the people on your list like it and read it. Then work up to a hybrid or combination newsletter, where there is some material that comes from you and some that comes from a template. If that goes well, create your own newsletter. Don't go all out with a custom, created from scratch newsletter from the onset.

Become Larger than Life on the Internet

There are thousands of stories of companies that have become larger than life through their Internet strategies. These little companies have secured Internet presence, position, and power and look much larger than they actually are in real life. Anyone can look substantial on the Net.

Use Pay per Click

More and more agents are getting into pay per click as an answer to their online marketing. Pay-per-click advertising on search engines and other sources can be effective, or it can be a bust. Most search engines have pay-per-click areas on the right-hand side of their Web site. People bid for these spots on a pay-per-click basis, and the cost can range from a few cents to a few dollars each.

The truth is, only about 10 percent of searchers go to the pay-per-click section. The vast majority of people use organic methods to find what they are looking for. Organic methods involve using a search engine to search for a specific phrase and then clicking on the top-ranked sites.

Keep in mind that you are not paying per prospect. You are paying per click. A click doesn't mean that you are going to get anything. Pay per click can be used effectively if you know the conversion numbers for your Web site—meaning that you know how many people take a free report, sign up for your newsletter, ask for more information, identify themselves as a lead, or are willing to book an appointment with you once they get to your Web site. To make pay per click profitable, you need to know your numbers, both online and through your standard sales process. Until then, you will only be guessing that pay per click works and is profitable. Perfect those conversion ratios before you spend a whole bunch of money on pay per click.

Search Engine Optimization

The more tentacles you have out all over cyberland, the more traffic you can generate. There are a number of different ways to create the outreach that you want in cyberspace. Having all of your properties on www.realtor.com and your company Web site is the right start, but it's not enough. A recent survey was done of the properties on the Internet. Over 50 percent of the properties listed did not have a picture attached to the property. You might generate traffic that way, but visitors will probably not click through with inquiries about any property without a picture. It shows how far we still need to go to master marketing on the Internet.

If you sell real estate in a resort area, linking up with agents who sell resort real estate in other areas can drive traffic. Linking up with resort Web sites, tourism Web sites from your area, and the Chamber of Commerce will also help to drive traffic. The objective is to choose strategic links that will help drive traffic.

Another strategy is to link up to other sites and sources to increase your search engine ranking. There is a difference between quality and quantity. Search engines give weight to the relevance of a link. If you go out and link to anyone and everyone, it probably will not be very beneficial. Your links should be focused on real estate and/or your specific market area. Anything else would not be viewed by the search engine as useful or valuable.

A word of caution: before you run out and hire someone to implement search engine optimization (SEO) on your site, do your homework. Implementing an SEO strategy is tricky business. You need to make sure that you are working with a reputable firm that will stand behind its work. You also can't have the philosophy of one and done—fix it once, and it will last forever. Effective SEO strategy is never-ending. Everyone is fighting for that front-page position. It changes each day, so you have to work to maintain your ranking.

You also want to make sure that the SEO firm is using reputable techniques. There are a lot of firms that use what the industry calls "black hat tactics." The problem with this strategy is that it works only for the very short term. Once search engines find out that you used black hat tactics, they won't just drop your ranking; they are likely to ban you. By that time, the SEO Company has your money, and you probably can't find it. (Another trick these companies use is to they get you ranked in terms that no one searches for; this succeeds only as long as it takes for you to figure out that you have zero Web traffic.)

Coach's Tip: *If you recognize the value of finding a company that can deliver a turnkey solution for you, and you would like a contact, I highly recommend that you go visit my friends and colleagues at www.realestatewebsiteseo.com. Tell them that you're a referral from Dirk's book, and that I sent you. They will give you not only preferential treatment but a better price on their services.*

The truth about technology is that it can be employed very effectively to increase the number of leads that are generated. What it can't do as well is produce high-quality leads. In the end, there is an unlimited number of prospects in the world that you can work with if you and your team are willing to work for free.

14

Generating Leads through Live Events

The growing challenge for salespeople in real estate is securing a face-to-face audience with a prospect or prospects. Putting yourself in front of live people is really the most significant challenge in the life of a real estate agent or real estate team. The live event model creates a number of positive opportunities for your real estate team. In fact, accessing all of the opportunities that are created through a live event program almost requires a team. The process of marketing the program consistently; following up on the marketing to increase attendance; delivering a high-quality program with a PowerPoint presentation, professional handouts, a quality room venue, refreshments, and information collection materials; and effectively following up after the program is an immense undertaking. There are numerous parts of the process of preparing and presenting a program that are production-supporting activities or at best indirect income-producing activities. You, as the Champion Team Leader, don't want to invest your time in those tasks.

Coaching Tip: *You don't need to be the greatest orator in the world to make live events effective. Designing the right format, scripts, and support pieces will be more than adequate… if you practice, practice, practice!*

You must decide on the type of event you want to engage in. Fundamentally, you can do events in two categories:

1. Public lead-generation events
2. Private appreciation events

There are advantages to each of these models. I would first caution you that you must select only one of the two categories. I really believe that the establishment of an event division in your business needs to be approached with caution. The learning curve on either of these categories is steep.

The public lead-generation avenue carries a greater risk, as the costs are higher and more consistency is required than with private events. You will also need to do a public lead-generation event more frequently than a private appreciation event. The private event will be larger in scope and complexity. It will require a longer planning period because of the quality of the event. You probably would not want to do a private event more than quarterly, while you might do a public event weekly (or even more often). I have a client who does buyer seminars a few times a week!

Public Lead-Generation Events

Events of this type, which can be buyer seminars, seller seminars, or investor seminars, are solid ways to attract prospects to meet with you. The most common of the three is buyer seminars. Buyer seminars develop a steady stream of leads that will enable your buyer's agents to have a constant supply of fresh leads to work. I have one client in Canada who generates over 4,000 buyer leads a year from his buyer seminar programs. There are really four benefits to establishing public lead-generation events.

1. *Increased personal leverage.* As your business grows, you won't be able to interact, talk with, or convert all of the leads that your team generates. The advantage of the public model is that you will dramatically raise the number of people that you can see personally. This approach saves you time and energy because your presentation and sales process is being delivered to multiple people at once. You can't meet with all these people individually to tell them about the marketplace and market trends; explain the home-buying process; introduce them to your affiliates; and explain the whole lending process, how you work, and how they will benefit by working with your team. But you can do all this in a group format.

2. *Convey your expert status.* Someone who has a physical platform from which to speak or who is the author of a book is automatically granted expert status. There are many people who have either or both of these credentials who really shouldn't be considered experts, but they are viewed that way nevertheless. By establishing a lead-generation model through events, you will be able to separate yourself from the competition. Can you imagine saying to a seller, "Everyone does open houses; everyone puts homes on the Internet; everyone does some newsprint advertising. We are all the same in that regard. Wouldn't you like to focus in on what I do differently?" They almost lean in when you talk like this.

The most common mistake for new presenters or speakers is to over-use PowerPoint. I was speaking at a program a number of years ago when one of the speakers ran long. The meeting planner came to the rest of the presenters (including me) and asked if we could each shave 15 minutes off of our talks.

I watched as the solid producing agent who was to speak after me turned ashen. He ran to his laptop and began cutting his PowerPoint slide presentation. I saw him a few minutes later—worked into a lather and stressed out. I asked him how many slides he normally had when he did an hour on the platform. His response was about 85. Then I turned ashen! A normal presentation with too many slides is like sitting through 400 frames of your neighbor's recent trip to Yellowstone!

---

3. *Exclusivity and sense of urgency.* It's easier to build both a sense of urgency and an aura of exclusivity in a public event. People look around the room and understand that there are other people who want the same things they do. They know that only a select group of people is here to hear your message. This is true even if one of your advertising media is the home magazines that everyone has access to.

You can explain exclusivity: you don't work with everyone, you work on a contingency-fee basis, and you select your clients carefully. If you have made a wonderful presentation and your listeners see value in your services, they are likely to act because of scarcity. They will have a feeling of safety as well, because they are not the only ones in the room.

You can build a sense of urgency, especially when you are conducting investor seminars. You can share stories of past success with other investors. Using the exact equity, down payment, and cash flow numbers that advertisers use on the late night, no-money-down infomercials is a wonderful strategy. Tell your audience about a couple of currently available properties that represent a tremendous opportunity. Then tell them that, at present, you don't have enough of these properties to go around if all of the attendees want one. You will have people in the room looking at each other and competing to act and act now.

This process also helps you establish your value at a higher level. It allows you to maintain your full fee when you represent both the buyer and the seller, rather than having the buyer try to negotiate some of your fee away. You can calmly tell him that you are not forcing him to buy the property. If he doesn't want this opportunity, you are fine with that; you will just sell it to someone else. The public format carries a strong measure of power.

4. *Aiding the transition to the buyer's agent.*   If the designated buyer's agent is present at the public event, you can allow her to speak for a few minutes. By doing so, you are raising her credibility and expert status as well. The passing of the prospect from you to the buyer's agent will be easier and smoother. The prospect will not feel as much like he has been shuffled off to the second banana or worse.

Select a Target Prospect

In selecting the right target, you must consider the type of prospect you want to work with. You can do this by evaluating the sophistication level you want in the prospects you work with, price range, commission earned per transaction, geographic area, and experience of the buyer. There are a number of factors that you need to evaluate. For example, if you are giving first-time home buyer seminars, you will generate more referrals from these people than you would if you conducted investor seminars. First-time home buyers usually have large circles of friends who are in the same age group and economic position as they are. If you have done an outstanding job for them, they will want to share this information with others. Investor clients are less likely to send you referrals. They don't want to share their secret weapon—you. They feel that if you are helping others, it will mean more competition for the best deals. They will worry that you might sell one of those great deals to someone else. Evaluate all your options and all the factors involved to make sure that you select the best match for your short-term and long-term goals and business philosophy.

> **Coaching Tip:** *In the live event model, you will attract what you are looking for. Be sure you are attracting the right target.*

First-Time Home Buyers.   The strategy for first-time home buyers is different from that for investors. A large number of these people are less flexible in terms of time because they are often dual income. You must offer your seminars at multiple days and times. You might even find that Saturday evenings are the most preferred times for your events.

The delivery of the program is more basic. You must create a sequential order for the process of purchasing and closing a property. You will have to deal with the basic misconceptions that first-time home buyers have when they purchase a home. The misconceptions include the following: If I look long enough and hard enough, I will find the perfect home. Never offer full price. Sellers always make counteroffers. I need to see a lot of homes. I don't need an agent. I don't need to be exclusive to an agent. It will be cheaper if I find my own lender. As an expert, you need to convey to these people the clear benefits of buying a home through you. You will also need to educate them on the negatives of doing it the wrong way. They must feel the pain and consequences of doing it wrong.

Investment Buyers.   You must demonstrate a very thorough knowledge of the marketplace when working with investors. They need to know, without question, that you are an expert and that you can find properties for them to acquire that no one else will be able to find. You must read every report created by the NAR that is related to investment property. You might want to search regularly for articles and studies that you can access via the Web or that appear in newspapers. Being able to use statistics on appreciation, rent increases, wealth creation through real estate, and appreciation by type of property or geographic location is extremely helpful.

Champion Example

I have one client who does investor seminars in the greater Los Angeles and San Francisco markets, but who sells real estate in Tucson. He compares the capital needed, rental payments, cash flow, cap rates, and appreciation in Tucson to those in the markets that his prospects live in. He builds a strong case for investment in his area as opposed to their investing locally.

Select Affinity Partners

You must broaden your group of experts beyond yourself. Prospects need to see someone else on the platform with you for 90 minutes to 2 hours. There is a long list of people that you could engage to speak. You could have a lender, an attorney, an accountant, a home inspector, or a title representative, to name just a few. While it might seem advisable to have all of these parties represented, does the phrase "too many cooks spoil the broth" sound familiar? Another advantage of having a larger number of presenters is that it allows the costs of the event—marketing, advertising, room rental, staff time, refreshments, and handouts—to be borne by more people. The platform time must be shared as well, however.

When you are doing an investment seminar, you might want to include an accountant and your lender as speakers to join you in presenting. The accounting issues with regard to investment property are complex—much more so than with an owner-occupied, single-family residence. You also might need to have two lenders presenting at the program because most lenders don't handle both residential loans (up to a fourplex) and commercial loans for larger units. There might be some people in the crowd who are ready for the more complex nature of a transaction larger than the fourplex.

With each affinity partner you highlight in your presentation, market with, or give a presentation slot to comes a bill for shared expenses. Affinity partners should expect to share in the wealth, but they must also share in the expense of the program. To me, that is a prerequisite for their involvement in the new transactions you are trying to create.

You also want to select your affiliates carefully based on three criteria:

1. *Quality of their service.*   Remember, client satisfaction and your future client referrals are tied to their ability to deliver what they promise.
2. *Level of buy-in.*   Your affiliates must be willing to ride the wave of trial and error for a long enough period of time to work out the kinks. To adopt a one-and-done philosophy is shortsighted. One and done means that if it doesn't work on the first try, you dump it. Both you and your affiliates must be willing to test these events for six months or six events before you junk the program.

3. *Quality of their presentation.*   If you are giving someone a spot on the platform, she has to be able to speak. She doesn't have to be world class and get the audience members chanting and standing on their chairs, but she does have to be able to connect with the crowd.

> **Coaching Tip:** *Work with affinity partners who are willing to pay most or all of the costs between them.*
> *Remember, your labor invested is larger than theirs, so their financial investment should be greater than yours.*

Promote Your Event

The success of these events, whether they are public lead-generation events or private appreciation events, is determined by your marketing beforehand. Preparation beginning weeks before the event is mandatory. The timeline you establish through your advertising, marketing, and calling will be a factor in determining how many people attend and the quality of those people. You want a large enough crowd to be successful. If the crowd is smaller, you must hope that each person in the room is better qualified to take action now.

You will need at least four weeks to promote an event properly. You can use direct mail, newspaper advertising, Web sites, home magazines, and even voice broadcasts to targeted lists. These lists need to target the prospects you want for the type of seminar topic you are delivering. For a first-time buyer event, acquiring a list of renters is effective. You must be sure the list has been scrubbed for do-not-call list numbers, though.

The whole marketing effort must be focused on driving participants to register for the event. You don't want people to just show up. You want them to register, so that you know how many people will be attending before the program. You also want to harvest their information, so that you can call them to remind them of the event. You want to be in regular (probably weekly) e-mail contact with all registered attendees before the event. This regular contact can be put into an autoresponder, so that it is launched automatically once it is set up.

You can use a service like Aweber to handle that for you. Then two business days before the event, a call should be made to the attendees. The call is to remind them of the event and urge them not to miss it. If your team is unable to reach some of those who have registered on that call, another call should be made the day of the program as a final reminder. The job is to get people to both sign up and attend.

Objectives for the Event

Each agent who does events might have different objectives. I have one client who does investor seminars where his objective is to sell a few of the properties sight unseen to the people in the room. He wants to sell properties that evening with a potential condition of visual approval of the property within so many days. That visual approval runs concurrently with the property inspection. At the very least, he wants to capture lead information on the prospects and book an appointment to meet with them to do a consultation in his office.

You want to at least have prospects sign up for a buyer consultation interview at predetermined times and days. If you can't get them to take that step, at least have them give you more information about themselves and agree to allow you to e-mail them properties based on their desires, needs, and wants. You could incorporate this strategy as a separate document or series of documents that they are asked to fill out. You could also incorporate it into the survey that you hand out at the completion of the program.

Setting an Agenda

There are a number of different ways you can arrange to have the information in your agenda delivered. I suggest that you open and close the program personally. You may not want to be master of ceremonies for the program, however. That could be a role for one of your buyer's agents if he can do it credibly. This technique elevates you to a higher level of expert or celebrity status.

Here is a sample agenda you might want to follow:

Opening warm-up	*2–3 minutes*
Overview of the current market	*3–5 minutes*
The home-buying process	*10 minutes*
Benefits of exclusive buyer agency	*10–15 minutes*
Benefits of working with your team	*5–10 minutes*
Lender: Mortgage 101	*20–30 minutes*
The steps a buyer takes	

Terminology clarification
Documents a lender needs
How I can help you
Short break
Possible other topics: title, escrow, tax advantages   *10 minutes*
Recap of services and benefits, marketplace opportunities   *10–15 minutes*
Give away door prizes
Close for surveys, buyer consultation appointments

You will note that this agenda also includes a suggested length of time for each segment. These are not etched in stone, but I would caution you to not make any segment too much longer. You want to finish in less than two hours. There are two reasons for this. First, most people will not want to be there for more than two hours. They will be tired and nonresponsive if you go longer than that. Many will also need to hire a babysitter for their children.

The second reason you want to keep your presentation to less than two hours is that some of the most valuable time for securing leads and interacting with people will be after the seminar is over. If people are lingering, they are the best prospects in the room. You and your team want to spend a lot of time at the end of the presentation trying to collect surveys and contact information and booking appointments for buyer consultation interviews. Your goal should be to meet and greet everyone before the program and also before they walk out the door. Before they walk out is your last chance for a face-to-face meeting with some of these people.

Coach's Tip: *I recommend not having a formal Q&A session at the end of your presentation. You want your attendees to linger and ask questions after the program. Announce that you will be staying after the program to answer any questions that they might have.*

Be sure to avoid the two biggest killers of the event model. The first is dragging on for too long. The program should move briskly and should be informative and entertaining. It should start and finish on time—every time. The second is becoming an infomercial. If your presentation sounds too much like a commercial or constant pitch, you will lose your prospects. You want to deliver a powerful close at the end and even a few trial closes in the process.

Go for the Close.   A great close is a natural ending to a great presentation. If your presentation has enthusiasm, conviction, and confidence, the assertiveness you need to show at the end will come more naturally. It's time to tell the attendees that you believe that you and your team can help them, that you are the agents for the job, and that you guarantee their total satisfaction in working with you and your team.

The Final Key

The follow-up after the sale is where your profit is really created. Anyone or any team can convert the really motivated people at the program. These people could be described as the low-hanging fruit that is easy to pick. The ability to convert some of the other people through effective lead follow-up after the sale is where you turn a good event into a great event.

The follow-up system after the program is more than inputting people's wants and desires into a property match system in your MLS service. The day after the program, every buying unit must be sent a handwritten thank-you note. (A buying unit would be defined as a husband and wife or a person and his or her significant other—any people who intend to purchase together.) A follow-up call is made on the third day after the event. When you make this call, the note should have arrived the day before. You want to ask whether the person has any questions after pondering your information and then ask for an appointment. In five more days, you want to call each buying unit about a really wonderful property (or even a few properties) that meets the couple's needs. These need to be good values that stand out. The objective of this call is to secure a face-to-face buyer consultation, not to show the homes.

If you are unable to secure an appointment to do a buyer consultation, you need to categorize the lead in terms of time frame, motivation, and level of commitment to you. Then apply the normal lead follow-up system that you have created to serve that client over time. Don't neglect to call these leads frequently enough (e.g., once a month) to check in.

Private Appreciation Events

Client appreciation events are quite different from public events. They are designed to be a slower but steadier process for generating listings and sales. Unlike with public events, you can't expect a certain number of face-to-face consultations after the event. You do need to set a specific objective for the client event in terms of attendance, communication before and after the event, atmosphere, and the buzz generated afterward. The objectives are a little more subjective and specific to you and your team.

My view is that a client event gives you an excuse to call. Inviting clients to something special and fun for them and their family makes connecting or reconnecting with them easier. It lowers your and your team members' call reluctance when you are calling friends, past clients, and sphere members. The excuse to call applies both before and after the actual event takes place.

Make It a "Can't Miss" Event

Whether you are planning a gala or a picnic in the park for a client appreciation event, you have to make it memorable and unique. Some client events, by the very nature of their timing and venue, compel people to come. Setting up an exclusive screening of an early showing of a new blockbuster movie for your clients compels them to come. If it is a family event like the grand opening weekend of *Cars*, *Shrek*, or some other guaranteed winner, you will pack the house. You will also get really excited and appreciative people.

Event Marketing Strategy

The approach to a private appreciation event is much more personal than that to a public event. You still want to secure the appropriate number of attendees and commitments, but the method should be more intimate. Printing creative invitations is the best strategy for direct mail. You can use e-Vite, but I wouldn't recommend it. You want to make the statement from moment one that this is going to be something they don't want to miss.

You might even indicate on the invitation that seating is limited. In most cases, it probably will be limited. A movie theater has only so many seats, for example. The special gathering area for events at your minor league baseball park might have fire-code restrictions on the number of people in that area. Building exclusivity builds excitement about the event.

The call is where the magic begins. Whether they can attend or not, you can touch all your clients and make them feel special through your call. The value of the call supersedes the value of the event. If you have a reasonably sized database of sphere members and past clients, it could take your team four to six weeks to contact everyone personally. If you do even two events a year for this large group, that is 24 weeks of calling your database before and after the event. When you add the more frequent contact that is needed for your top-level or platinum-level past clients and sphere members and calls to everyone on a house anniversary, personal anniversary, or birthday, you have most of your whole year of telephone prospecting allocated. The best part is that these are really fun and rewarding calls for you and your team to make.

During the Event.   Even though your guests are there to have fun, you have a limited opportunity to address them personally. Your address should be brief and centered on these topics:

1. Thank them for giving you the opportunity to serve them
2. Market update
3. Your need for referrals
4. Thank them for their attendance

The length of time for this address should be less than five minutes. If you go longer, your commercial infringes on what your guests came for. Be sure to put yourself in a strategic place before and after the event so that you can personally meet and greet each person that comes. You are running for mayor in their real estate life. You need to be shaking hands and kissing babies.

Tickets to Events

Another wonderful strategy to implement with your best group of referral sources is taking them to events. I had a client once who had four season tickets to the Dallas North Stars. This was a husband/wife real estate team, and both of them were big hockey fans; they never missed a game. They always had an extra pair of tickets, so they could take their best customers. When they got their season tickets, they would sit down and call their clients to arrange to take them to the games for the whole season.

I told them that they were working too far in advance. With every call they made, they found a time in the season to take the person they called. We worked out a system where they called only a few days in advance. The outcome was that they had to make far more calls to give the tickets away. On average, they had to talk with five couples before they found someone who was able to go with them. The truth is, the four couples who couldn't go felt as good about the agents as the one couple who did go. The agents generated five times as much relationship value from the same ticket costs!

15

Turning Leads into Dollars

The real objective of lead generation is to move a prospect quickly to an appointment, so that you can avoid lead follow-up all together. Making the transition from prospect to client quickly will do wonders for your income. It will also lower your frustration and the frustration of your buyer's agents and listing agents.

When salespeople are required to participate in lead follow-up to secure sales, their attitude will deteriorate over time. There isn't a buyer's agent, listing agent, or any type of salesperson alive who hasn't complained about the quality of leads. I guarantee that, as a lead agent, you will hear from your sales staff, "These leads are garbage," at least sometimes (if not regularly).

One of the best and most immediate actions for you to take when this happens is to turn a few of these "garbage" leads into sales. I remember the first time this happened to me; it was within the first six months after I hired a buyer's agent. The buyer's agent was complaining that the leads were no good. My first mistake was that I initially believed him.

Champion Team Rule: *Just because one of your team members says it doesn't mean it's true—check it out for yourself!*

I worked diligently for the next 30 days to produce more and better leads by expanding my marketing efforts. At that time, I heard again, "These leads are garbage." I then decided that I needed to work them myself for a few weeks. I am very competitive, and I wanted to show my complaining buyer's agent that sales could, in fact, be made even from these leads. I had them give me a dozen leads that they were working. Out of those twelve leads, I booked four face-to-face presentations in the next two weeks, and in less than a month, I had three accepted contracts to purchase homes from those "garbage" leads.

The Real Objective in Lead Follow-Up

Your objective in lead follow-up isn't to build a relationship. It isn't to send people more stuff about you or about the marketplace. It isn't to bond, connect, or any other typical view of salespeople. It is to book a face-to-face appointment to make a presentation of the value of your representation services. This is true whether the prospect is a seller, a buyer, or both.

Barrier to Success

I coach one of the most successful real estate teams in Canada. This team closes in excess of 275 transactions annually through its buyer's agents alone. That is a solid amount of production, on average, for the 10 buyer's agents that the team has employed. Through working with this team, the problems that agents have with leads became obvious to me.

In the fall of 2005, we were reviewing the numbers to execute a business plan for 2006. We evaluated the volume of leads generated during the last 12 months. The volume was over 5,500 leads. The team's closed units were just over 275. At first glance, 275 units seems wonderful, but compared to the volume of 5,500 leads, it's pretty small. It's approximately a 5 percent conversion rate for every lead generated. In real numbers, it is 5 deals out of every 100 leads. That should put it in perspective. The truth is, this rate is OK compared to that of typical agents, who are probably at around 2 percent.

Coaching Tip: *The bottleneck for agents' revenue is the increase in conversion ratios of their leads. You must remove the bottleneck by setting appointments.*

When I dug deeper into the numbers of each buyer's agent, I found that once an agent got prospects to a face-to-face buyer consultation, the lowest conversion rate to contract was 46 percent and the highest was 67 percent. The results went from 5 percent to 46 percent instantly.

It's easy to see where the biggest barrier to success in lead follow-up and conversion lies. It's the appointment. Once an agent with even average skills and abilities can bring the prospect to her office, the odds of conversion go up almost 10 times. It's in the area between lead and appointment that the waste occurs.

The final piece of the story came when I asked this highly successful team leader, "What's your goal for this next year in units?" He shared with me that he wanted an increase of 100 units, which was a 36 percent increase. My question was, "How are you going to do it?" He proudly replied, "I need to generate another 1,600 leads to get there." He had put pen to paper and figured it out. My response was, "That's one way to get there, but why don't you consider increasing your conversion rate by 2 percent? Then you would add 110 units in production."

Why market, process, call, mail to, e-mail to, and advertise to generate more leads when conversion is at 5 percent or lower? This team leader had more than enough leads to sell 375 homes. In fact, he probably had more than enough leads to sell 700 homes. Most successful real estate teams have figured out how to create leads. Lead generation has made them successful. They have more leads than they know what to do with, so they get sloppy and complacent. They don't have the conversion systems and strategy to match their prowess in lead generation.

For a number of years, I coached an extremely successful Champion Lead Agent of a team on the East Coast. He is truly one of the best agents in all of North America. We were evaluating his direct-response advertising and marketing strategies and their results. His marketing strategy had paid for itself and created a small profit of $50,000 for him after he factored in his costs. This was a respectable return, but not outstanding. I wanted him to consider dropping the strategy because it wasn't worth the effort, in my opinion. He had large sales numbers from this direct-response strategy, but the cost of his time, advertising dollars, and staff time and the low conversion rate held the profit to the $50,000 level.

To convince him, I asked him to call all the leads in his database that he had gotten through this strategy. He had been dripping on them and calling them infrequently, based on the length of time to move date that the client had indicated. In the next two weeks, he proceeded to call all of his direct-response advertising leads. Two weeks later, he informed me that he had just found 62 people who had bought and sold with other agents in the last year. They were long-term leads that he had failed to meet with. He had sent them marketing pieces regularly, but he had not booked an appointment to secure the relationship. We calculated that he had lost in excess of $500,000 in listing-side revenue alone through not aggressively trying to book a face-to-face appointment with these long-term leads. Their motivation had changed, and he hadn't. He hadn't secured the relationship or at least gotten a commitment that these people would interview him when they began considering agents.

Using the DNA² Method

(Desire, Need, Authority, and Ability)

Desire relates to wanting to do something. Desire also relates to a time frame—do it now! There is a difference between desire and interest. Anyone can have interest. Interest doesn't indicate a high probability of doing something. We really don't have to care about interest. Interest is a way for prospects to evade making a commitment. We need to zero in on whether they want it (desire) or need it (Figure 15.1).

Need refers to a void you have identified that your service can help prospects overcome. There are some areas of real estate sales where it is easy to spot need. That is one of the reasons I liked expired listings. There was a clear need on the part of the sellers. My job was to convince them that I could fill their need. They can't just have interest. They have to have need.

Authority involves asking the following questions: Is this person the ultimate decision maker with regard to this decision, or is there someone else involved in the decision? Is there anyone else's guidance that the person will be seeking before making this decision?

Ability relates to financial capacity. Does the prospect have the financial ability to move forward? Does the prospect have enough equity in her current home to sell at this time? If she doesn't have enough equity, can she personally make up the loss out of her other assets? If not, is the bank willing to take a short sale?

Desire	-It is essential for someone to move forward.
Need	-You have identified a void that your service can help them overcome.
Authority	-Are they the ultimate decision maker with regard to this decision or is there someone else involved in the decision? -Will they be seeking guidance from anyone else to make this decision?
Ability	-Do they have the ability financially to move forward? -Do they have enough equity in the home to sell at this time? -If they don't, can they personally make up the loss out of their other assets? If not, is the bank willing to take a short sale? -Do they have the necessary credit score to secure financing? -Do they have the necessary down payment? -Can they make the projected monthly payment based on the income to debt ratio?

Figure 15.1 DNA method.

If the prospect is a buyer, the following ability-related questions arise: Does he have the down payment necessary? Does he have the necessary credit score to secure financing? Can he make the projected monthly payments based on the income to debit ratio?

Typical Agent's Approach to Leads

The truth is that in selling, it's challenging to create rapport in this day and age. Most consumers know exactly what you are trying to do. They see through many of the rapport-building techniques that real estate sales trainers have taught for years. In our fast-paced, instant, results-driven society, our prospects have been family, occupation, recreation, and dreams (FORD) systemed to death. While the FORD system has a place in establishing clients and maintaining past clients, it's a tired and overused system or technique that a high percentage of people have been overexposed to.

> **Coaching Tip:** *Consumers and prospects are too smart and too cautious to be bonded into a business relationship of high trust—quickly. In fact, these old techniques can often have a result opposite to what you want.*

To use the FORD system, you ask questions centered on topics like these:

- What's going on with your family?
- How's everything at work?
- What do you do for fun?
- What would you do if you won the lottery?
- What are your hopes and dreams?

We do want to know where the client is employed, so that we can reach her at work or know her financial capacity. Fred, the cardiologist who works at the hospital, probably has a greater financial capacity than Bob, the dishwasher who works at Elmer's Steak House. In turning leads into dollars, however, sitting face to face with either Fred or Bob is really our objective.

Agents become Champion Agents, and Champion Agents lead Champion Teams through lead management, lead categorization, and lead conversion systems and strategies that are stellar. One of the reasons you have a team or are considering building a team is that you have too many leads for you to work. If you allow your buyer's agents to take the typical agent route to lead conversion, your results will be lacking. You also may be losing money.

> **Champion Team Rule:** *You can't achieve unconventional production by using conventional means.*

Since leads are the lifeblood of your business, your systems, strategies, techniques, scripts, dialogues, and accountability must be accurately focused on wringing the most out of every opportunity. I was so focused and sparked by the concepts of this chapter that I was up very late last night. I just couldn't sleep for thinking about all the leads, conversion ratios, and challenges that salespeople face. It caused me to spend about six hours in the middle of the night, calculator in hand, personally crunching the numbers of all my sales staff. I spent hours analyzing the sales ratios of leads for each salesperson in Real Estate Champions. I evaluated each lead category or source that we generate leads from and compared the conversion rates. I reviewed all of the leads that each one of my salespeople had in his bucket in the top two lead classifications we use.

I then created a report of a dozen or so pages giving my findings with explanations of my conclusions from the facts for my sales manager to implement. I also gave my sales manager action steps and accountability numbers and systems for each salesperson at Real Estate Champions. After all of this analysis, I found that we were very good in some areas and not so good in others. I have probably been doing this exercise at least twice a year. Because of last night, I am now going to do it every six to eight weeks. Are you willing to do this so that your people are not typical agents, but Champion Agents? Do you care enough about them to help them become Champions?

The Desperate Agent Model

Too many agents operate with buyers from a desperation or scarcity mentality. They use the four-step desperate agent model, applying it over and over again in hopes that the odds will somehow miraculously swing in their favor at some point.

Keep the Prospect on the Phone

Often, we believe that if we can keep the prospect on the phone longer and find commonality or common ground, we will be able to secure his business. We feel that if a prospect likes us or thinks we are nice, we raise the probability of a sale. We want to keep prospects on the phone long enough to secure their phone number, so that we can follow up with them. Our objective as a desperate agent is to secure a lead. A Champion Lead Agent's focus is not on securing the lead but on securing the appointment. The lead has limited value; the appointment has significant value.

Offer to Send the Prospect... Stuff

The average agent wants a phone number and an e-mail address so that she can send the prospect stuff. There is nothing wrong with acquiring a prospect's full contact information.

The problem arises when that, rather than getting an appointment, is our primary objective. When sending prospects properties via e-mail becomes our be-all and end-all form of prospect conversion, we have lost the game of sales. The conversion ratio for e-mail contact is significantly lower that for face-to-face or even a phone contact.

I recently began working with a dynamic young couple in the Atlanta area. They are effective Internet marketers. They had about 300 leads that they even had phone numbers for. These 300 leads were getting property match information based on their preferences as homes came on the market. This couple produced a couple of deals a month from this Internet strategy.

When I began to work with this couple, I asked them why they hadn't called all 300 of the people that they were "working" with. They said, "We get a few deals a month from this; why bother?" I told them to call all 300 in the next week. They called 79 and reached 39 people at home. Of the 39 that they talked to, they set 16 face-to-face presentations. That is a 41 percent close ratio. They conducted 11 face-to-face buyer interviews and committed 7 to a buyer's agency contract. That is a 64 percent close ratio. They had already sold 2 homes, and they expected to sell several more in the next few weeks. They ended up selling 6 homes in a 30-day period out of their 7 clients, 11 appointments, and 39 leads. They also found out that many of the 40 people they tried to reach for a few weeks, when finally contacted, had already bought and sold with another agent.

Hope that Your Stuff Is Better than Everyone Else's.   Unless you can prove and clearly show that your marketing materials, philosophy, sales strategies, and track record are superior, it will be rare for you to convert a buyer by e-mailing him properties based on a profile.

If you secure a prospect through an ad call, a sign call, an open house, or the Internet, you must assume that other agents have all the information you do. If you manage to convince the prospect to share his e-mail address, you must assume that five other agents have it as well. Whoever meets the prospect face to face wins. We are all sending the same property matches, so he is receiving the same properties from every agent he comes in contact with.

Pray that You Eventually Get an Appointment

There was a huge difference in results when my couple from Atlanta went after the business by scheduling appointments. They stopped waiting for prospects to call when they were interested in a home. They went after the prospects that other agents knew about but were waiting for a call from, just as they had done previously.

When I say appointment, I am not talking about an appointment to show property. I am talking about an appointment to conduct a buyer interview in order to determine the prospect's DNA[2] and to assess the odds of your servicing this client and earning a commission. Pretend for a moment that you are a personal injury attorney. As a personal injury attorney, you offer a free consultation. The reason you want the consultation is to determine the probability or odds of your winning the case. We are evaluating prospects based on the odds of our achieving their goals and serving them well. We also are evaluating how much we will earn, how soon we will earn it, and what it will cost us in time, effort, energy, emotion, and dollars invested.

The truth about lower-performing agents is that they are too much in need of "the deal." As a team leader, you must deal decisively and aggressively with agents who are in need or even desperate. Their view that they don't have enough income is merely a symptom of a greater disease.

They don't have enough closings or enough income because they aren't working with enough committed prospects who want to buy now. In short, they don't have enough people who have signed exclusive right to represent contracts. They don't have enough committed clients because they fail to hold enough buyer consultation interviews. In order to achieve an exclusive representation commitment from a prospect, you must conduct enough buyer consultation interviews. No one can sign exclusive right to represent contracts with all the prospects she meets with. However, your buyer's agents should be able to achieve a minimum of a 50 percent close rate.

The lack of enough buyer consultation interviews results either from a lack of sufficient high-quality leads or from a lack of skills in converting, categorizing, and providing clear, definable value to the prospect, so that he has a desire to meet with you. A lack of leads can result from failure to execute a high-quality marketing strategy. The most likely source of the problem is not enough prospecting by individual members of the team. That can be traced to buyer's agents, telemarketers, or even you. Certainly, one of a Champion Lead Agent's primary roles is to be the rainmaker for the team.

Reasons for Deficiency in Prospecting.
1. Lack of confidence in our face-to-face sales presentations.
2. Poor preparation and scheduling of time for it.
3. The salespeople don't know what to say.

Lack of confidence in our face-to-face sales presentations is a large issue that stunts prospecting activity. Most salespeople want to avoid direct personal rejection. There is nothing that is more likely to produce direct personal rejection than a face-to-face presentation. Requiring your salespeople to perfect their face-to-face presentations will lead to increased prospecting.

Poor preparation and scheduling seems like it would have an easy fix. The truth is, it's harder than it looks. You must prepare for your prospecting the day before to enhance the odds of your taking action the next day. You must train your sales agents to determine the calls, people, prospects, and leads that they must be contact the day before they intend to make these contacts. Without this small action, the odds of their completing all the prospecting and lead follow-up that need to be done for the day drop to less than 50 percent. You will see a further drop to less than 10 percent when they do not assign a set time each day for this activity. In order to increase the quality and quantity of your lead follow-up and prospecting calls, you must have a set time in your schedule, and you must prepare for each day of prospecting. Hitting the daily contact goal can be accomplished only by using these two techniques together.

Salespeople not knowing what to say is a big problem. When on a prospecting and lead follow-up call, a salesperson must have a plan. If she doesn't, her lack of skills will come through loud and clear. The other thing that usually comes through if she doesn't know what to say is her desperation and need.

Many salespeople lose it right away on the call. In fact, they lose it in the first seven seconds. They lose it by opening up the dialogue with, "And, how are you today?" That opening reeks of salesperson, salesperson, salesperson… danger, danger! The prospect's defensiveness and guard go up immediately. You have just announced to him that you are like every long distance, charity ticket, heart association, or windshield repair salesperson out there. Improving what you say and how you deliver your message will dramatically influence the team's income, as well as your sales agents' personal income.

> **Coaching Tip:** *Reread the three deficiency problems. Make a decision right now about which of these three you need to address for yourself and your team.*

Three Cs of a Buyer

When working with buyer prospects, they must posses what I call the three Cs of a buyer:

1. Commitment
2. Compromise
3. Competitiveness

A Champion Lead Agent expects her agents to get a commitment from the client. Most trainers will tell agents to ask buyers, "Are you working with another agent?" That really isn't the right question or the right wording. The word *working* has too broad a definition. *Working* could mean that a prospect met an agent at an open house, that he is receiving property matches from an agent, or that there is an agent who farms his neighborhood. None of these things means that the prospect absolutely will buy and sell with that agent.

The proper question is, "Are you committed to another agent?" The prospect will either know exactly what you mean and respond with a yes or no, or he will ask you for your definition of committed. Either way, you gain clarity and avoid wasting your time with a prospect who could be disloyal in the end. Investing your resources in prospects who have a low or limited return is a clear recipe for disaster. Not only are the odds of getting a commission from this type of prospect long, but your agents will often beat themselves up later over not recognizing sooner that they were poor prospects. This can affect their attitude, lowering their confidence and production. Gaining commitment from a prospect at a high level is the only thing in which a Champion Agent invests her time.

A Champion Lead Agent requires her agents to work only with clients who are willing to compromise. If a prospect has the objective of achieving an "I win; you lose" type of transaction, the agent's job will be far more difficult. If the prospect is unwilling to compromise on what he wants in a home, you both will be looking for the "perfect" home for a long time.

A Champion Agent counsels her clients that there are no perfect homes, that most people end up with about 80 percent of the things on their wish list in terms of amenities, and that she is working to find the client the best possible home, based on his needs, wants, and desires and given the current market conditions and market competition.

A Champion Agent also makes sure that the prospect is willing to be competitive. Many buyers are hoping to be the exception rather than the rule. They want to be the one buyer to buy a home at 80 percent of the asking price, when the market average is 95 percent. They are unwilling to offer full price to anyone, even when the low inventory of homes, large volume of buyers wanting homes, and market conditions dictate otherwise. A prospect or client who is unwilling to be competitive or take competitive action when the circumstances dictate will increase the amount of time you have to invest, increase your frustration, lower client satisfaction, and lower the probability of your compensation.

The Mental Roadblocks of a Buyer

The biggest roadblock for buyers is fear. The size and scope of the decision to make an expensive purchase or an exclusive commitment to an agent creates fear in even the most risk-tolerant buyers. There are really six types of fear that an agent must be ready to address to raise her performance to the Champion level.

Fear of Making the Wrong Decision.   This fear can be seen in people who have to rally a group of advisors, friends, and family in order to feel comfortable with moving forward. This army of advisors can pick up on the fear and feed it, so it increases. That is the usual result when the advisors have too much power. *The best technique to use is assurance, backed by facts, that this decision the prospect is making is the right one. In extreme cases, you might use the fear of loss of security if the client doesn't act now.*

Fear of Making Any Decision.   These are the people who say they want to think it over. They are generally the slow-moving, analytical type. You must pinpoint what they need to think about. You might even want to consider quantifying the worst results possible because the worst-case scenario in their imagination is much worse than anything you could explore logically on paper. *You will want to build urgency in these prospects through the fear of loss. You might even consider the time-tested Ben Franklin close where they compare the pros and cons logically on the left and right sides of one piece of paper. Another advanced technique would be to ask the odds of each negative that you write down. You might find that prospects are getting their knickers in a wringer over a 5 percent chance of a negative consequence.*

Fear of Change.   Most people are change-resistant. They don't try to be catalysts of change in their personal or professional lives. *The best technique is to ask people questions about times in their past when they made a decision to make a change like this and it worked out well for them. Help them focus on the positive feelings from that experience. Then link the impending decision to make this change with those positive experiences. Say to them boldly, "Well, this situation seems exactly like the situation you just described."*

Fear of Being Cheated.   Some people have had a negative experience in the past that is clouding their decision and raising their fear. In many cases, it comes down to, "Will you do what you say you will?" Will you, as their exclusive service representative, deliver the goods? *By conveying conviction in yourself, your services, and the quality of the outcome that they will experience, you will remove that fear. Boldly stating with passion, energy, enthusiasm, and confidence that you guarantee your personal performance will move them quickly through this hesitation.*

Fear of Looking Bad to Others.   This fear is ego-centered. The most motivating factor for most people is recognition. We all want status and recognition. This fear is based on the need of our ego to maintain or even grow our personal power and personal recognition. *Use examples of other high-profile people you have served. If you don't have any clients who are recognizable by name, use a title. By title, I mean state the person and his title, like*

CEO of _____ or senior vice president of _____ or Dr. Johnson, the long-time heart surgeon in this area.

Fear of Acting without Sufficient Thought and Knowledge.   These are the people who want more and more information. This fear can often be linked with other fears to forge an impenetrable barrier that only wastes a salesperson's time. These people must be spotted quickly and dealt with accordingly. *The proper approach is to quantify and specify the types of information that they need. What type of knowledge do they need to acquire to make the decision? In the past, when they were making decisions like this, what was required?*

Leads are the lifeblood of any sales business. Your personal ability and skill along with that of your team will be one of the biggest factors influencing your income. Your can still make money if you are sloppy, but your margins and your net profit will be minuscule. You will run the risk of going out of business quickly when you face a negative market change.

PART IV

TAKING YOUR TEAM TO THE CHAMPION LEVEL

16

Effective Marketing Strategies for the Team

While there is alignment among some of the marketing strategies for individual Champion Agents, there are a number of additional strategies that need to be implemented to increase the exposure and positioning of your team. There are also some unique messages and benefits that need to be conveyed clearly, so that general consumers as well as specific prospect groups see the competitive advantages of doing business with you and your team.

In marketing to a general consumer population, I believe it is advisable for you to have a niche. Even as a team, you don't have the advertising budget of McDonald's, Coca-Cola, or Chevrolet to get your name out there. It is advisable for you to define your market area, market segment, geographic niche, property type, or client type to increase the odds of your gaining a dominant market position or market share. Your volume of units and sales along with your production ranking does have its advantages in exposing your team. Even with favorable numbers and comparison to other agents, however, production differences in large areas can look small, even when you are using a bar graph. You must engage in niche marketing to be as effective as you can be. Once you have established your niche, applying an effective marketing plan will yield even more results.

Coaching Tip: *When it comes to marketing and marketing messages, consistency is better than being fancy. In the end, consistency is king!*

Three Core Marketing Messages

To be effective in marketing yourself and your team while still protecting your value and fees in the marketplace, there are what I would describe as three core marketing messages that you need to establish. When you use these three messages effectively, you can create a larger, more established image of success, positive results, and delighted clients.

We Are in the Business

The first core message is that your team is in the business. Too many people forget that you are a real estate agent. You can advertise how great you are on every billboard in town, but there will still be people (even in your sphere) who will forget that you are an agent—let alone a successful one leading a Champion Team. A Champion Team uses repetition of its message to drive its point home. In the end, it's more important to be consistent than it is to be perfect. In school terms, it's good enough that your marketing piece is an A-. It will take you as long to bring the piece up to an A+ level as it took you to create the A- piece in the first place. If the cost of perfection is failing to get your message out the door frequently and consistently, then the cost versus the return is too high. A Champion Team doesn't leave to chance or luck the possibility that people will remember it when it comes time for them or their friends to buy or sell.

We Are Good at What We Do

The second message is that your team is good at what it does for your clients; that you possess skills, abilities, and knowledge that few other agents and teams possess. You have to be cautious about how you convey this message. You don't want to come across as arrogant or self-absorbed.

When you are larger than life and more successful, some of your prospects will assume that you are arrogant or self-absorbed. Therefore, when you are larger than life, you will sometimes need to be more human in your marketing. This is a more dangerous position for a team than for a sole agent because when you are highlighting the team rather than yourself exclusively, the message tends to be less personal. You do need to exude the confidence of a successful salesperson and a successful business that achieves results that your clients can count on. You also need to show that your clients are highly satisfied with the service they receive.

When a service offered by different providers has a similar cost to the consumer, as the service of a real estate agent or real estate team does, the quality of the service and the expertise of the provider are truly important. Your message of successful results for clients through statistical satisfaction surveys and testimonials can help you break free of the crowd. It allows you to use empirical documentation for your argument of, "pick me to represent your interests."

It Matters Whom You Select to Represent Your Interests

Finally, you need to demonstrate that it really matters whom people select to represent their interests. This is the message of a Champion Agent and Champion Team. Together, if you can ingrain that message in the consumer's brain even before he has need of real estate services, you increase your odds dramatically. When I talk about increasing the odds, I mean the odds of your team being selected to make a sales presentation. One of the key mistakes lead agents make regularly with their marketing is trying to accomplish too much with it. Your marketing should be designed to get your phone to ring. The most fundamental objective in marketing is to produce leads. The way to effectively gauge the value of the marketing that your team is doing is:

- What is the cost versus the number of leads created?
- What is the conversion rate of those leads to appointments?
- What is the conversion rate of appointments to clients?
- What is your average gross revenue per unit from the marketing?
- What are your costs for your business?
- Is there a net profit when you get to the bottom line?

Champion Agents and Champion Teams must project the message that it fundamentally matters whom the consumer selects to represent his interests. The reason that commission rate decreases and discount real estate companies have become prevalent in North America is the poor job that we have done in getting this marketing message out. We have not conveyed to the public that it really makes a difference whom you list with or buy through. It makes a difference in down payment, sales price, purchase price, net equity at close, ease of transaction, level of satisfaction, after-sale service, and countless other areas.

It matters to the consumer who his agent is. The people doing the discounting are trying to convince sellers and buyers that all agents are the same. We must explain to people that a Champion Team can have a large effect on sales price and the smoothness of the transaction. A Champion Team will have a positive influence on sellers' and buyers' short- and long-term equity position.

Key Team Marketing Messages

There are some very strategic and effective marketing messages that teams can use but individual agents cannot. An average team can use these marketing messages with great success. *A Champion Team can use them to dominate.*

My list of marketing messages is by no means all-encompassing. There is truly an unlimited supply of possible messages if you do the work to search for, evaluate, and design them. The expensive part is the investment of dollars and time to test your messages in the open market and then track the results, so that you can consider their impact on sales and on your team's status in the marketplace.

It Doesn't Cost More to Get More Service

The cost of high-quality real estate representation services is fundamentally the same. While good agents, teams, and companies can choose any commission rate they want, the most professional providers are all within a reasonable range of one another. This is true of most professional services. Most dentists, doctors, and accountants are also within a reasonable range of one another in fees when they are providing comparable services.

As a Champion Team Leader, the cost the consumer pays for your service is the same, but the value of your service is not. You are providing prompter attention in most cases and more significant expert counsel because of the volume of transactions you see annually. Maybe you have marketing and exposure services that raise the probability of the sale of someone's home. There are numerous benefits to the higher service model that your team structure can create.

We Raise the Probability of Your Success

A team has the opportunity to swing the odds in its clients' favor. With a team, there are more people working together toward a clear objective, which increases the odds of a favorable outcome. There are more salespeople, both buyer's agents and listing agents, who are out creating leads in a personal way through more open houses, broker open houses, ad calls, sign calls, larger sphere of influence reach, and past clients. With a team, you can be more responsive to the hot prospects by getting with them faster to show the property more promptly. In a competitive market for listings, you can get the buyer into the home before any other agent can. Your team also has sufficient staff to work with prospects with a medium or lower motivation level or a longer time frame in a more personal way. This means that you always have a larger pipeline of leads to show your new listing to than other agents.

One Individual Agent Can't Provide as Much Value

The economics of additional staff are clear. One horse cannot pull as large a wagon for as long a period of time as a team of two horses can. The same is true for the individual agent. This argument is especially effective when a marketplace takes more effort to sell in—when inventory is up, days on the market are increasing, and absorption rates are increasing. You could also argue that a team provides more value through greater exposure, more marketing, more effective Web sites, more frequent open houses, an increase in sign calls because of more for sale signs in the ground, a greater ability to cross-market your home with other homes, and more showings by a listing agent team that has a higher level of motivation to sell your home rather than just any home.

We Reduce the Risk of an Unsuccessful Outcome

Because a team is more responsive to your clients and new leads, you can convert prospects at a higher rate than other agents. Your additional staff provides better customer service, so your clients are more satisfied. You may be able to prove that by comparing your satisfaction ratings and percentage of business that is repeat or referral with NAR national statistics on overall consumer satisfaction ratings and the percentage of sales that come from repeat or referral business. You can develop a positive marketing message using your statistics on average listings taken to listings sold. Combine that with a series of services that only a team can provide—and you've got a winning combination.

Build the Appearance of a Large Service Team

One of the best strategies to make your team appear larger is to include all the people who assist you. In the marketing materials you create, insert a picture of the team that includes your lender, title representative, home warranty representative, attorney, home inspector, repairperson, and anyone else you work with regularly to facilitate your service to your clients. You can also create a list of your team members with their job titles and roles. This list can then be turned into a marketing piece to send to your clients and prospects. You can probably also split the cost of this piece with all of your service providers, since they have a vested interest in increasing your sales. Use this approach in your direct mail, Web site, prelisting package, and buyer counseling session package, and as a handout at open houses. There are numerous forums you can use to help expose your new team.

Create a Marketing Strategy to Appear Larger

The best strategy I have used with clients is described as the blitz and retreat strategy. You make a commitment of dollars to blitz a specific geographic area or segment of the marketplace in which you want to increase your market share. You blitz the marketplace with marketing pieces at close intervals. You blitz it with your team, your statistics, client testimonial pieces, benefit offers, free report offers, and free market update offers. All the while, you are promoting the team and the value of the team.

In the blitz, you are mailing something at least every two to three weeks. You continue this for at least six months, but no more than a year. While you are blitzing people with mail pieces, you also need to be on the phone or face to face with the people in your target area. It doesn't work as well if you just mail stuff.

Then, after 6 to 12 months, you retreat to half of what you were sending before. If you marketed to the people in your area every two weeks, now you do it once a month, for example. The amazing thing is the people who were blitzed still think that you are sending them pieces every two weeks—and that perception can last for years!

Position Your Team Members as Experts

Becoming the expert in the marketplace is one of the most significant challenges facing agents and their teams today. This is mostly because of the dynamic changes in marketplaces over the last few years, with rapid expansion in appreciation in most marketplaces, more people using real estate as an investment vehicle, the changing financing options for consumers, the currently increasing interest rates, the commoditization of our services in the marketplace, rampant commission cutting and discounting of fees by agents and companies, and the massive influx of new licensees. As a Champion Team Leader, these problems are multiplied exponentially as you try to position yourself as the expert. The truth is, one false move, miscalculation, misstep, or error by one of your staff members can undermine all of the work you have done to position yourself and your team as experts.

With the advent of the Internet, information about properties on the market is available to anyone who wants to search for it. People have maps, charts, pictures, virtual tours, and neighborhood and school information. In many cases, in fact, consumers have too much information and get bogged down by information overload. The value we offer as experts is the interpretation of that information, coupling the analysis of it with the proper questioning to pinpoint the client's wants, needs, desire level, and expectations. We save the prospect time, money, and frustration and provide protection and security when we are experts.

Be an Expert in Your Market

You have to be the expert in the marketplace. Webster's definition of expert is, "One who has acquired special skill in, or knowledge and mastery of, something." One key word that I want to point out is *acquire*. To acquire something, you have to apply some action and effort. In other words, it takes work. You have to do something to become the expert. You have to take action and change your thinking and your actions. To be an expert is to be adept, an authority, a master, professional, a wiz, or maybe even a specialist.

Champion Team Rule: *A relationship with a prospect or client is not enough. As an expert, you must bring a tangible value to each transaction.*

When you are the expert, past clients can explain that the value they received from you clearly exceeded the cost of your services.

Elements of Expert Value.

1. *Saving them money on a down payment.* You had a better counseling approach and better contract-writing skills that reduced the initial cash investment they had to make in their new home. You secured a better lender that was able to stretch their dollars further, so that they didn't have to part with as many for a down payment. This allowed them to buy new furniture for cash, rather than on a payment plan at a higher interest rate.

2. *Selecting the best long-term investment for them.* You and your team really understood the marketplace, so you counseled them from a historical perspective on what has happened and what might continue to happen to their investment. You cautioned them when you saw signs of overheating. You factored in how this purchase will better position them in the future and how this particular home and this neighborhood will be a better investment vehicle.

3. *Educating them on the marketplace.* Through more effective education strategies, you increased their comfort in making the decision to work with you to buy or sell their home. When they decided on a home, they had a higher level of trust and comfort in moving forward with you. The angst we all feel as a result of buyer's remorse was lessened because of your market knowledge, so their home-buying experience was better.

4. *Helping their financial future through investment property.* Few agents are adept enough to take advantage of this vast opportunity. Your clients all want financial independence for themselves. Most of them don't understand the vast leveraging power of a real estate investment.

Coaching Tip: *As the marketplace for real estate services becomes more competitive, the value for agents who have expert-level market knowledge will increase.*

Convey Market Knowledge and Credibility

Experts not only understand the marketplace but study the marketplace. They possess and use empirical evidence concerning the marketplace to clearly articulate their positions and beliefs to prospects and clients. They advance viewpoints or professional opinions with confidence and conviction because they know they are right. They are able to counsel their clients better because of their increased knowledge of where the market is today and where it will head in the future.

Price Point Comparison.   Most people, real estate agents, and the media view the marketplace as one entity (or possibly a couple, based on geography). That is too narrow an approach. Price is a significant factor. Once you decide on a geographical area or segment, you also need to segment by price point. You need to divide your marketplace into five key price segments: entry, lower middle, middle, upper middle, and upper. Each one of these segments can be vastly different from the others.

Your sellers and buyers say that they want to know the overall health of the marketplace. What they really want to know is what's happening in the specific marketplace that they are trying to buy or sell in. The only way to convey that information to them is through price point comparison.

1. *Know your available inventory levels.*   All markets are influenced by inventory levels. The inventory levels, in turn, affect the percentage of homes that sell every month. The higher the inventory, the lower the percentage of homes that sell each month. Another term used for the percentage of homes sold is listings sold versus listings taken ratio. In a normal or neutral market, the listings sold versus listings taken percentage will run 65 to 70 percent. In an inventory-short, robust, high-level seller's market, the number will be well above 90 percent. You need to know the level of competition that sellers and buyers will face based on the marketplace inventory levels.

2. *Determine the number of sales in the last 30 days.*   I did not say sold or closed properties. I said sales or pending sales. You want an accurate analysis for the previous 30 days. If you count closed transactions, you are really reflecting the marketplace inventory from 30 to 60 days ago, not 1 to 30 days ago. A property that closes, for example, on June 30 was really a pending sale in May or April, depending on the typical time in your market to complete the paperwork, inspections, appraisals, repairs, document writing, and all the other behind-the-scenes work for closing. Always reflect the activity from 1 to 30 days ago.

3. *Calculate the absorption rate or the number of months of inventory.*   This last calculation is the lynchpin of the whole analysis. Take the current inventory levels in each price point and divide them by the pending sales for the month. This will give you the number of months of inventory left if sales remain constant. (You are using the best-case situation in this calculation by making the assumption that no new available homes will come on the market before the entire present inventory is sold. It is unlikely that this will be true, but you want to deal only with solid data. This calculation will always need a qualifier.)

Champion Example

1. *Let's say you have 100 homes for sale in the entry-level price point. On average, 20 of these sell every month. You clearly have five months' worth of inventory left. A seller will need to be competitively priced if she is to sell during the next month. What you are doing with this calculation is providing a clear picture of the current supply and demand mix in the marketplace.*

2. *Let's say there are 300 homes for sale in a given geographic area, and 30 of them are pending this last month. Divide 300 by 30 and end up with 10 months.*

3. *In contrast, one of my clients in southern California sent me her market statistics from a year ago. They showed 98 properties available with 176 pending on a monthly basis. That's quite a bit different; this marketplace is far more robust than one with 300 actives and 30 pendings. The latter has ten months of inventory, and the former has about two to three weeks. Your strategy, tactics, and counseling of clients would be very different for these two marketplaces.*

- *Which marketplace allows the seller greater control?*
- *Which marketplace do you think is appreciating faster?*
- *Which marketplace inspires the greatest seller greed?*
- *In which marketplace will homes spend fewer days for sale?*
- *In which marketplace do buyers have the least control and the greatest need to meet seller demands in order to make the purchase?*
- *In which marketplace do the sellers put more pressure on agents to cut their commission rate?*

The marketplace with only two to three weeks of inventory is the correct answer to all these questions. The other marketplace is behind on all counts. The seller has to be informed, or you are wasting your time.

The trends in the marketplace are determined by the inventory of listings, pending sales, and the number of months of inventory. Your marketplace will not magically go against the law of supply and demand. The key is knowing what the law is saying about your marketplace. Don't leave your office without your monthly analysis!

Figure 16.1 illustrates how to use your evaluation of the market trends to your advantage. I have included a market trend report for your use.

Real Estate Market Trends

Monthly Report

Month: _____

Price Range	Current # Of Listings	Avg # of Sales Per Mo.	Selling Price % of List Price	Avg Days on Market	Remaining # Months Inventory
$ Entry					
$ Low Middle					
$ Middle					
$ Upper Middle					
$ Upper					

Previous Month's Statistics

Month: _____

Price Range	Current # Of Listings	Avg # of Sales Per Mo.	Selling Price % of List Price	Avg Days on Market	Remaining # Months Inventory
$ Entry					
$ Low Middle					
$ Middle					
$ Upper Middle					
$ Upper					

Same month last year's statistics

Month: _____

Price Range	Current # Of Listings	Avg # of Sales Per Mo.	Selling Price % of List Price	Avg Days on Market	Remaining # Months Inventory
$ Entry					
$ Low Middle					
$ Middle					
$ Upper Middle					
$ Upper					

Figure 16.1 Monthly report of real estate market trends.

Figure 16.2 is an example of one of my clients' marketplace trends grid for a month.

Example Real Estate Market Trends

Monthly Report

Month: _____

Price Range	Current # Of Listings	Avg # of Sales Per Mo.	Selling Price % of List Price	Avg Days on Market	Remaining # Months Inventory
$0 - $300K	125	201	99%	6	.62
$300K - $500K	337	286	98%	14	1.20
$500K - $650K	247	179	96%	11	1.40
$650K - $800K	101	15	95%	37	6.70
$800K and up	75	6	95%	68	12.60

©2006 Real Estate Champions, Inc.

Figure 16.2 Actual client's monthly market trends report.

There is a significant difference once you cross the line between the middle segment of the marketplace and the upper-middle and upper segments. Agents, consumers, and media are reporting only the good news right now. They are describing the robust nature of the marketplace—that there is no inventory and that homes are selling fast. The truth is that things are quite different in the middle and the upper-middle sectors. The inventory levels are 6 to 12 times greater. While homes are still selling, sellers must be competitive.

Define Your Competitive Points of Difference

A Champion Team wants to dominate the competition and gain a larger market share in the process. A Champion Team wants to create competitive points of difference that lead to a competitive advantage over its competition.

A Champion Team's focus should be on a steady increase in market share. Your objective is to compete with intensity and focus to gain more prospects, clients, and profits. The outcome will be a significant gap between your competitors and you. Your next objective should be to exploit that competitive advantage. In the game of real estate sales, success requires creating and achieving a competitive advantage over your competition and being consistent in applying that competitive advantage to eventually achieve a decisive advantage or a sustainable decisive advantage.

What Is a Competitive Advantage?   A competitive advantage is the use of specific strategy, tactics, and resources to gain the upper hand over your competitors. It is exploiting the difference between your products and services and those of the competition to attract more prospects and clients. It leads to market share growth, increased revenue, and profits. It eventually causes your competitors to be weakened in the marketplace.

The best method for teams to use to create a competitive advantage is a cash investment. There are plenty of teams that try to achieve a competitive advantage, get halfway there, and run out of cash or resources. They spend ever-increasing amounts of marketing dollars to try to achieve a competitive advantage.

In the end, a Champion Agent who leads a Champion Team achieves a competitive advantage by applying discomfort to others and being able to tolerate it herself.

Law of Supply and Demand.   Let me throw out this question for your consideration. Do we, as a real estate community, significantly influence the number of homes or overall real estate units that are sold annually? When I ask agents this question, there is usually confusion. Let me further clarify it. Did we, as a real estate community, significantly influence the fact that 7.2 million transactions were conducted in 2005, while only 6.8 million were done in 2004? Did we create the extra 400,000 units sold?

Too many of us think that the answer is yes, but the truth is that it's no. The law of supply and demand dictates the number of units that are sold in any marketplace at any given time. The inventory of homes, inventory of buyers, consumer confidence, and interest rates can all be factors in the law of supply and demand. We don't have a role here. Our limited role is to influence *where we generate our sales*. This limited role involves better conversion of the leads that we have now. This effectively allows us to attract a greater portion of the leads in the marketplace. We don't really create more leads overall; we are just better at attracting and converting the ones that are there. In order to increase your sales in a marketplace that is static or even dropping, you have only one option for growing your business. In a real estate marketplace that is expanding and robust and that has increasing sales numbers, you still have only the same one option if you want significant growth. Drum roll, please: you have to take business from somebody else! The only way to achieve sustainable and continued growth in sales units is to take those units from some other agent, team, or company.

Features of Your Service Are Benefits to Your Customers.   Your goal, as a Champion Team Leader is to climb the ladder of competitive success, to clearly understand the features of your service. Then you have to turn those features into clear, distinguishable benefits to the consumer. You must also be certain that those benefits are things that consumers are willing to pay your team for without concern. Then you will need to turn those benefits into competitive points of difference and be able to demonstrate a high level of benefits relative to your competition. You will need to transform those competitive points of difference into competitive advantages. You do that through clear and quantifiable differences that you and a very small group of other teams provide. Then you morph the competitive advantage into a decisive advantage.

By this point, the features, benefits, and competitive points of difference should be so clear and compelling for you and your team and so provable in nature that a prospect would, in effect, be faulty in his thinking if he chose to work with anyone else. Finally, you have attained a sustainable decisive advantage, and your competitors will never be able to catch you or do what you do as well as you do it. They almost have to concede the territory to you. There are very few companies that attain a sustainable decisive advantage because of the nature of our capitalist society.

Attaining this takes some time and real thought. You have to be willing to sit quietly for a chunk of time staring at a blank piece of paper. Ask yourself the following tough questions:

- What is your team good at?
- What do you do better than the rest of the agents?
- What have your clients said about services that they really appreciated and assign significant value to?
- Are there key statistics that you can use?
- Do you have a competitive advantage in a geographic area?
- Do you have a market share in a specific point or geographic region?
- Is your competitive advantage your Big 3 statistics?
- Average list price to sale price
- Average days on the market
- Average listings sold versus listings taken ratio
- Is it the percentage of delighted clients in your customer surveys?
- Is it a quantifiable increase in the sales price of the homes you list?
- Is it a quantifiable savings for the buyers whom you represent in terms of
- Average sales price against the list price?
- Average down payment against the industry average?
- Average savings secured to your clients?

A Champion Team that has a competitive advantage can back it up with statistics. It's an empirically proven advantage, not a nebulous feeling. It's an accurate advantage in a comparison between the team and the Realtor community at large or a specific Realtor the team is competing against. Invest time to determine and evaluate your competitive points of difference—no matter how long it takes. Once you have identified them, use those points and your competitive advantages in marketing strategies to create a long-enduring dominance in your marketplace niche.

17

Your Team Members Must Master the Telephone

The telephone will be the tool that, if mastered by your team, will create the greatest lever for your success. How real estate salespeople handle the phone determines their income. Everyone who is in sales needs to be a pro with the phone. Most people have the misconception that only people who complete the final sale over the phone need to have exceptional telephone sales skills. The truth is, we all are selling something over the phone. Whether we are selling an idea, a product, or a service, we use the phone as one of our primary tools to create a contact, lead, or appointment in order to make a face-to-face presentation.

A little over a year ago, I was interviewed by the National Association of Realtors for an article it wanted to publish. The interviewer asked me this question: "What is the very best sales tool currently available to real estate salespeople?" Before I gave the interviewer my response, I warned her that she would be stunned by my answer. She was expecting me to expound on the virtues of a Web site, targeted marketing piece, personal brochure, or BlackBerry or Treo. When I told her that the greatest sales tool for the last 30 years has been (and still is) the telephone, she dropped the phone on me.

She proceeded to rattle off what some of the other experts she had talked to had shared with her: Web site, personal brochure, marketing pieces, BlackBerries. The truth about all of those sales tools is that they don't make sales. They aid in organization, competitive differentiation, or even lead generation, but none of them will actually directly help you make a sale. The telephone is still the only tool that will enable you to convey your sales message in a personal way so that you can inject emotion, urgency, passion, and conviction into your message and can handle questions and objections in a way that guides your prospect to an appointment or final purchase.

It is my belief that for any profession in the business world, there is one primary tool and multiple secondary tools. If you are successful as a business professional, mastering that primary tool will separate you from the competition and will position you as world class in your field in earnings, prestige, and recognition.

The quality of the words that you convey and how you convey them over the phone will enable you to rise to the top of the field in any sales profession. It doesn't matter whether you are selling rain gutters, windshield repair, real estate services, insurance, or financial services; your ability to thrive (not just survive) will be determined by your mastery of the sales techniques you use over the phone to create sales or book appointments.

Why We Struggle to Master the Telephone

Most real estate salespeople don't view themselves as salespeople at all. They view themselves as consultants, counselors, marketing consultants, Realtors, blah, blah, blah. Just look at your business card. What does it say? Does it say real estate salesperson? We are in sales, my friend.

A great consultant is really a great salesperson. Just evaluating situations, marketplaces, and strategies effectively doesn't make you a great consultant. You must organize your recommendations and clearly identify the benefits of those recommendations to your client. Then the magic part, if you are among the most successful consultants, is selling those recommendations to your client. If your client doesn't act on your recommendations with enthusiasm, passion, and resolve, she won't be as successful as she expects to be. If you don't sell your clients, they won't require your services again or refer you to others who could benefit from your services.

Our skills and our focus, as real estate salespeople, are centered on building a relationship. Because relationships are best created face to face, where we can use the visual and nonverbal cues of communication, we focus our time and attention on interacting and connecting face to face. The truth is, it's almost impossible to get enough face-to-face time with people to drive your business without at least an introductory phone call. You have to use the phone to book appointments with prospects to make sales. It's rare for real estate salespeople to be able to make the complete sale, from first contact through contract, face to face without some use of the phone.

It's also impossible to complete the sale exclusively over the phone. You will usually need the support of your face-to-face skills. The only exception to this might be real estate salespeople in resort markets or sales to investors. The point of contact with the most motivated prospects is generally the phone. You might get an initial hit on your Web site, but your team's objective must be to secure a phone number so that you can use the art of verbal persuasion.

Listen Your Way to Success

Our ability to serve our customers and prospects well is determined by our ability to listen. Most real estate salespeople were convinced by some friend or relative to get into sales because they had the gift of gab rather than the gift of listening. In all sales situations, the gift of listening far outweighs the gift of gab.

To become a better listener, you need to understand why you want to improve that skill. What's your desire or motivation for improving? If the why is large enough, the how becomes much easier. The why includes more sales, shorter sales cycles, higher conversion of leads, and more referrals because your client service is better.

On any sales call, there is one party who has the most important and relevant information, opinions, and comments. Hint: that person isn't you. What the other person has to say, along with how you receive it, process it, and respond to it, will determine your income. This truth must be embedded in your brain.

Three Mental Mistakes That Block Listening

Sometimes one of the best ways to learn how to do something is to evaluate how *not* to do it. By knowing how not to do something, we can apply the 180-degree theory to success.

1. *"I've got this nailed."*   Too often, we get entrenched in our scripts and dialogues and don't listen as well as we should. We are so focused on getting to the sales presentation or the closing section of our script that we forget to listen along the way. We miss the nuances that any good real estate salesperson must pick up on to make the script come alive. We need the preparation, scripts, and dialogues; what we don't need are the blinders from overpreparation, the preconceived ideas of what the client needs based only on our research, and rigidity to a fault in our scripting.

2. *"I'm the expert; just ask me."*   Often, we are looking for opportunities to flex our mental muscles. We are listening for openings where we can impress our clients with our knowledge and preparation, rather than really hearing their needs. We get antsy to demonstrate to our clients how much we know. This anxiousness can lead us to interrupt prospects because of our excitement for the sale. When you feel that anxiety, it means that you really aren't listening. What the prospect has to say is always more important than what the salesperson has to say.

3. *"Enough about you; how about me?"*   This is similar to the "I'm the expert; just ask me" problem. The difference between the two is that when we are in the "Enough about you; how about me?" mode, we are looking for openings to make our presentation or pitch. We are scanning the conversation exclusively for the cue to leap into our sales pitch. The minute we hear something that resembles the opening we are looking for, we start the windup and throw our pitch.

Three Steps for Effective Listening

1. *Always take notes.*   The act of taking notes forces you to focus on the prospect and what he is saying. Just jotting down the key concepts, problems, issues, and company information directly from the prospect will do. An effective technique is to tell the prospect that you are taking notes. This will raise your status with him instantly.

> *Mr. Smith, I'm taking notes because I don't want to miss anything, and I need this critical information that you are sharing with me to better serve you.*

If you tell the prospect this in advance, he will understand when you ask him to repeat something or to slow down or give you a moment.

> *Mr. Smith, I am sorry, but my shorthand needs a little help. I want to clarify the information on _____. Could you please go over that again, so that I can get it on paper?*

When you do this, your prospects will experience the warm feeling that you really care about meeting their needs. They will think, "This guy is different from the other real estate agents I have worked with in the past."

2. *Ask more questions.*   Whoever is asking the questions is in control of the conversation. The asker turns into the receiver of the information. If you want to learn, you need to ask. You don't learn anything by talking. You already know all that you know.
    Let me share with you a few general questions that are effective.

   * Can you elaborate on that?
   * Can you give me a little more perspective on that issue?
   * Can you explain to me how this works?
   * Can you review that again for me?
   * "Bob, I'm not quite sure what you mean."

3. *Instant replay.*   As real estate agents, we need to make sure that we have it right, both on paper and in our brain. The only way to do that is to instantly replay or summarize what we have heard and understood the prospect to convey.

> *So, Bob, let me see if I am on the right track. You want to increase the size of your home and need a fourth bedroom. You feel that moving into the Arrowwood neighborhood would be a big step in accomplishing those goals. Being able to acquire a home in the $400,000 price range, so that you could keep your overall payments under $3,000 a month, would be a big plus for you. Is that correct?*

You don't want to repeat what the prospect said word for word. Your job is to summarize accurately and interpret what you heard, not to become a mynah bird and repeat everything he said.

When you engage in instant replay, your prospect will often do one of these three things:.

- Confirm that the instant replay was correct.
- Correct your instant replay in the areas where you didn't have it right.
- Give you new and additional information.

All of these are terrific outcomes because you know you have the information right when you hang up the phone. As a bonus, you might also get more information. When people add information after the instant replay, it's usually something really important. You got into their inner circle, and you have inside information that most of your competitors will not have gotten. Because this information is so valuable, you want to increase your focus on listening

When people share more information, you will want to repeat the instant replay process again and use a phrase at the end like:

> *Do I have it right?*
>
> *Bob, am I on the right track?*
>
> *How does that sound?*

Reading Between the Lines.   There are times when pauses and muted responses like "oh," "I see," "that's interesting," "how so?" and "really" don't spur information. When that occurs, you will need to read between the lines. Ask yourself these questions.

1. Was my presentation off?
2. Did I miss a need that the prospect expressed?
3. Is my timing off?

You will have to evaluate the situation quickly because you want to be able to move on to the next step without losing the sales conversation. To get between the lines, use any of these questions:

1. Bob, what did I miss?
2. How do you feel about that?
3. Is there anything that can be done to reverse your decision?
4. Where do we go from here?

Listening is the glue in any prospect or client relationship. The only way to know and serve the prospect or client better is through listening. There is an interesting bonus that salespeople who are effective listeners receive. As you flex your listening muscles, the prospect or client gets to know you as well. He begins to develop a clear picture of you and your company and what you stand for. Most people will conclude that you are caring, trustworthy, professional, and reliable. You have opened the door to a quality, long-term service relationship.

Using Scripts to Improve Performance

Close your eyes and imagine there is a technique or process that will make each call more effective. This process has the effect of improving your communication with the prospect, creating a stronger impact, increasing your sales, and reducing your individual call times. The net result is that you can increase the number of calls you make in a day, resulting in more contacts made, so your sales goals can be achieved more quickly with a higher probability of success. For someone on full commission compensation, like a real estate salesperson, it would mean more money.

I have just described the benefits of using scripts. Most salespeople (especially real estate salespeople) would rather have their skin eaten off by ants than use scripts. This is even truer when real estate salespeople are communicating via the telephone. The hard truth is that well-constructed, practiced, and perfected scripts work. In fact, they work exceptionally well when a salesperson has practiced them enough to internalize their use.

Internalizing a script doesn't mean that you don't have it in front of you anymore when you are delivering it. It means that your practice and memorization of it have been at such a high level that the script is now part of you. As an example, if I delivered my listing presentation today, about 10 years after I delivered it the last time in front of a seller to secure a listing, I would still deliver it with high quality. It would be better than the listing presentations of probably 99 percent of the agents licensed today. That's because of my commitment and work for more than eight years to practice, memorize, and internalize its delivery. When a salesperson achieves that level of perfection of delivery, it doesn't sound or seem like a script—but it is.

Seven Rules for Using Scripts

1. *Don't have a negative attitude toward scripts.*   The right attitude with a mediocre script will generate better results than the perfect script delivered with the wrong attitude.
2. *Know your overall goal for the call.*   The scripts you use will be far more effective when you are clear about your goals and objectives for the call. Know the target before you invest your time in the call.
3. *Always use feedback response techniques.*   The statement "that's really exciting" is a feedback response statement. It links or bridges the client's response with your next question. It demonstrates to the client that you care, and that you are listening. When you use this technique, the script will come out like normal conversation. Use phrases like "that's exciting," "terrific," "great," "wonderful," and "wow" as your positive response. Of course, you also need negative phrases to express feedback. If the prospect is telling you that his dog just died, you can say "I am sorry" or "that's unfortunate" to bridge to your next question.
4. *Don't blow through pause points.*   In most scripts, there are pause points. These are places where you need to wait or pause for a response. It could be after you have asked a more challenging question that requires the prospect to think. It could be before you answer if your script leads to a more open exchange. (A good pause point is a terrible thing to waste.)
5. *Listen attentively.*   It is easy to be so focused on the script and the next question that you fail to hear the response to your current question. The connection you create with the client comes first through the skill of listening. (You can talk your way out of making a sale to a client, but you can't listen your way out of making a sale.)
6. *Make sure your script has open-ended questions.*   You want the prospect to talk 80 percent of the time. You can't achieve that with closed-ended questions. You also can understand the parameters of the prospect's wants and needs better with open-ended questions.
7. *Don't forget to script the close.*   If you excel at every other step on the script but fail in the closing, your results will be poor. You must have a scripted process to close for your goals or objectives for the call. If you are trying to gain a referral, you have to close and ask for one. If you are trying to book an appointment, then you will need to

close for that as well. You don't need elaborately worded closes for the telephone. In fact, a simple, straightforward close like a summary close or a feedback recommendation close is most effective.

> *Mr. Jones, if I understand you correctly, if you could find a one-story home with a three-car garage in the Riverdale area, you would consider meeting with me. Based on my market knowledge and experience, there is no doubt that I can find you a house that meets your requirements. All we need to do now is simply set an appointment to explore this further. Would _____ or _____ be better for you to meet at my office?*

As you can see, this summary close is quite different from the following recommendation close.

> *Mr. Jones, based on what you have told me thus far, I would like to recommend (insert the solution or service you are offering). Would _____ or _____ be better for us to meet to discuss these options?*

Powerful Opening Statements

Your opening statement in a lead follow-up makes all the difference. The first 10 to 15 seconds of your phone call are the most critical. Some studies have indicated that a salesperson has 8 seconds before the client shuts her down or shuts her off. The client might be on the phone with you longer, but she won't buy. You set the mood and the tone of the call in the first 8 seconds. The prospect will decide, even on a lead follow-up call, if she will listen further.

Opening statements have to be scripted word for word. Here are the rules for powerful opening statements.

1. *State your name.* I know this sounds fundamental, but it's amazing how few people do it. To really be good, state the client's name at the beginning of your opening state-

ment. When people hear their name, they tend to listen to the next few sentences more carefully. If you are making a call to an unknown prospect, however, be careful. An unknown prospect is someone whose name you don't exactly know how to pronounce. If there is a chance that you are going to butcher the client's name, don't use it. There is nothing that says *salesperson* faster than a mispronounced name.

2. *State your company name.*   Again, this seems like common sense, but it often gets omitted. Also, try adding a tag line.

> *We specialize in Eastside properties.*
>
> *or*
>
> *We specialize in selling homes that failed to sell previously.*
>
> *or*
>
> *We specialize in helping families net a higher amount from their home than the market average.*

3. *State why you are calling.*   This is where a lack of scripting often affects us. We tend to fall apart right here. We can go into long explanations that totally overwhelm and confuse the prospect. Begin each call with, "The reason for my call is… " This technique will force you to focus on your call objectively and get you quickly to your preplanned offer.

> *The reason for my call is that we met at the open house on Chestnut last week.*
>
> *or*
>
> *The reason for my call is that you called us about the property on Chestnut a week ago.*
>
> *or*
>
> *The reason for my call is that you had called us about our new home listed in Fairway Meadows.*

4. *Hook in the benefit statement.*   This tells the prospect why he should even listen further.

> *Hello, Mr. Smith. I'm Dirk Zeller with Real Estate Champions. The reason for my call is that we met at an open house on Chestnut last Sunday, and there have been some changes in the marketplace. I was wondering if I could take a few minutes of your time to update you on the new developments.*
>
> *or*
>
> *Hello, Mr. Smith. I'm Dirk Zeller with Real Estate Champions. The reason for my call is that you contacted us a week ago about a home on Chestnut. We have had considerable success in helping families like yours achieve the home of their desires with a low financial investment. I was wondering if I could take a few minutes of your time to see if there is a possible fit.*
>
> *or*
>
> *Hello, Mr. Smith. I'm Dirk Zeller with Real Estate Champions. We specialize in helping homeowners who have failed to sell previously achieve a sale. The reason for my call is that we have had considerable success in getting homes sold that were previously on the market with another company. I was wondering if I could take a few minutes of your time to see if there is a possible fit.*

Tape or record the reason for your call. If you want to be a real professional, tape or record your lead follow-up call as well. Then review, critique, and evaluate your calls.

"Kiss of Death" Opening Statement.   The worst opening statement is, "And how are you today?" If you want to have no chance whatever of making a sale in the next year, use this opening statement. Many newer salespeople and lower-skilled salespeople fall back into its use more frequently than others. You will need to watch, monitor, and record the opening statements of your sales team regularly to ensure that they don't backslide into its use.

Transforming from Canned to Planned

The reason most salespeople sound canned is a lack of preparation and practice. They are unable to inject emotion, changes in tonality, and pauses into their scripts and dialogues, so they come across as canned. We get the visual image of their being trapped in a can of soup with the lid resealed, with no hope of getting out. This "canned" existence doesn't allow for any room, flexibility, or creativity on their part. This is especially true in the case of agents who have the extra dose of entrepreneurial spirit that is required to build a team.

Salespeople who are highly skilled are never confined by their scripts. They use bridging statements, stories, testimonials, personal guarantees, and analogies to enhance the effectiveness of their basic scripts. These additions are not in lieu of the script, but in addition to it. A Champion Salesperson will inject a story at a strategic moment in the script based on where she is in the sales process and what the prospect just shared with her. The key is that the presentation remains planned. She may at times stray from the script for strategic reasons, but she knows when to get back to the comfort of her scripting.

Exploring and Collecting Information

The real job of any salesperson is to explore a prospect thoroughly. We need to explore the prospect's beliefs, experiences, expectations, desires, wants, needs, ability, and authority. The most successful salespeople are collectors of valuable information.

Your questions for exploring need to center on trying to identify your prospects' problems. What problems do they have? How significantly are these problems affecting their lives? How long have they had these problems? This will help you determine the size and cost of the problems. The decisive question is: —is the problem large enough to cause the person to take action and either buy or sell?

My objective with a prospect was to acquire as much understanding of his situation and philosophy as I could before our meeting. This gave me an almost unbeatable edge over the competition. It's hard to lose to buyer or seller apathy or another agent when you have more information than your competition because you explored more effectively than the next guy.

Take Powerful Notes

Your job, as a salesperson, isn't to write down every word the prospect utters. You want only the client's most valuable concepts, ideas, problems, hopes, dreams, wants, needs, and expectations. You might even create a script for that by listing these segments on an 8 1/2 × 11 piece of paper. Then allow yourself some room to write the responses, placing them under the key topic headings you have predetermined (Figure 17.1). This technique moves you out of the linear tracking and recording mode and into a mapping and thinking mode.

Mapping Your Prospect

Valuable Concepts		Ideas
	Expectations	
Problems		Hopes
	Dreams	
Wants		Needs

©2007 Real Estate Champions, Inc.

Figure 17.1 Mapping your prospect.

Pinpoint Wants, Needs, and Sales Barriers

In this book, I have shared with you a number of techniques and proven scripts to uncover wants and needs. The complementary book, *The Champion Real Estate Agent*, has even more of these resources in its pages. Another success option would be our complete scripts and dialogues book. I have assembled the most comprehensive scripts and dialogues book for real estate sales ever created, *The Champion's Guide to Real Estate Sales Scripts*. As the team leader for your team, you will find it to be one of the best investments in your business that you could ever make. You can pick it up at our Web site, www.realestatechampions. com/scripts.

Take Control of the Conversation

Remember, the only way to take and keep control in a telephone sales situation is to ask questions. The one who asks the questions has the power. If you feel, during your call, that you are losing power, ask another question.

Controlling and guiding a prospect can be done only through questions. When you feel, at the end of a call, that you lost control of the call, review the questions you asked. When did you lose control? For some real estate salespeople, the answer is that you never had it. What are the questions that you need to ask on your next call in order to keep control? You need to create or decide upon these questions now, while the feeling of loss of control and the conversation are fresh in your mind.

18

Building High-Performance Teams

There are many twists and turns on the path to success when you are building high-performance or Champion Teams. In this last chapter, I want to give you the final piece of the puzzle of team building. I am going to share with you general strategies, tactics, and philosophies that any Champion Team can use to achieve a competitive edge in the marketplace. What I am sharing with you is universal; it applies to any Champion Team, whether in sports, business, or real estate sales. Live these!

The Myth of One

"If you want it done right, do it yourself." "Look out for number one." These are quotes we have heard frequently throughout our life. While your personal effort will be a significant factor in your initial success, your long-term success is determined by the people you have surrounded yourself with and what they do.

The belief that one person can do something extraordinary is a myth. It takes one person to have the passion to start something. However, it takes others to catch the passion and finish it. When we examine significant accomplishments, they aren't achieved by one person's actions alone. You can't create something great by yourself. The great Wright brothers were just that: brothers—a team. The sum of the two of them together was greater than their individual parts.

Our great nation moved away from the horrid practice of slavery because of one man's passion and resolve. That man was Abraham Lincoln. Lincoln instilled that passion and unity of purpose by beginning to take action with his cabinet and General Grant, who then conveyed it to the officers below him. The course of our nation was forever changed by the beginning inspiration of one man, who then built a Champion Team around him to help him carry out his inspiration.

If you look, you will find a team behind each of the individual players who dominate at high levels in most sports. Annika Sorenstam, arguably the greatest women's golfer in the history of the sport, is clearly a female version of Tiger Woods. Behind the cool exterior of this fairway assassin is a team of people who support her goals and those of the team. She has an agent, business manager, swing coach, behavioral psychologist, personal trainer, and caddie. All of them work in concert to win golf tournaments and maximize the Annika Sorenstam brand. What looks like one person is really a team of people.

Get Your Ego Out of the Way

For most successful people, their ego has helped them to achieve the measure of success that they currently have. Having a strong ego will lead you to achieve individual success. The problem is that your strong ego can stunt your ability to build a Champion Team. Often, our greatest strengths can also be our greatest weaknesses.

One of the first steps in getting your ego out of the way is to admit that you aren't good at everything. You can't do everything, but why should you? In my youth, I thought I was good at everything. I was sure that there were only a few flaws in my skills and character. The definition of that view is immaturity. The older I become, the more I realize that I am not skilled or good at everything. In fact, I am skilled at a few things and unskilled at many.

I have come to the realization that I have reached the Champion Level of skill, ability, and passion in about half a dozen areas of my business life. I have to accept that fact and control my ego, so that I don't assume that I am at the Champion Level in anything beyond those half-dozen things until I have verifiable, empirical proof of this. In the interim, my objective is to increase the amount of time that I invest in those half-dozen areas. This will create the greatest personal satisfaction for me. It will also create the greatest value for my company, Real Estate Champions. Another action I must take is to make a direct investment of my time in improvement. I need to be reading books, listening to CDs, and watching DVDs. I need to be working to perfect my half-dozen things at a higher level, while also trying to add more areas to the list.

I believe that Champion Performers who lead Champion Teams recognize their limitations and work within the boundaries of those limitations. This doesn't mean that they resign themselves to those limitations and give up; it means that they have the ability to be honest with themselves about where they truly are right now. The question isn't whether you think you are great at everything; the real question is how soon you are going to realize that you aren't.

Most of you who are trying to build and lead Champion Teams can be challenged by insecurity. This insecurity is most likely linked to your need to feed your ego; it holds you back from the realization that you aren't good at and can't do everything. It causes you to take on more and more, which leads to more pressure and lower performance. The truth is, spinning more plates in the air doesn't increase your likelihood of success. Adding more plates only increases the probability that you are going to drop one.

This insecurity can manifest itself in your philosophy and actions when you are building your team. My view has always been that I should hire people who are better and smarter than I am. The more people I can put on my team who meet those criteria, the more successful the team will be. Your clear mandate is to hire people who are better than you. Since most of us are good or world-class at only a few things, that shouldn't really be that hard to do. (The most challenging part isn't finding these people; the most challenging part is dealing with our ego and insecurity.)

We Are Good—But We Are Not *That* Good

Most people who lead teams that don't have members who are better than the leader in key positions aren't in this situation because of poor hiring judgment on their part. It isn't because they fail to attract the right people. It isn't because of a lack of intelligence that they don't hire them. It boils down to their ego and insecurity. Too many team leaders surround themselves with weak players on the team to make themselves look good. They are incapable of hiring people who are smarter and better than they are. This approach is guaranteed to fail.

> *The first method for estimating the intelligence of a ruler is to look at the men he has around him.*
> —*Machiavelli*

You can't maintain control over everything in your business and your life. You have to give up something. The question is, what? While you may want to control everything, that is not a good foundational philosophy if you are trying to build a Champion Team. You must want others to gain advancement, recognition, and success. You have to be willing to take a back seat to others at times if you want to continue to sit in the front seat.

Establish a Play-to-the-Limit Culture

Educating, training, and coaching your team members to play all out and give it their best is what will separate you from the competition. When you have a group of high performers who give it their very best at all times, you will win over time.

Achieving success in your personal or business life requires you to pay a price. Success sets the price; you and I are merely required to pay the price that it demands. If I want to be a Champion Dad to my children, there will be a price to be paid in terms of time, attention, personal interest, activities, special actions, prayer for them, learning what really makes them tick, encouragement, mentoring, studying successful fathers, reading to them and about them, and just hanging out. Whether or not I achieve the status of Champion Dad will be entirely a payment issue. I don't lack the ability, desire, money (it doesn't take much), energy, or passion to accomplish the goal. Am I willing to invest what I need to invest and pay the price on the installment plan to be a Champion Dad? The installment plan means that it's not a one-time payment; it's an all-the-time payment.

The same philosophy holds true for your real estate business and your team-building efforts. The only difference is that in your business, not only do you have to pay the price of success personally, but you also have to get everyone else on the team to pay it with you. If you fall short of your objective, it will be because you didn't get the whole team to make the payment that success requires. The whole team must be willing to pay the price on the installment plan every day.

If You Want to Win Big, the Price Will Increase

Whatever got you to the level of success that you currently enjoy will not be enough to keep you there. To even maintain the status quo in earnings, production, and quality of life in the future, you and your team will have to improve. You will have to be willing to invest more resources and exert more effort. The more successful your team becomes, the more people will be gunning for you. The more your team stands out above the others, the more of a target it becomes.

When athletic teams achieve the pinnacle in their sport for two consecutive years, they are always asked which world championship was more difficult. I have never heard anyone say it was the first. They always say that the second one was more challenging. The truth is, becoming a Champion Team has a high price tag attached. The highest price is the price you will have to pay to repeat your success or to continue winning because the risk is higher and the improvements are smaller and more refined.

Coach Your Team to Success

The way to create sustained growth and success in your organization is through coaching. By becoming an effective coach, you can improve your team's performance consistently over time. With coaching, you have a chance to build a Champion Team; without it, you have no chance.

As a team leader, you have three avenues available to you for improving individual and team performance. These are education, training, and coaching. *Education* is fundamentally information. In some cases, the first step toward improved performance is new information or a reminder of information that is already known. Sometimes it's more valuable to relearn something that you already know but aren't doing than to learn something new. You must instill the value of education into your team culture. The culture of personal learning or education will help build your Champion Team. Your staff and you must make the commitment to read, study, listen to CDs, watch DVDs, and attend seminars. The challenge with education is, once you have it, what do you do with it? It's still up to you and your team to use it.

The next avenue is *training*. Too many people view training and education as the same thing. Training goes into far more depth than education, although there are always elements of education in training. Fundamentally, training is focused on raising your skill or your team's skill in specific areas of the business. It could involve the sales functions or service functions of the team. Most people decide to engage in training when they spot a deficiency, and they create training or contract for it through an outside source to deal with the deficiency in that area. At its core, training is more action-oriented than education. The objective in raising the skill level through training is using action and repetition.

Lastly, and most importantly, you must provide *coaching*. Again, you can provide it yourself or hire an expert like our Team Performance Coaching program to coach you and your team. Coaching is a personal process of performance improvement. Effective coaching analyzes who you are, where you are going, your skills, your business, your goals, your values, and your envisioned future and connects those things with a plan for skill development, using a customized format of execution and accountability to raise the odds of your success dramatically.

Coaching for peak performers has been around for years. For many decades, the most successful athletes have been coached to win the big event. Tiger Woods would not be the golfer he is today without his golf coaches. In fact, Tiger did not have a coach during the period a few years ago when he didn't win a major championship for over 24 months. Once he started to work with a coach again, he won a major championship within six months.

Michael Jordan, John Elway, and Michael Johnson all had coaches. Leaders of some of the most successful companies in the business world have coaches. Behind each great milestone or accomplishment stand two people—the one who executes the task or carries out the game plan, and the one who helps create the game plan and teaches and coaches the one executing it to reach his goals and objectives.

Traits of a Good Coach

Because you are going to need to be a coach to your team in some capacity, I want to share with you what makes a good coach. When these traits are used to help you move forward in your life, the results are amazing. A coach can help you increase your production and enjoyment of life and help you craft a life of long-term success.

The first trait of a great coach is the ability to listen and help you with your goals. The difficulty for most people is not achieving their goals, but setting those goals in the first place. We can truly accomplish anything in life provided we truly decide to do it.

The second trait of a successful coach is guiding you to understand that all goals must have deadlines. Deadlines get one's juices and thoughts flowing to create the desired result. Determine effective deadlines for all areas of your business. A Champion coach will take the goals and vision that you set for yourself and teach you to achieve them. She will help you create a step-by-step game plan to achieve the future you envision. Even big projects that seem like mountains can be broken down into bite-size pieces, and a coach has the objectivity to help you do this.

Let me share my secrets of success in coaching. I founded Real Estate Champions in 1998 as a coaching company. My only vision at that time was to provide the highest level of coaching to the real estate community. That is different from all of the other speakers who have now moved into coaching because of the business opportunity. There is a significant difference in quality, expertise, execution, and results between a company like Real Estate Champions, which is and was a coaching company first, and a company that evolved into doing coaching because it had a platform from which to sell coaching services. Our tenure in the coaching field and this distinction make us the unequivocal experts in real estate coaching.

Commitment.   As a team leader, you will have to make a commitment similar to the one that I made almost 10 years ago. Coaching your staff will not be enough to achieve success. You must make a commitment to becoming a coach. You have to decide to be a coach— that is the first step. The next step is to design a framework, systems, action plans, and accountability measures. The biggest challenge will be pausing to devote enough time to define your structure and objectives. Then you must design the coaching tools, action plans, and accountability systems to ensure your team's success.

You must do this consistently and on a regular schedule. Coaching can't be hit or miss. You will need to include coaching time in your time-blocking schedule for each person you are making a commitment to coach. There will be stuff that happens, and you will want to move, adjust, or even cancel your coaching time with your team members, but that is a shortsighted approach. You may be able to make more money today by doing that, but over the long haul, allowing yourself to do it even once opens the door to danger.

Hire a Coach for Yourself. Get some help with coaching, either through education or through training. There are a number of companies and organizations that provide generalized coaching training. You can take a skill path seminar on coaching or join the local chapter of the International Coaching Federation and receive some training from it. You can take courses online at Coach U. My only caution is that few of these programs are specific to sales coaching, and none of them is specific to real estate sales coaching. Too many of them are centered on what I would describe as discovery or life coaching. Discovery or life coaching involves leading a client to uncover or discover what he should do. This type of coaching is too broad.

In sales coaching, you don't need as much discovery. There are only four ways to increase a salesperson's performance and production. You know what they are because I have referred to them frequently: (1) increase the number of contacts, (2) improve the method of contact, (3) increase the quality of the prospect, and (4) improve the quality of the message. The type of coaching a salesperson needs is more like that provided by an athletics coach. Your swim coach doesn't help you discover how many laps you need to swim today and each day to reach your goals. She tells you how many laps you need to swim. She helps you make your stroke more effective by removing wasted motion and effort. When you are working on sales coaching with your team, the smallest piece is self-discovery.

The ultimate buy-in is to hire a coach for yourself. You have blind spots and unresolved problems that you don't have the solutions for right now. Some of them have probably plagued you for some time.

- What are they costing you?
- What if someone could solve them now?
- What would that be worth to you?
- How much more money would you have in your pocket?
- What would the improvement of your quality of life be?

The specialization that occurs in the real estate industry is a rarity in the coaching industry. Most coaches are generalists; they work with anyone from any profession. I don't believe this is the correct approach. When you look at the roots of coaching in athletics and entertainment, you find people coaching only in their field of expertise. An acting coach doesn't coach you to be a better singer; you get a vocal coach for that. A football coach in college or at the professional level doesn't decide to coach college or professional baseball instead. He might coach his son's or daughter's Little League team, but not at a higher level of skill than that.

My advice is, make sure you select a coach who specializes in real estate sales, or at least in sales. You also want to select a coach who has personally achieved a high level of performance in real estate sales.

Selecting a coach who has played at the highest level of real estate sales is paramount if you want to be a Champion. You need someone who has been in the trenches and has sold a lot of real estate. This is true from the top of the company to each and every coach. There are large coaching companies that hire anyone off the street to coach their technology or referral programs. Some of these coaches, as opposed to the CEOs or speakers who are the public face of the company, have never sold real estate as a career. They will be able to take you only through grade school. Check the credentials of the individual coach, as well as those of the company. If the outfit you are considering doesn't offer a complimentary consultation with the coach you will be working with, be very wary. Always interview before you commit. It is easy to get wrapped up in the emotion of a seminar where someone does a call to action to buy coaching at the back of the room. That's what those seminars are designed to do—get you to the back of the room to buy.

Evaluate and interview a few companies and the individual coaches for each company. The differences are even larger than the few that I have mentioned. Don't rush; make the right selection the first time.

Becoming a Champion yourself and building a Champion Team is a process that you must commit to and work toward each day. It's a decision that is connected to action. It isn't merely an intention. If we all received a reward based on our intentions, we would all be wealthy and thin. We must be focused on our commitment to excellence. Without it, we will fall far short of the Champion level. There is a delicate balance between striving for excellence and perfectionism. I believe that Champion Performance is attainable for everyone—for you and your team.

****

I am delighted to have had the honor of sharing my personal journey to becoming a Champion in my life and building a number of Champion Teams. I hope your results match or exceed those of my other clients. Please feel free to share with us your journey and how you are doing. One of the best parts of my career is the stories I hear from people like you. I am here to continue to serve you in your journey. You can reach me through Real Estate Champions at 1-877-732-4676, or www.realestatechampions.com or at 5 NW Hawthorne Ave., Suite 100, Bend, OR 97701

My belief is, everyone deserves to be a Champion!

Index

About the Author

Dirk Zeller has been recognized throughout his real estate career as one of the leading agents in North America. He has been described by many industry insiders as the most successful agent in terms of combining high production with life balance. His ability to sell more than 150 homes annually, while working only Monday through Thursday and taking Friday through Sunday completely off every week, is legendary in the real estate field.

Dirk has turned his success into significance by founding Real Estate Champions. Real Estate Champions is the premier coaching company in the real estate industry, with clients worldwide. Dirk has created such revolutionary programs as "Protect Your Commission," "The Champion Listing Agent," and "Positioning Yourself as the Expert." These programs, and others like them, have changed the lives of hundreds of thousands of real estate agents worldwide.

Dirk is one of the most widely read and quoted authors, speakers, and coaches in the real estate arena. His three books (and counting), *Your First Year in Real Estate, Success as a Real Estate Agent for Dummies*, and *The Champion Real Estate Agent*, are the quintessential books for real estate sales success. His free weekly newsletter, "Coaches Corner," is read by more than 350,000 subscribers. Dirk has spoken to sales agents and sales managers in all of the major real estate companies all over the world. He is an international authority in the field of real estate and sales success.

With all the blessings and success Dirk has attained, his faith and his family are still the primary focus of his life. He and his wife of 18 years, Joan, are active with their children, five-year-old son Wesley and two-year-old daughter Annabelle. He and his family reside in Bend, Oregon.

You can contact Dirk at:
Real Estate Champions
5 NW Hawthorne Ave.
Bend, OR 97701
1-541-383-8833
Info@RealEstateChampions.com